City in Common

SUNY series in Latin American and Iberian Thought and Culture
—————————
Jorge J. E. Gracia and Rosemary Geisdorfer Feal, Editors

City in Common

Culture and Community in Buenos Aires

JAMES SCORER

Published by State University of New York Press, Albany

For information, contact State University of New York Press, Albany, NY
www.sunypress.edu

Production, Eileen Nizer
Marketing, Kate R. Seburyamo

Library of Congress Cataloging-in-Publication Data

Names: Scorer, James, 1978–
Title: City in common : culture and community in Buenos Aires / James Scorer.
Description: Albany : State University of New York Press, 2016. | Series:
  SUNY series in Latin American and Iberian thought and culture | Includes
  bibliographical references and index.
Identifiers: LCCN 2015020844 | ISBN 9781438460574 (hardcover : alkaline paper)
  | ISBN 9781438460581 (e-book)
Subjects: LCSH: Buenos Aires (Argentina)—Social life and customs. | Buenos
  Aires (Argentina)—Social conditions. | City and town
  life—Argentina—Buenos Aires. | Commons—Argentina—Buenos Aires. |
  Community life—Argentina—Buenos Aires. | Buenos Aires
  (Argentina)—Intellectual life. | Politics and culture—Argentina—Buenos
  Aires. | Dictatorship—Social aspects—Argentina—Buenos Aires. |
  Neoliberalism—Social aspects—Argentina—Buenos Aires. | Buenos Aires
  (Argentina)—Politics and government.
Classification: LCC F3001.2 .S36 2016 | DDC 982/.11—dc23
LC record available at http://lccn.loc.gov/2015020844

10 9 8 7 6 5 4 3 2 1

For Jordana and Luca

∾

. . . y sobre todo porque, lo piensen con palabras o no, la calle recta que van dejando atrás, está hecha de ellos mismos, de sus vidas, es inconcebible sin ellos, sin sus vidas, y a medida que ellos se desplazan va formándose con ese desplazamiento, es el borde empírico del acaecer, ubicuo y móvil, que llevan consigo a donde quiera que vayan, la forma que asume el mundo cuando accede a la finitud, calle, mañana, color, materia y movimiento—todo esto, entendámonos bien para que quede claro, más o menos, y si se quiere, mientras sigue siendo la Misma, ¿no?, y en el Mismo, siempre, como decía, pero después de todo, y por encima de todo, ¡qué más da!

—Juan José Saer, *Glosa* (1985)

Contents

Illustrations

Acknowledgments

The origins of this book lie in the period I spent in Buenos Aires between 2000 and 2002. Arriving soon after the resignation of Carlos "Chacho" Álvarez, I left in the midst of the crisis, some months before the election of Néstor Kirchner. Though it was a period of intense political and social conflict, on a personal level it was also a time of great friendships and solidarity. I am forever grateful to Paula Porroni, Alex Pryor, Marcelo Topuzian, and particularly Carolina Favre, who welcomed me so warmly to their city. Since that time, many other people in Argentina have been extremely generous in helping me toward the completion of this project in all sorts of ways. I would like to thank Ana Amado, Ana Dinerstein, Beatriz Flastersztein, Julio Flores, Andrea Giunta, Roberto Jacoby, Ana Longoni, Federico Lorenz, Federico Reggiani, Mariana Santángelo, and Sebastián Touza. Javier Trimbolí was particularly generous in the time he gave over to me to talk about Argentine history and culture. Bernardo Blejmar and Graciela Shvartzman have always been prepared to help me throughout the past decade and a half. I would also like to thank Juan Giménez for his kind permission to reproduce artwork from *Ciudad* (Barreiro & Giménez, 1992) and Eduardo Risso and Puro Comic for their kind permission to reproduce artwork from *Parque Chas* (Barreiro & Risso, 2004). Heartfelt thanks also to Paula Eleod for permission to use one of her photographs for the cover of this book.

In the United Kingdom, I am grateful to the Institute of Modern Languages Research, University of London, for permission to reuse material from my essay, "Recycling the City: Streets: Walking, Garbage and Cartoneros," which appeared in Elisha Foust and Sophie Fuggle's *Word on the Street* (London: IMLR, 2011 [igrs books]). Many of my current and former colleagues have offered sound advice and support over the course of the project, particularly Carmen Herrero, Parvathi Kumaraswami, Leandro Minuchin, Christopher Perriam, Karl Posso, Lúcia Sá, Patience

Schell, and Peter Wade. Jens Andermann and Jon Beasley-Murray gave helpful input on the direction of my research at a time when it needed it most. Equally important has been the companionship (often at a distance) of Matthew Allen, Troy Blacklaws, Roman Buss, Mariana Casale O'Ryan, Emanuele D'Onofrio, Glyn Fry, Stefanie Gänger, Charlotte Gleghorn, Gwen MacKeith, Paul McAleer, Ana Moro, Aike Müller, Anne Paffenholz, and Vijay Tymms. Caroline Davis, Richard Ford, and June Taylor were also kind enough to support my travels. My family, particularly my parents, has been unfailingly supportive in more ways than I can list here. Without all of you, the process of writing this book would have been a whole lot less grounded and a whole lot less enjoyable. Above all, I would like to thank Jordana Blejmar, who saw this book through from start to finish and who is deeply inscribed in it and the life that lies beyond.

Introduction

Rife with despots, rapes, and killings, the postcity landscape is ruled by might and inhabited by bodies that have become fighting machines, objects of exchange, and outlets for sexual use and possession. Outsiders are regarded with suspicion; insiders fear for their lives. Under perpetually rainy skies, the urban landscape has become an endless stretch of wasteland, contaminated water, and rubbish, such that the only site of commonality is survival—to outlast the threatening others living in the same threatening landscape. At times, the world of Rafael Pinedo's novel *Plop* (2004) appears to be our urban destiny. Trapped in a cyclical, predetermined, and inescapable future, we are unable to flee this apocalyptic cityscape that has been turned into a nightmarish post-urban terrain. Like the protagonist Plop, named after the sound he made falling into the mud as his mother gave birth during a forced march, we too will be submerged in the grime of this corrupted city.

Some would have us believe that dystopian cityscapes such as Pinedo's are our only urban future. Violence, fragmentation, and fear dominate our urban imaginations and are inscribed into the material cityscape. For many urban dwellers and theorists, positive sites of commonality are simply no longer part of our increasingly conflictual formulations of urban territory (Korn, 2007, p. 33). Without ignoring the pressing reality of urban fragmentation and its material and social impact, this book addresses some of the ways that cultural imaginaries can and do point toward alternative urban futures, because beyond such discord, disaffection, and enclosure, the urban remains a privileged site of links, connections, and encounters that exist alongside and sometimes undermine the divisive and alienating trends of the city. Such encounters are the basis of what I call the *city in common*. Swelling from below, the city in common disrupts the imposition of an imposed urban spatial order. Of course, the common itself is not inherently democratic. It can also be divisive, such

1

that shared spaces or identities can be used to reinforce inequalities and promote exclusion as much as to construct equality or togetherness. As a consequence, an important step toward creating democratic, inclusive cities is to rethink the ways that the common is imagined and put into practice: The negative traits of the common must be rejected in favor of its more affirmative attributes, ones that can foment and support the real and imagined meeting places that make of a city a shared space.

I focus on the way that the city has been variously constructed as a commons through quotidian actions and habits and, more particularly, the role that cultural practices and imaginaries play in imagining such commons. The cultural common is part of social production since envisioning the urban aids both understanding of the city and the possibility of change. The frequently splintered materiality of the contemporary cityscape poses serious challenges for culture's ongoing attempts to construct urban communities. Urban fragmentation threatens to disenfranchise the urban imaginary, which, in the words of urban historian Adrián Gorelik, increasingly "swims in its own impotence" (2004, p. 279).[1] But culture can still be a productive force in the construction of the city in common. As a process of engagement, culture is an active insertion into the flow of meanings in the city, meanings that themselves have an impact on material space and practices. Culture transforms the way in which urban dwellers use the city, which in turn produces urban settlements that are not a series of (de)finite pieces that fit together like a jigsaw puzzle to create unified wholes but which are palimpsests of simultaneous times and spaces. In that sense, they are built on a set of singular urban practices and encounters that work constantly in common. In that commonality the city can be understood as a whole once again, not an exclusive or excluding whole, but one which is identifiable as such precisely because it assembles many encounters. Thus the cultural texts discussed here all contribute to the construction of a kindred and shared locale through and in which urban dwellers produce the city.

The city in common that I analyze in this book is Buenos Aires between the military coup of 1976 in Argentina and the aftermath of the country's economic collapse of 2001, a period of radical transformation of the city's commons. My analysis considers the major urban trends and developments in Buenos Aires from the beginnings of the neoliberal model until the crisis that culminated in the upheaval of 2001 and the subsequent election of Néstor Kirchner in 2003. In Chapter 1, I draw on contemporary theories of "the multitude" to introduce the concept of the city in common. The multitude, in tension with the national-popular politics of "the people," has been a constant presence in Buenos Aires, from the British Invasions at the beginning of the 19th century, prior to the formation of the nation-state, to the uprisings of 2001. Reading the history of Buenos Aires through the multitude reveals how it is the city itself, whether physical or imagined, that emerges as the salient protagonist of struggles over the common in Argentine history. That historical reading feeds into a discussion over how the notion of the urban commons might offer an alternative to the paradigms of urban fragmentation and enclosure that dominate readings of the Latin American city.

Chapter 2 analyses how the 1976–1983 military dictatorship transformed the urban commons and then how, post-dictatorship, memory practices attempted to overturn that transformation, restoring a more inclusive commons based on remembering in and through the urban landscape. To demonstrate how the dictatorship created a commons based on the incorporation of exclusion and violence, I focus on Martín Kohan's *Dos veces junio* (Twice June), a novel that highlights the common and everyday nature of the exception. During the post-dictatorship era, one means of overturning the exception can be seen in the way that diverse memory practices, namely the use of silhouettes and forms of popular justice, deploy the urban commons as a means of overturning the exception. In Chapter 3, I demonstrate how culture wrestled with the aftermath of a dictatorship that had problematized both the nation and the urban representation of that nation—Buenos Aires—as sites of belonging. Beginning with the contentious proposal to move the national capital, I highlight how comics, one of the few thriving cultural products of the 1980s, struggled to find a way to escape the national city of Buenos Aires.

Chapters 4 and 5 focus on the city of the 1990s, transformed into an object of consumption populated by the citizen-turned-consumer and the rise of the shopping center. Both chapters deal with the conflict over the urban commons that developed during this decade, highlighting how the loss of traditional markers of identity, not least that of work, fueled the growing importance of territory for identity construction, political expression, and cultural imaginaries. In Chapter 4, I look at two different kinds of exclusionary commons that emerged as responses to an increasingly isolating and dangerous city: the commons of the gated communities that came to dominate the urban periphery, and the enclosed communities depicted in Argentine cinema. In Chapter 5, I turn my attention to the way the neighborhood emerged in the neoliberal city as a privileged and highly localized frame of reference around which a disenfranchised youth could confront urban neglect. Focusing particularly

on Gran Buenos Aires—a term I use in this book to refer to the metropolitan area of the city that lies outside the autonomous central urban
district of Capital Federal—and the musical form most closely associated
with that vast urban cordon, *rock barrial*, I go on to indicate how one set
of literary imaginaries, for all its neighborhood specificity, turns the local
into an open, expansive commons.

Chapters 6 and 7 focus on the challenge posed to the notion of a city
in common by the urban poor. In the former, I look at the influence of
informal rubbish collectors known as *cartoneros* on the use of the city and
its urban imaginaries. Focusing on three kinds of commons connected to
cartoneros—the street, movement, and garbage—I show how the activities
of these workers and their interactions with garbage, both of which are
"out of place" in the city, disrupt established urban imaginaries. Whilst
cultural engagements with *cartoneros* always run the risk of romanticizing
poverty, they are still important reminders of how the city houses very
different recycling processes to those evident in large-scale gentrification
projects. Chapter 7 traces the history of shantytowns in Buenos Aires,
looking at the problems posed for the city in common if informal dwellings are excluded from the urban imaginary or if they are included only
as spaces of exoticism and mystique. When urban dwellers both within
and beyond the shantytown display a common understanding of space
rather than engaging in an unequal relationship of solidarity, glimpses
emerge of the way dichotomies of inside and outside can be left behind,
opening the door to a city in common.

Buenos Aires is a meeting place that foments encounter, not just
among its inhabitants, but also as a city that is no longer simply a
"European" city misplaced in Latin America. Buenos Aires is itself in
common, a city that holds within it the legacy of imaginaries drawn from
European, North American, and Latin American urban traditions. Recent
urban theory has recognized the importance that cities of the global south
have when addressing the problems and possibilities of the city, reminding
us of the way "the south" constantly inhabits and inscribes "the north"
within the global network of urbanity. Cities should be seen in terms of
their shifting points of commonality and individuality within that network. Writing on postmodernity in Latin America, John Beverley and
José Oviedo set out "less to present a 'regional' variant of postmodernism
than to resituate the concept itself, which risks being colonized by Anglo-
European provincialism" (1995, p. 1). I believe that Buenos Aires can similarly inform readings of the urban commons. The situational knowledge
and development of one particular place is not employed in an attempt

to construct Latin American cities as a site of resistance to global trans-formations, but rather to inform our understanding of the global city.

If I began this book with an apocalyptic vision of the urban future—a post-urban shantytown characterized by unbridled individuality, slavery, and survival—I want to end it with a story that imagines a more affirma-tive urban future. "El fin de la palabrística," included in Marcelo Cohen's collection *Los acuáticos: historias del Delta Panorámico* (2001), highlights how bodies working in common can combat the fragmentary tendencies of the contemporary city. The story is set in a city called Ajania, located on the Delta Panorámico, a series of interconnected island cities, which places the story within the imaginative topography of Buenos Aires and the delta formed at the head of the River Plate. The choice of the delta symbolizes the fragmentary nature of a city of islets, mirroring the equally fragmented truths of an unreliable narrator who constantly corrects him-self, reassessing his own comments, even admitting that he lies (p. 30) and that he likes "misinforming" (p. 37). The alienating solitude of indi-viduality in the city of Ajania produces languid, world-weary citizens who exist in a kind of drug-induced trance. That narcotic effect is a result of the "Panconciencia," an all-pervasive, indeterminate force that links the delta's islands like the waves of neoliberal mass media. Addiction to the Panconciencia leads to the glazed state of "porcelainitis" (p. 19), creating a city that exists in a perpetual present in which creativity and historicity are suppressed by inaction. In the defense of their own space, the inhabitants of Ajania relinquish control over their own bodies. The collective effort to control panic in the city suppresses suicide, the ultimate act of self-control, such that citizens are subject to the sovereign's godlike authority, and urban life is regulated by pills and edicts on movement, with energies channeled into fear of those outside the city: "The sharpened, terrifying energy was applied to the decoration of a gleaming camp of exclusions: *So that those outside don't enter here*" (p. 19).

In the same vein as the inside/outside dichotomies that mark Buenos Aires, whether in terms of nationhood, poverty, or race, Ajania is here built around an exclusive commons, a "we" that stands in stark opposition to the amorphous mass of "those outside." Its "outside" is comprised of derelict factories, a postindustrial landscape marked by rubbish dumped by the city, symbolic of the way that the city excludes its unwanted social waste. But like Domingo F. Sarmiento's famous 19th-century description of Argentina as being caught in a dichotomy between urban civilization and provincial barbarism, one that continues to inscribe the urban imagi-nary of Buenos Aires, Ajania is dependent on what it constructs as its outside, suffocated by the product of its own fear: "The more the outskirts were dying, the more circumscribed the inside" (p. 19). How can this fragmented city of citizens who are afraid to place their bodies to work in common be overcome? How can the fear of the outside be overturned into an inclusive urban commons? And, since the story relates a detective's investigation into the disappearance of a character called Viol, how can the post-dictatorship Argentine paradigm of a crime without a corpse be resolved?

Cohen's story imagines an alternative city via the "palabrística" of the story's title, an urban intervention in which people come together in the street and climb on top of one another to form human towers that spell out words and phrases. The original inventor of this "human graffiti" is Viol himself, whose body remains disappeared. Resolving the case, however, becomes secondary to the activities of "la Palabrística," such that Viol's disappearance is overcome not by the discovery of his body (which never occurs) but by the way he is remembered by the bodies that enact the practice he invented: The disappeared body is surpassed by bodies acting in common, transforming the absence of the disappeared body into presence. In contrast to regulated urban bodies, "la Palabrística" also encourages a deregulated use of creative bodies, turning the drugged city into a celebration of urban elevation created by these human towers, which are reminiscent of the ancient practice of building "castles" made of bodies during festivals in Catalonia. The participants create a mechanics of encounter in which they depend on each other's mutual stability. "La Palabrística" replaces the multiplicity of disconnected urban bodies with a multitude of bodies working in common. Not just a human tower, though, "la Palabrística" is simultaneously a writing machine, as the human castles also form letters. Viol has thus created language through bodies and bodies through language, indicating how culture, like many of the works analyzed in the rest of this book, can enact an urban future in which an inclusive commons can be put into practice. Thus, one day Viol discovers that the tower enables him to see beyond the edge of the city, his gaze breaking down the division between inside and outside (p. 50). Following Viol's lead, the narrator imagines a space full of the possibilities of bodily sensation, fecundity, and baroque excess. Escaping the false consciousness of the pills that impose equilibrium on the bodies of Ajania, here bodies can become unregulated, fluid, and unlimited, escaping the perpetual, narcotic present to open the door to memory and forgetting. Believing that Viol will be venerated for this new freedom, the narrator imagines a commemorative monument—a four-sided tower with each face stating THE END. But the story does not finish with "THE END," the words themselves expressed in capital letters in the text. Speculating about Viol's possible death, the narrator fears that his own narrative report is partially responsible: "My hypothesis would be a snippet of a weave that goes beyond me" (p. 59). The influence of culture is thus not the end of the narrative, but "THE END" of "la Palabrística"—the end that comes before the end, comprised of bodies standing firm, turning enclosure into encounter and breaking down insides and outsides to create a city in common.

Chapter 1

The City in Common

On 10 August 1806, British invaders under the command of Colonel Beresford found themselves trapped in Buenos Aires. Ill prepared for street fighting, particularly in a city of flat roofs, the British soldiers were forced to surrender under a barrage of stones, boiling water, and sniper fire from above. This act of defense was Buenos Aires's first insurrection. The second came only a year later, in 1807, when Lieutenant General Whitelocke invaded the city with some 7,000 men. Again, the inhabitants of Buenos Aires put up a determined defense, repelling the invaders in another act of urban resistance. In 1806, with the Spanish Viceroy Rafael de Sobremonte retreating to the city of Córdoba, the arriving British forces were not initially repelled—the Audiencia and the Cabildo preferred to surrender rather than follow Sobremonte's order to resist. But spurred on by the French-born Santiago Liniers, the inhabitants of Buenos Aires formed secret urban resistance groups. Certainly some of those revolting were dissatisfied Spanish businessmen unhappy with British plans for commerce (Ternavasio, 2009, p. 29), but the militias of both 1806 and 1807 were by no means merely Creole, as subsequent narratives would suggest in an attempt to establish these events as the first truly *national* acts; rather they were comprised of a hodgepodge of urban dwellers, from Creoles to slaves, from Catalans to those from what is now Paraguay. A British officer subsequently described the stalwart defenders of 1807 as being "of every description, from the original Spaniard down to the Black: some of them were clothed in uniform, others not" (Whitelocke, 1808, p. 370). As the vanquished made clear, the defenders were a multinational and multiracial mix of slaves and freemen, of trained soldiers and ad hoc combatants; this group, not the Viceroy's forces, defeated the British.

The defense of Buenos Aires in 1806 and 1807 is a key moment in the city's history. It was a rejection of European military and economic imperialism, and also of Sobremonte's order to withdraw and surrender.

9

Ignoring the security of the fort, which, like Sobremonte, was the local manifestation of the Spanish Crown, the city relied on its own streets and inhabitants to repel the invaders. Looking to France and the United States, the inhabitants of the city demanded a Republic via public marches and graffiti, a demand that highlights that this was a city in limbo—it had rejected the Crown, but an alternative Republican government would not materialize until 1810. The period was, in the words of historian Marcela Ternavasio, "a crisis of authority without precedent" (2009, p. 29). Different to Manuel Belgrano's declaration of "amo viejo o ninguno" (old master or none) when he left for Uruguay in 1806, an act of exile undertaken to avoid swearing allegiance to the British Crown, the defense of Buenos Aires rather revealed a desire for neither old master nor new: It was a spontaneous declaration of liberty from and through a city held—albeit briefly—in common. The crowds that gathered outside the town hall on 14 August 1806 to demand the removal of Sobremonte, a "cabildo abierto" that prefigured the more famous open council meeting of 1810, finally got what they wanted: Santiago Liniers as military chief of Buenos Aires. Together, in and through their own city, they had built their own destiny.

In 2001 an assortment of inhabitants of Buenos Aires gathered to affirm their constituting power. Already tired of a government that was unable to control a growing economic crisis, that was forced to rely on loans from international monetary bodies to sustain a currency that had been fixed to the U.S. dollar at the rate of one-to-one by the 1991 Ley de Convertibilidad, and that was dogged by allegations of corruption, Argentine citizens were then confronted with an austerity measure known as the *corralito*, a restriction on access to cash in private bank accounts, introduced by Fernando de la Rúa's administration to avoid a bank run and subsequent financial collapse. After days of strikes, supermarket sackings, marches, and roadblocks, the protests came to a head throughout Argentina on 19 and 20 December. A huge crowd gathered in downtown Buenos Aires to demand the removal of President De la Rúa, ignoring the implementation of martial law with the cry, "De la Rúa, boludo, el estado de sitio te lo metés en el culo" (De la Rúa, you dickhead, stick the state of emergency up your arse). On 20 December, after 2 days of violent struggle with the police in which five people were killed in Buenos Aires alone, the crowd was successful and the president fled ignominiously. In the wake of De la Rúa's resignation, three more heads of state were forced out over the following 2 weeks.

These two civic uprisings, occurring almost 200 years apart, could not be further apart in the narrative of Argentina and its capital city.

Colonial Buenos Aires at the time of the British Invasions was a small trading outpost, a far cry from the Buenos Aires of the new millennium, a vast metropolis that not only lays claim to having a major political and cultural role within Latin America but also to being a significant player in the region's interactions with a globalized economy. And if the first act of resistance was one against colonial invaders, the second was a rejection of an elected president and economic policies that encouraged foreign investment and financial regulation at the expense of middle and lower classes. Nevertheless, these two moments in Argentine history—these two Buenos Aires—are not merely two ends of an historical spectrum. They also share a number of traits that highlight other possible readings of the city's history and its role in the formation of the Argentine nation. Both of these cities were experiencing troubled national identities: The colonial city wanted to become an independent national city; the postmodern city expressed a desire for greater autonomy in the context of post-dictatorship trauma and neoliberal globalization, both of which had destabilized the nation as a site of belonging. Both cities experienced successful insurrections that placed them in unresolved states: The colonial city was not only defending itself against foreign invaders but also liberating itself from colonial rule; the rallying cry of the city of the new millennium was "¡que se vayan todos!" (get them all out!). And, crucially, both insurrections were formed by a mix of peoples and groups who came together to utilize the nature of their own urban environments to bring about change.

Just like 200 years earlier, the protestors' ability to utilize the city in 2001—breaking up asphalt for missiles, setting up lines of bodies at key vantage points—enabled them to get a foothold in the streets. Like the British Invasions, the area in and around the Plaza de Mayo was essential to the geography of conflict, symbolized by the death of a protester at the intersection of Avenida de Mayo and Chacabuco, for example, or the police barricade set up outside the Banco de la Nación. Protesters and police variously used all the downtown streets during their battle for the Plaza de Mayo, the symbolic heart of Buenos Aires and, indeed, of Argentina. Of the streets fought over in and around the Plaza de Mayo, two key arteries were Calle Defensa, the street that runs from Parque Lezama in the neighborhood of San Telmo to the Plaza, and Calle Reconquista, the continuation of Defensa on the other side of the square, running to the bottom of Plaza San Martín. Both streets had been named after the lines of defense taken by those defending the city from the British invaders almost 200 years earlier. By using the very same streets as part of their rejection of the government's curfew, the protestors created a topographical bond between these two cities. Given that Buenos Aires has forever been shaped by a tension between the "people" and what, following Michael Hardt and Antonio Negri, I will call the "multitude," the links between these moments in the city's history highlights that December 2001 was not the genesis of the multitude but rather a moment when it once again emerged into the spotlight.

Buenos Aires and the Multitude

Writing in 1899, the historian José Ramos Mejía analyzed the British Invasions alongside the Primera Junta of 25 May 1810 and the dictatorship of Juan Manuel de Rosas in an attempt to understand the politics and violence that lay behind the latter's period of rule in the mid-18th century. Ramos Mejía believed that to truly understand a figure like Rosas, the *caudillo* whose presence dominated 19th-century Argentine political thought, the historian should address Rosas's followers—the ordinary citizens that formed his power base. Ramos Mejía's work, *Las multitudes argentinas*, therefore, is an attempt to grapple with the importance of the general populace in Argentine history and not just the individual. The term that he uses for this general populace is *multitud*. On the one hand his description of the meeting that declared independence from Spain in 1810 as formed by "more *multitud* than simple group, because it is of a more uniform . . . level" (1977, p. 58) suggests that he is describing the uniformity of the entity known as "the people." But as Ramos Mejía states, "the *multitud* is not what we commonly call *the people*, the group of inhabitants of a city or a country, even if that does not mean that it can not, in specific circumstances, present itself to us as *multitud*" (1977, p. 99). Highly conscious of the differences between group, people, and *multitud*, Ramos Mejía emphasizes the *multitud*'s heterogeneous makeup, its animalistic, biological characteristics and its nature as an antagonistic force of protest, forever threatening violence, all of which distance the *multitud* from the people (1977, pp. 32–40). And his portrayal of its molecular nature, the aptitude that "simple bodies have for forming more or less complex combinations with another simple body" (1977, p. 36), is not sufficiently explained by the crowd, which tends to oneness rather than multiplicity. Thus, *Las multitudes argentinas* is an early attempt to grapple with the notion of the multitude within Argentine historiography.

Ramos Mejía anticipated the philosopher Paolo Virno's more recent discussion of the struggle between multitude and people, a struggle that,

Virno argues, lies at the heart of the birth of modern sovereignty and nation-states in early modern Europe. Virno has argued that post-Fordist transformations such as the collapse between public and private spheres, the amalgamation of producer and citizen, and the development of intellect, perception, and linguistic communication as productive resources all contribute to the contemporary return of the multitude. But Ramos Mejía's text highlights that the multitude does not only belong to the postmodern globalized world order. In the examples taken from the history of Buenos Aires that I refer to briefly in this chapter—the British invasions, the immigrant city, the Peronist city, and December 2001—the multitude emerges as a potent force, problematizing Virno's belief that the multitude is a concept without a history (2004, p. 43) and Horacio González's suggestion that the multitude has no future (Moreno, 2002b, p. 146). Not just tied to the neoliberal economic policies of the 1976–1983 dictatorship and rejecting the implied post-dictatorship truce of "dictatorship or democracy" (Colectivo Situaciones, 2002a, p. 9), December 2001 has a far longer history that predates the founding of a specifically Argentine people.

The foundation of Latin American nation-states was also dependent on the creation and institutionalization of the people (Williams, 2002, p. 4). Jon Beasley-Murray's analysis of posthegemony (2010), in which a case is made for the political potential of the multitude, begins in 1492 and the precarious, even fictional, relationship between constituted and constituting power that highlights the tensions between multitude and people. Ramos Mejía saw that tension in the forces unleashed in Buenos Aires—he saw the plurality of the multitude, its commonality, rather than simply the single, unified will of the people. The inhabitants of Buenos Aires were often very different from each other, even speaking different languages, and yet they were able to act in common. Still unable to lay claim to an alternative nation-state, they rejected their status as a Spanish people and rejoiced in the city's newfound lack of sovereignty. As such, they rejected the sovereign's ability to rule *over* the people by constructing a multiplicity that countervailed sovereign authority, giving the city democratic potential.

Buenos Aires at the end of the 19th century and beginning of the 20th century was a city similarly inhabited by the multitude. Large numbers of European immigrants began to transform the social, cultural, and physical assembly of the city. Whilst intellectuals tried variously to conceptualize the nature of Argentine national identity, this city of immigrants destabilized that vision. As Adriana Bergero shows, Buenos Aires at this time was linguistically and culturally very diverse, inhabited by what she calls the "heteroglossic multitude of the grotesque city" (2008, p. 47). In the face of a proscribed and exclusive set of commonalities proposed by nationalist thinkers such as Leopoldo Lugones, the cultural expressions of urban dwellers offered a synchronous city in common. Over the course of the coming decades, intellectuals and politicians wrestled over what kind of a national "people" could be fashioned from this diversity. In *El hombre que está solo y espera*, first published in 1931, Raúl Scalabrini Ortiz put forward "el Hombre de Corrientes y Esmeralda" (the Man at Corrientes and Esmeralda) as the archetypal figure of Argentine national identity. Despite writing that "the *porteño* man has a crowd in his soul" (1933, p. 27), Scalabrini Ortiz's white man from Buenos Aires was hardly representative of the nation in gender, class, geographical, or racial terms (Garguin, 2007, pp. 171–172). Nevertheless, it was precisely that lack of representativity, suggests Enrique Garguin, that enabled thinkers like Scalabrini Ortiz to build a vision of Argentina in which the oligarchy was in opposition to a people that still included the middle classes. With the growing recognition and visibility of the racial and class diversity that came with Peronism, however, Garguin argues that the "people" was subsequently reconfigured as being specifically working class, causing, in turn, the emergence of the middle class as a discursive category (2007, p. 179).

Whether Garguin is right about this late emergence of the notion of the middle class as such, his argument highlights the conflictual nature of the development of an Argentine people at this time. That conflict was symbolized in the events of 17 October 1945, the day when vast numbers of Peronist supporters descended on the center of the city to demand the release of Juan Domingo Perón, then Minister of Labor. Scalabrini Ortiz himself celebrated this multitude as "the most heteroclitic crowd imaginable" (2009, p. 29). Ivana Incorvaia suggests that Scalabrini Ortiz moves here from the solitude of his earlier book to delight in these collective forces, and she emphasizes the importance of the fact that he uses the term "multitudes and not the category of people" to describe these forces (2012, p. 2). But Incorvaia ignores the one reference Scalabrini Ortiz does in fact make to the "people," which appears in the final paragraph of his short piece: "the substance of the Argentine people . . . was present there" (2009, p. 31). His shift in terminology reveals precisely how the multitude is not an end but rather what precedes the formation of the people. That shift from multitude to people is what, in many ways, defines Peronism: the need to bring under control the unruly constitutive force that brought

Perón to power. This narrative, which dominates the period between 1946 and 1955, is described by Daniel James as the "attempt to institutionalise and control the heretical challenge it had unleashed in the earlier period" (1993, p. 34), and by Beasley-Murray as the desire to curb the excesses and energies of the "unrepresentable, overwhelming and fanatical" multitude and transform it into a people (2002, p. 39).

Like the British Invasions and the Peronist city, December 2001 likewise reveals the tension between multitude and people. Those seeking further examples of global unrest in the wake of the protests against the World Trade Organization that took place in Seattle in 1999 quickly inscribed the Argentine crisis of 2001 and especially the days of 19 and 20 December within a global narrative of resistance. Advocates of the multitude, perhaps the most hotly debated theoretical intervention of the left at the time following the publication of Michael Hardt and Antonio Negri's *Empire* in 2000, pounced on the events in Argentina as the manifestation of a force that could combat the new form of globalized sovereignty Hardt and Negri called "Empire." Though the driving forces behind theories of Empire and multitude were external to Argentina, the concepts spread quickly and with considerable enthusiasm within a country that has strong connections to Western philosophical and political thought, particularly that from Italy (e.g., Virno, Negri, Giorgio Agamben, Roberto Esposito). Negri, for example, was invited to give a talk via videoconference on 14 December 2002 about the Argentinazo and it seemed to matter little that the philosopher himself seemed somewhat uneasy at being asked to comment on the situation in Argentina, stating in his very first sentence that "there's not much I can say" (2003, p. 27).[1]

There was—and still is—considerable debate as to whether the multitude is an appropriate term to apply to the events of December 2001. After all, the palpable presence of national flags and the protestor's discourse of saving the nation ("la patria no se vende, se defiende" [defend the fatherland, don't sell it]) is evidence of the persisting force of the people and an accompanying national identity. The canvas of Hardt and Negri's work, furthermore, especially with the addition of *Multitude* in 2004 and *Commonwealth* in 2009, is huge, taking in vast tracts of World—though especially European—history and philosophy and discussing class, labor, and war in contemporary society. Thus, when using the notion of the multitude in other contexts some elements fit better than others, which is one reason it is so contested. Nevertheless, it is striking that Negri, Giuseppe Cocco, Aída Quintar, Perla Zusman, Colectivo Situaciones, Virno, and Horacio González all, to a greater or lesser extent, saw the multitude in the events of 2001 and beyond, highlighting the manner in which diverse bodies, groups, and singularities had been brought together into a period of collective, self-determined action. The expressions of autonomy and political protagonism voiced by *piqueteros, asambleas barriales,* and *cacerolazos* were read by some as a movement of movements.[2] The protests were a moment of popular insurrection that made visible feelings of discontent that were already in existence, as Quintar and Zusman affirm: "from the December event onwards, diverse expressions of collective action, which, until then, had only been noticed and valued sporadically, become visible" (2003, p. 63).

Critics of such readings in the immediate aftermath of the events tended to highlight that the so-called "collective" nature of the multitude was nothing more than, on the one hand, working-class poverty stirred into supermarket sackings by opposition parties trying to de-stabilize the incumbent government and, on the other, a middle class awakened by an economic crisis that, in the shape of the *corralito*, was suddenly knocking at their doors. It was in this line that sociologist Alejandro Kaufman argued that the suggested anticapitalist traits of the pots and pans *cacerolazo* protest was undermined by the protagonists' belief in private wealth and property generated out of social exclusion and the appropriation of national wealth (Moreno, 2002a, pp. 138–141). Kaufman saw in Buenos Aires the cities of Sodom and Gomorrah, destroyed, according to certain rabbinical readings of the bible, for wickedness, inhospitality, and the veneration of personal property. Likewise, Ignacio Lewkowicz further refuted the notion that supermarket sackings, roadblocks, *cacerolazos,* protests against military impunity, and local neighborhood assemblies be seen as part of a coherent political movement, suggesting instead that they reflected a disbanded desire for "good capitalism" (2004, pp. 84–88). Even if, as María Moreno points out, accusing the middle classes for acting only when the crisis affected their pockets is somewhat disingenuous since the *piqueteros* were also motivated by personal economic concerns (2011, p. 13), the subsequent economic growth and concurrent manner in which the middle class have embraced representative politics once again appears to lend credence to perspectives such as those of Kaufman and Lewkowicz.

Many of the protesters were reacting to the immediate economic crisis of 2001 and to specific government measures such as the *corralito* that affected mainly those reliant on cash savings and who managed their finances through the banks. But Olga Onuch (2014) also makes the point that many of those who participated in the events of 20 December did not return to the streets for subsequent protests, leading her to conclude that it was a political demand and not material deprivation that was the prime driver for the mass mobilization that took place on that day. The observation is an important one, even if neoliberalism makes it increasingly difficult to differentiate between the economic sphere and other areas of social existence (Fornazzari, 2013). Nevertheless, it would be misleading to see 19 and 20 December 2001 as events in isolation. The diversity of protestors and the forms of protest demonstrated how economic and social policies introduced over the previous two-and-a-half decades had drawn together many sectors of Argentine society—the sense of anger that exploded in December 2001 had been building up not just over the previous months but over an entire decade during which the vast majority had seen rises in unemployment, undernourishment, and the cost of living. The protests against, for example, the government's desire to repay its increasingly expensive loans and to rely on emergency payouts from the International Monetary Fund emerged equally from a disenfranchised working class desirous of reclaiming a stake in national politics and from middle-income earners. Likewise, the supermarket sackings that took place during December 2001 highlighted that the crisis had affected far more than just bank account holders. In Buenos Aires, the sackings took place predominantly in the working-class districts of Avellaneda, Quilmes, San Martín, Boulogne, San Miguel, Ciudadela, Moreno, Lanús, and Lomas de Zamora. The supermarket sackings harked back to similar protests that took place in 1989, undertaken by a similar sector of the populace in the face of the uncontrolled hyperinflation that brought down the government of Raúl Alfonsín. Thus, whatever the specific motivations behind the various waves of protest and the assembly of protestors during 2001, they were united by a shared discontent specifically related to the context of neoliberal Argentina and expressed in the joint maxim "¡que se vayan todos!" ("get them all out!"). Ana Dinerstein has described the cry as "the joyful collective energy of civil disobedience and rebellion" (2014, p. 116), its creativity producing "a surplus or *excess* that has no grammar in the logic of state power" (2014, p. 117). It was, for a time at least, a demand for a complete overhaul not just of politicians but political representation in general.

The more recent widespread commitment to national elections, the gradual dissipation of neighborhood organizations, the decline in worker-owned factories, and the alliance between the government and many *piquetero* groups has encouraged some to see the cry "¡que se vayan todos!" as a failed political project. Beatriz Sarlo, for example, has argued that the failure of the *asambleas* to provide a viable form of action led the majority to return to a desire for political representation: "the majority wanted a 'normal' president, who would take difficult decisions and take responsibility for evaluating the consequences. They wanted someone with whom they could take a break from a lack of certainty seen by those who were mobilized as productive unrest but which bewildered those who weren't" (2011, p. 173). Sebastián Carassi is even stronger: "the December 2001 outburst can be read . . . as the end of the 'end of politics,' as a spontaneous and untidy reaction against the desertion of politics that took place during that long decade of the 1990s" (2007, p. 53). Quintar and Zusman suggest that the 2003 elections in which Néstor Kirchner was elected might be read as "a means of once more posing the rejection of an exclusionary economic and social system and a system that underestimated the more participatory alternatives of citizens, prioritizing, instead, the politics of spectacle" (2003, p. 65). The key point about "¡que se vayan todos!" is, however, made by Colectivo Situaciones, who point out that the act of enunciation itself highlights that an enunciator remains (2002a, p. 172). The phrase acts not as the expression of a political void, nor simply as an expression of disgust and a rejection of the past, but as an affirmation of the desire for autonomy in the present.

The figure of the multitude persists in analyses of the consequences and implications (or lack of them) of the Argentinazo. Carassi has argued that the Argentinazo was simply an expression of "the impulse to participate in the political life of the country in a more active way than that prescribed by electoral democracy" (2007, p. 50), suggesting that the only quality held in common by the protestors was that of "being against" (2007, p. 47) and leading him to argue that "a multitude may be formed by a huge collection of angry solitudes" (2007, p. 48). But we should not be so quick to dismiss the multitude out of hand when thinking about December 2001 or, indeed, the Kirchner era that followed. "Being against," if indeed this was the only point of commonality, is already a powerful shared site of politics. In any case, the discussions over the multitude both at the time and now indicate that the multitude remains a useful tool for thinking through the last decade of Argentine politics. Theorizing the multitude is a sustained and affirmative attempt to tackle the nature of political life and to advocate a means for establishing democracy. Thus, even if the Argentinazo was recognizably not a Paris Commune, the multitude provides a prism for thinking through exactly what it was.

Though the specificities of the acts listed above in terms of political and social motivations, origins, and protagonists should not be collapsed into sameness, they do have many things in common. Like the insurrections of 1806 and 1807, they demonstrate how diverse political and economic motivations can work together toward a common goal and, indeed, through shared practices and uses of the city. The events of 2001 illustrate how a multiple social body built its own destiny, drawing strength not from sameness—their protagonists, motives, and past histories were not all the same—but rather what they shared in terms of aims, methods, and historical consciousness. One key site of commonality for these struggles has been the city itself, both material and imagined. The British Invasions, fin-de-siècle immigration, Peronism in the mid-20th century, and December 2001 are all moments of Argentine history when the city, specifically Buenos Aires, plays a leading political role. The historian José Luis Romero called the British Invasions the first urban experience of Buenos Aires (2009, p. 302). That urban experience was the first moment when the city saw itself as such, the heterogeneity of the multitude creating a common space from and through Buenos Aires, a city that desired to be neither a British nor a Spanish colonial outpost. Not yet Argentine, the city had its first moment as a city in common. The immigrants that later came to Buenos Aires transformed the city center, turning the mansions that used to belong to the urban rich into multifamily tenement housing. The day the crowds bathed their feet in the fountain of the Plaza de Mayo in 1945 violated expectations about who had the right to do what in Buenos Aires. These new working-class political actors turned the city into "the space of the unknowable, threatening 'other' and the locus of an epistemological crisis" (Podalsky, 2004, p. 4). This Buenos Aires, made strange for the urban middle and upper classes, was precisely "foreign" because it was a city in which those normally excluded from urban politics began to stake a claim to political ownership; this was a city to which the wealthy were not accustomed.

Like the new urban protagonists of 1945, the protesters of December 2001 also used the fountain in the Plaza de Mayo to refresh themselves (Zibechi, 2003, p. 187), a further symbol of the urban narrative established by these uprisings. Thus, even though Lewkowicz expressed his skepticism about there being ties between different social movements during the crisis, he himself argued that the rebuffal of De la Rúa's curfew on 19 December 2001 turned the city's streets into spaces of inhabitation (2002, p. 22). Also advocating the figure of the neighbor as a new form of commonality that connects bodies with other bodies (2002, p. 134), Lewkowicz argued that one form of potential shared commonality in Argentina during the crisis was, even when contested, precisely "being in the street" (2002, p. 132). Occupying these spaces, whether on marches or as part of neighborhood assemblies, resulted in bodies gathered together in acts of urban encounter that put into spatial practice urban commoning and political autonomy.

The City, Enclosure, and the Commons

The prevailing trend of urban planning in recent decades has been toward greater private capital investment, the private management of public spaces, and the development of a range of initiatives to safeguard private property. Neoliberal economic policies, the reduction of state involvement in urban design, and the expansion in urban populations have all contributed to cities dogged by extreme poverty, unemployment, crime, and fear, creating an atmosphere of social division and disunity. As David Harvey writes: "This is a world in which the neoliberal ethic of intense possessive individualism, and its cognate of political withdrawal from collective forms of action, becomes the template for human socialization" (2008, p. 32).

Overturning the postmodern celebration of the fragment as a means of dismantling overarching narratives of power (Kozak, 2008), contemporary urban theory has tended to describe these trends in terms of negative fragmentation. Analyses of Latin American cities in particular are characterized by the discourse of fracture. Already in 1976, the Argentine historian José Luis Romero wrote that rapid urban growth in Latin America had brought about a transformation in the urban landscape, such that cities "stopped being cities in the strict sense and became a juxtaposition of isolated and anomic ghettos" (2005, p. 322). Such a reading of the Latin American city has continued over subsequent decades. More recently, Teresa Caldeira's seminal *City of Walls*, for example, a study of crime and policing in São Paulo, analyses the way in which "privatization, enclosures, policing of boundaries, and distancing devices create a public space fragmented and articulated in terms of rigid separations" (2000, p. 4). Jaime Joseph has written of how Lima, particularly on its urban periphery, is fragmenting both as a consequence of enclosed, private neighborhoods and the ghettoization of the city's poorer areas (2005, p. 209). Jaime Lizama has looked at the transformations of public space, city neighborhoods, and transport networks in Santiago de Chile under the title *La ciudad fragmentada* (2007), a city in which the wealthy flee urban encounter, denying the city as dwelling place and using it merely as a provider of services. The collection edited by Kees Koonings and Dirk Kruijt, *Fractured Cities* (2007), includes essays that look at the deteriorating, divisive effect of urban violence and insecurity on various Latin American cities, including, for example, "divided Caracas" (Briceño-León, 2007, p. 86) or the "fortified network" of Managua (Rodgers, 2007, p. 71). And Tom Angotti has recently written of "enclave urbanism" in Latin America (and beyond) as "the conscious design and development of fragmented cities and metropolitan regions (2013, p. 11).[3]

The Buenos Aires of the new millennium has been described in similar terms of damaging urban fragmentation. It has been variously called a de-collectivized "multiplicity of societies, like islets" (Svampa, 2005, p. 296), an enclosed city dominated by "territorial insularization" (Tella, 2005, p. 66), a "city of islands" (Janoschka, 2005, p. 102), and "various cities, one inside the other" (Wagner, 2008, p. 8). Despite the possibilities opened up by the crisis of 2001, Adrián Gorelik argues that Buenos Aires has gone back to being an archipelago, a form of urban growth that was established in the city during the 1990s (2006, p. 34).[4] And Beatriz Sarlo wrote an essay on urban imaginaries in Buenos Aires with the subtitle "Buenos Aires from Integration to Fracture" (2008). Following the nostalgia for the modern city often expressed in her writings, Sarlo constructs a narrative that culminates in the wistful reflection that "a proud city that had managed to develop its style through a combination of European influences has found its Latin American destiny" (2008, p. 46). She indicates how, for many Argentine critics, Buenos Aires is far from being the Paris of South America and has become all too Latin American. That urban Latin American destiny, it seems, is fragmentation.

Urban fragmentation can take many forms: physical barriers within the city, such as the grilled fences that surround the Casa Rosada; political fragmentation, such as *barrios*, which are partially self-governed; social fragmentation, such as the peripatetic red-light district, which was relocated from the highly visible area around Godoy Cruz to a considerably less visible part of the park Bosques de Palermo; racial fragmentation, in which access to spaces is limited as a result of racial difference (Williams Castro, 2013); and in conjunction with all these is the city imagined in terms of frontiers and barriers. In many ways, not least when remembering the physical, architectural layout of Buenos Aires, organized into blocks and squares, fragmentation appears to be the very definition of the city itself. Fragmentation is a useful concept for thinking through the threats to the shared nature of urban spaces and encounters, particularly when understood in conjunction with the notion of enclosure, a term that highlights how the transformations in the urban landscape described here are a threat to the productive potential of commons. Thus, the increasing trend of urban dwellers to resort to material and imagined means to resist perceived threats to their way of life, such as the "conflict" being played out on the urban periphery of Buenos Aires between enclosed neighborhoods and shantytowns, might be better understood as a tension revolving around the enclosure of the urban commons.

Despite genuine concern for the city's future, narratives and analysis of fragmentation do run the risk of focusing only on the darker realities of urban living in Latin America. When Koonings and Kruijt ask whether there is an "antidote" to the "social and spatial fragmentation of Latin American cities" (2007, pp. 4–5), such terminology frames Latin American cities as diseased or poisoned spaces. There is no doubt that Latin American cities are highly divisive and violent, and we should not be blind to such traits, which have a very real, material impact on the lives of a staggeringly high number of urban dwellers who live below the poverty line. Moreover, within the network of Latin American cities, Buenos Aires is often safer and more integrated than many other urban areas in the region. Nevertheless, Buenos Aires, like these other cities, can remind us that other readings of the Latin American city are possible and that those readings should find a place alongside discourses of fragmentation. If not, the danger is that, as Angotti argues, Latin American cities are caught within the dualism of "urban Orientalism," in which experts either express "dire predictions of a catastrophic urban future" or promote urbanization as a means of steering urban Latin America toward a misleading promise of North American urban prosperity (2013, p. 5). Moreover, as Dennis Rodgers, Jo Beall, and Ravi Kanbur argue, sustained and overwhelming focus on the fractured city has led to what they call "a Latin American urban 'impasse,'" in which we are blinded to the ongoing ways in which cities remain unified entities (2012, p. 5). Buenos Aires is a place of extreme inequalities and conflict and has its fair share of despondent nightmares. But it also offers more affirmative readings of the urban, underlining how the city also produces spaces of togetherness in which productive commons can countervail the drive toward enclosure.

Historically, the commons was a concept pertaining to rural life, a reference to land held in common and used as a shared resource or to land held by an individual but which commoners had common right to use in certain designated ways. Thus the ancient commoning right to woodlands was of vital importance to subsistence as wood was used as fuel, building material, or to fashion footwear or tools (Linebaugh, 2008,

p. 32). But even medieval commentators were clear that the commons was not simply related to land but also to less obvious material commons such as air or intellect, both seen as gifts from God to be shared by all. Even such universal commons have been subject to conflict over use—more recently, tensions over these global commons can be seen in debates over the nature and management of entities such as the Internet, climate change, and intellectual property rights (McShane, 2010, p. 105). At the heart of these debates lies a tension between private ownership and common use. That tension between ownership and use harks back to the earliest notions of the commons, defined not in terms of ownership but how a particular resource is used. Following earlier theorists who argued that common was also a verb (i.e., "to common"), the historian Peter Linebaugh in his study of the Magna Carta stresses that "to speak of the commons as if it were a natural resource is misleading . . . the commons is an activity" (2008, p. 279). The emphasis on the act of commoning means that though the urban commons can be seen "as common pool resources resulting from the urban transformations of industrial economies—with roads, car parks, waste disposal facilities and recreation areas given as examples," the *shared* nature of the commons is better explained by a combination of the material and the social (McShane, 2010, p. 102).

Not all commentators, however, have seen the decline of the urban commons in negative terms. Garrett Hardin's famous and influential essay "The Tragedy of the Commons" (1968), in which he argued that humans' inherently selfish nature means that common use will inevitably lead to the irrecoverable decimation of shared resources, has influenced some contemporary urban theorists. To take one example, Shin Lee and Chris Webster echo Hardin by stating simply that "urban spaces as urban commons deplete with overuse" (2006, p. 27). They list the reasons why enclosure and privatization now dominate and order urban infrastructure and services:

> The weakness of the state, problems with raising local taxes, a revolt against high local taxation, an ideological shift towards lean government, problems with accountability, transparency, and responsiveness of municipal governments, the superior knowledge of the private sector in supplying capital, the superior knowledge of communities in organising and evaluating demand for shared goods and services, and the active divestment of state responsibilities. (2006, p. 29)

Aside from assimilating common property rights with "primitive communities," describing the shift from common rights to private goods as inevitable, and taking the market line by arguing that "clearer boundaries make for more efficient exchange (lower transaction costs) and the more efficient the exchange system, the easier it is for boundaries to change, usually by subdivision" (2006, p. 30), the danger posed by positions such as the one set out by Lee and Webster is that they construct communities that are necessarily private entities. In their vision, local enclosed communities are more efficient, less corrupt, and have a greater interest in action; but this positive enfranchisement of local politics does not envision a series of communities working a shared resource in common with other communities. Instead, it promotes enclosed communities using "private" commons as a means of bypassing the state in order to generate greater profit.

Lee and Webster's argument about local communities does, however, highlight the need for a more nuanced reading of the commons than mere celebration, for individual communities can build and use individual commons that perpetuate enclosure rather than expand access to the city and its production. As Margaret Kohn has illustrated, not all commons are alike: "The commons of a gated community is not the same as a Boston Commons" (cited in McShane, 2010, p. 105). And David Harvey, controversially suggesting that indigenous communities might need to be removed from their Amazon homelands to preserve the rainforest, has argued that "some sort of enclosure is often the best way to preserve valued commons," adding that "one commons . . . may need to be protected at the expense of another" (2011, p. 102). All these views emphasize that the commons is a site of conflict, a shifting entity to be negotiated over and through, and one that is not necessarily always in conflict with enclosure (or, indeed, fragmentation). How, then, is it possible to understand urban communities and urban commons in a way that confronts the negative elements of such enclosure? One answer might lie in the relationship between the multitude, (urban) space, and culture.

Commons, City, Culture

Urban communities, much like the commons, can promote enclosure and division. The centrality of private property and monetary consumption within contemporary citizenship does not simply produce a city in which individuals hoard their goods and defend them against other individuals;

rather, the city is more frequently inhabited by private communities that defend themselves in common against other private communities or entities. Nevertheless, the notion of the commons or the act of commoning is still one meaningful way of enabling greater democratic control of the city. In particular, when urban communities function as a multitude, they enable us to imagine a politically productive urban commons.

Community, as Jean-Luc Nancy has suggested, is not an essence: "Such a thinking constitutes closure because it assigns to community a *common* being, whereas community is a matter of something quite different, namely, of existence inasmuch as it is *in* common, but without letting itself be absorbed into a common substance" (cited in Berman, 2001, p. 14). The texts analyzed in this book portray a wide variety of different communities, many of which act in common. And yet some of them act in common to perpetuate enclosure. The distinction I wish to draw, then, is between those communities that are open and expansive—offering the potential for political encounter and commonality with a wide variety of potentially entirely different communities—and those that are introspective, built necessarily around fixed boundaries that encourage exclusion. To put it in the terms of philosopher Roberto Esposito (2008), if immunity protects the individual from common law, releasing them from the gift giving that lies at the heart of every community, then we can see the latter introspective communities as immune from the process of gift giving that forms the city as a whole. The commons that such communities create can be called "anticommons" (McShane, 2010, p. 104), or perhaps better, "exclusionary commons" (Harvey, 2011, p. 103).

The city lends itself particularly well to any discussion of the friction between inclusive and exclusionary commons. As Paul Chatterton argues, the city is "the ultimate contemporary common . . . thoroughly characterised by both the powerful forces of capital accumulation and the practices and potentials of the common" (2010, p. 627). Privatization, enclosure, and the commons are not solely urban concepts, but it is in the city that they are laid bare, not least because they are so often in such close proximity to one another. With ever-expanding urban populations, the capitalist city, which has always been the site of surplus of different kinds, is the prime location for surplus labor, one that can be transformed into an inclusive commons.[5]

Here too the multitude, one example of an entity that embodies the notion of being-in-common, emerges as a particularly powerful urban presence. As Hardt and Negri argue, the metropolis is "the skeleton and spinal cord of the multitude, that is, the built environment that supports its activity, and the social environment that constitutes a repository and skill set of affects, social relations, habits, desires, knowledges, and cultural circuits" (2009, p. 249). The city encourages people to act in common. Buenos Aires is particularly suitable as a space for thinking through such commoning not just because of the struggle between multitude and people highlighted in my abbreviated history set out above, but also because it is in the Argentine capital that the material and symbolic failures of neoliberal economic policies have come to the fore, putting (some) brakes on the drive toward enclosure. The period from the military coup of 1976 to the beginnings of the Kirchner era is emblematic of the contemporary trend toward privatization and enclosure, evident in such urban phenomena as gated communities, shopping centers, the citizen as consumer, and shantytowns. But how can the city in common—or, indeed, the multitude—be thought of in a specific place? How is Buenos Aires a city in common with Mumbai, Hong Kong, Madrid, and Mexico City, and yet still recognizably Buenos Aires?

Hardt and Negri have rejected struggles founded in the local, going in the face of the Left's emphasis on "place-based"—particularly nation-based—movements and their defense of local boundaries in the face of globalization (2000, p. 44). The limitless, boundaryless nature of what they call Empire, intensified by the flows of globalization, particularly of people, goods, money, images, and information, has disrupted fixed territorial entities such as nation-states and cities. Despite attempts by the nation-state and, indeed, the city, to regulate flows and reterritorialize boundaries, increasingly permeable borders and displaced "peoples" ultimately threaten the mutual constitution of the nation-state and its people. Such fluidity has intensified the power of the multitude, freed from the rigid impositions of the state and its fixed national boundaries. In sum, Hardt and Negri argue, in Empire there "is no *place* of power" (2000, p. 190; italics in original) because "we are confronted no longer with the local mediations of the universal but with a concrete universal itself" (2000, p. 19).

But the understanding of space set out by Doreen Massey (2005), who sees space as a sphere of constantly shifting, heterogeneous trajectories, allows the local and place-specific to be valued without the inscription of exclusionary boundaries. The fluid multiplicity of interrelated paths and narratives constantly reconstruct place, overturning its assumed dependence on boundaries, difference, and otherness. Place is thus created through the combination and intensity of "stories-so-far," the joining points of geometrical, abstract, imagined, and material trajectories, such that place is best understood as *"meeting* place" (2005, p. 68). As meeting place, Buenos Aires illustrates not only how power can be located but also how that power can be resisted without reinforcing insides and outsides. Buenos Aires is not a place apart but a place within simultaneous narratives of global urbanism. And yet, at the same time, Buenos Aires is also specific, local and historical, a city held in common and built around the shared intensity of a situational spatial praxis.

The concept of fluid place and encounter indicates why the city is such a potent site for layers of communities. Though advances in technology and virtual space are potent sites for resistance, they are ultimately at their most powerful when they facilitate the coming together of urban dwellers in material practices of resistance. It is within the commons of everyday life, habits, and practices, which Negri describes as "a great wealth of life styles, of collective means of communication and life reproduction, and above all of the exceeding of common expression of life in metropolitan spaces" (2002), that the city gathers together multiple narratives in a gesture of expansion. The political potential of public space has often been seen as one of the principal facilitators of physical encounters between citizens, frequently those who do not know each other. Such "moments of encounter" (Amin & Thrift, 2002, p. 81), based around an ontology of meeting place, are a large part of the process of building the city in common. As Amin has stressed, however, public engagement is also formed through the urban dweller's participation in a much wider range of experiences: "the collective impulses of public space are the result of pre-cognitive and tacit human response to a condition of 'situated multiplicity,' the thrown togetherness of bodies, mass and matter, and of many uses and needs in a shared physical space" (2008, p. 8). But the city is not only formed by the conglomeration of the people who live there, by its material objects or its habits; the city is also built through the imaginative dialogues constructed by its dwellers about their relationship to such objects, habits, and dwellers (Podalsky, 2004; Biron, 2009).

Here I follow Abril Trigo's definition of culture, or "the cultural" as he prefers, as the "historically overdetermined field of struggle for the symbolic and performative production, reproduction and contestation of social reality and political hegemony, through which collective identities evolve" (2004, p. 4). Given Trigo's emphasis on struggle and contestation, I would question Peter Linebaugh's suggestion that commoning is somehow inherently "a natural attitude" (2008, p. 45). Commoning (as his book demonstrates so powerfully) is historically contingent, a field of struggle forever shifting between enclosure and the commons. Commoning is not natural; it is to be learnt and to be built. As such, contested cultural imaginaries, themselves a kind of commons, offer a window onto the equally contested construction of the urban commons (whether material or imaginary). Cultural production is an act of commoning that thinks, imagines, and questions urban communities, and, as such, it is an inherent part of their very materialization.

Massey's aforementioned definition of place as "stories-so-far" intensifies the link between culture and the city. Her emphasis on the narrative construction of space, the writing of space that is geography, and of the constant change implied by "so-far," highlights how culture might have a role in thinking the urban future. Analyzing cultural geographies and urban imaginaries, as Arturo Escobar implies, is vital to analyzing the political nature of contemporary Latin America: "The geographies of responsibility that emerge from relationality link up with issues of culture, subjectivity, difference, and nature" (2010, p. 42). Culture both reflects and informs, and that ability to inform, to question, and to imagine a commons plays a crucial role in refashioning political imaginaries. Culture is thus an act of commoning (intellect was one of the earliest forms of the commons), creating an active link between culture and city that means urban imaginaries are themselves part and parcel of the urban commons; imaginary acts provide a common wealth of political values and visions.

Jessica Berman argues that "communities come into being to a large extent in the kinds of stories of connection we have been told or are able to tell about ourselves" (2001, p. 3). The particular power of such stories, she suggests, is that they can reinsert into political communities "the varieties of 'being-in-common' that are often relegated to the margins of the national discussion and . . . the kinds of voices, such as those often present within fictional narratives, that seem to speak outside of politics in general" (2001, p. 15). Like all forms of commoning, however, cultural acts are not by definition inclusive or desirous of imagining cities in which urban dwellers work in common with all; many urban imaginaries either celebrate private communities (whether consciously or unwittingly) or are pessimistic about the urban future in terms of togetherness and cohabitation. The chapters that follow, therefore, highlight both exclusionary and inclusive urban communities and spaces depicted in literature, comics, collective art acts, films, music, and photography. At the meeting place of these various cultural trajectories and imaginaries lies the city in common.

The interdisciplinary methodology employed by this book places it squarely within cultural studies. The nature and future of Latin American cultural studies has been the subject of some debate in recent years

(Beasley-Murray, 2010; Del Sarto, Ríos, & Trigo, 2004; Irwin & Szurmuk, 2012; McClennen, 2011; Richard, 2012), but it is my belief that a multi-disciplinary approach is the only way to capture the intertwined relationship between urban imaginaries, struggles over the commons, and the nature of political belonging in Argentina. Of course, as Nelly Richard has highlighted, interdisciplinarity runs the risk of producing "a pragmatic sum of reduced pieces of knowledge which, in their own partiality and diversification, adapt obediently to the divided nature of the functional crossovers between globalization, multi-culturalism, fragmentation, post-modernism and neoliberalism" (2012, p. 169). Nevertheless, though many of the texts discussed in what follows are in tension with each other in terms of the way that they respond to urban life, they are drawn together precisely by their engagement with the city and the different commons to be found there. In seeking out the links between very different kinds of texts, political philosophies, and urban history, I hope to avoid reproducing fragmentation and instead mobilize urban imaginaries into their own kind of commons.

Chapter 2

Dictatorship, Exclusion, and Remembering in Common

The film *Crónica de una fuga* (2006, dir. Adrián Caetano), which was based on Claudio Tamburrini's testimonial account of his experiences during the 1976–1983 dictatorship, relates the incarceration and escape of four detainees held by the military in the detention center known as Mansión Seré. Much of the film is concerned with highlighting the brutality of the military regime, emphasizing the exceptional nature of violence during this period of judicial exception, that is, a period in which the constitution is temporarily suspended. The film intensifies the exceptionality of torture by highlighting day-to-day elements that frame the violence of the dictatorship: the guards watching a World Cup game on television; the everyday activities that carry on in streets and houses; the game of football in which the protagonist is participating before his capture. These everyday activities do not represent what the dictatorship is not or offer a space that is external to the dictatorship. They are part and parcel of the way the period was normalized even within its exceptionality. Thus the apparent extraordinary nature of the period is overturned in a sequence that strikes at the heart of the urban experience during the dictatorship: Having escaped the building in which they are being held prisoner, the detainees make their way through the grounds and scale the perimeter fence. With their hands bound and their naked bodies exposed to the raging storm, they drop over the other side of the fence to find themselves on a built-up street. Failing to stop a bus by chasing it down the middle of the street, they look up to see a man in a suit getting out of his car. For a moment, the escapees and the businessman stare at each other, each exposed to the implications of discovery. Then the man nods to them from under his umbrella and the naked men scuttle off down the road.

This brief scene epitomizes a number of key points about the transformation of the city during the dictatorship. First, what appeared to be a space apart from the city—the detention center—is, in fact, located very much within it. The extensive vegetation of the grounds in which the building is located suggests that the house is in the country whereas, in fact, Mansión Seré was located on the boundary between Ituzaingó and Castelar, two suburbs of the city. Second, that the detention center is a former 19th-century mansion taken over by the military symbolizes the way that private, domestic spaces were reconfigured and appropriated by the repressive state. Finally, the businessman's reaction to the four naked bodies with hands tied standing in the middle of a road in a storm demonstrates how quickly he is able to assimilate what appears to be extraordinary into his urban landscape.

The last Argentine military dictatorship reconfigured the city in common in a number of long-lasting and far-reaching ways. Future chapters are inscribed by other ways in which the dictatorship transformed the city's future, such as problematizing the nation as a site for the commons, or laying the foundations for a neoliberal model that made consumption into the privileged site of the commons. But the dictatorship also made both the exception (in a legal sense) and the exceptional (what is extraordinary) commonplace. That is to say, the military made the paradigm of the exception the common ground around which citizenship, social relations, and urban life were constructed. This refashioned commons was based on the principal of the common enemy, an internal—rather than external—threat to a restricted and restrictive set of values based around a capitalist-Christian worldview. As a result, the commons of the dictatorship was one based on the principal of exclusion, creating a city in which sites of encounter were turned into sites of estrangement and distrust. It is easy to forget, therefore, that the businessman's reaction to the naked men in *Crónica de una fuga* should shock us not because he does not turn them in but because he does nothing to help them.

Despite the fact that the dictatorship transformed the nature of the city in common, Buenos Aires prior to 1976 was not an idyllic space of inclusion, and the kinds of transformations that took place under military rule certainly had their origins in pre-dictatorship history. The ideological rift of the Cold War, later intensified by the 1959 Cuban Revolution, combined with the divisive nature of Peronism, meant that after 1946 the "common" nature of Buenos Aires had been fought over in increasingly violent confrontations between and within Peronists and anti-Peronists. More important, one impact of the Peronist era was to transform the city itself into *the means* to express particular political standpoints: on the one hand, the military asserted their authority by physically invading hostile spaces, as they did in 1966 when, under the dictatorship of General Juan Carlos Onganía, they used brutal force to overturn a sit-in by students and faculty members at several faculties of the Universidad de Buenos Aires, an event that came to be known as "La noche de los bastones largos" (Night of the Long Sticks); on the other hand, students, workers, and, increasingly, armed left-wing militants saw the ideological struggle as one to be expressed, in contrast to Ernesto "Che" Guevara's theory of the rural-based "foco," via the urban, symbolized, for example, by the 1969 insurrection in the city of Córdoba, known as the "Cordobazo."[1]

The manner in which the dictatorship turned the exceptional into the everyday is clearly captured in Martín Kohan's 2002 novel *Dos veces junio* (Twice June). Published some 25 years after the start of the dictatorship and at a time of intense political upheaval, Kohan's novel was written following 2 decades of intense public debate over the most productive way to address the traumatic past. *Dos veces junio* turns away from the memory politics adopted by human rights groups during the 1980s and 1990s by freeing itself from the demands of testimony. Instead, the novel addresses the way the dictatorship transformed the exceptional into a commons by focusing on two recurring representations of the period, torture and disappearance, and the everyday experience of the exception. *Dos veces junio* draws these diverse experiences together to emphasize the commonplace nature of evil and the way that the "common man" assimilates the exceptional. If Kohan's novel demonstrates how the dictatorship made the exceptional ordinary, then other cultural practices in the post-dictatorship period used the everyday city to create an inclusive memory commons. The use of silhouettes in public art events in the 1980s and the call for an end to impunity enacted in the 1990s by the *escrache*, a form of popular street justice, were in some ways very different practices, not least because the latter was partly based on the mobilization of the local as a means to ostracize former perpetrators who had escaped justice. But both shared the desire to put bodies in space and to use the city to enact a memory politics that brings together the figure of the disappeared, other victims, family and friends, and wider urban society as part of the formation of a memory that is not collective so much as one that is constantly formed and reformed in common.

Spaces of Exception and Common Enemies

The 1976–1983 dictatorship was a state of exception, a suspension of the law that is notionally designed to uphold the law. As Giorgio Agamben has famously argued, during the state of exception *homo sacer*, his term for the figure of nonpolitical existence, can be sacrificed without consequence, an extra-legal act that means *homo sacer* is included within the polis even in the moment of its very exclusion (1998, p. 11). The detention centers during the dictatorship encapsulate this precarious positioning—despite their apparent exceptionality as spaces apart from the city, they were also turned into commonplace elements of urban life. Inside, inmates were *homines sacri*, subject to death (or disappearance) without consequence, a point epitomized by the military's proclamation to prisoners that "we are God" or their efforts to prevent suicide since that would have wrested away from them the Godlike control over death (Calveiro, 1998, pp. 54–55). The brutality of torture and rape was accompanied by techniques designed to further defamiliarize the space of incarceration, such as blindfolding prisoners and leading them on different routes around the prison to enhance disorientation. But at the same time, the detention center was also made disconcertingly banal and everyday: One detained militant, for example, was told by the officer who had murdered her husband that she need not worry as he had personally taken care to find a home for their pets (Di Tella, 1999, p. 98). Other prisoners expressed confusion over these bizarre introductions of the mundane: "I found myself talking to a torturer, the very one who tortured me, not about torture but about his family, the problems his son was having at school" (quoted in Di Tella, 1999, p. 85). And many detainees who were released put their survival down to the ability to engage in the everyday life and routines of the camp, with some inmates forced to "work" as mechanics, secretaries, or librarians.

Detention centers also formed part of what Hugo Vezzetti called the dictatorship's "geography of horror" (2002, p. 175). In Capital Federal alone there were over 50 sites directly connected to detention and/or torture, a little over one per *barrio*, illustrative of how the city had become saturated with such spaces (Memoria Abierta, 2013). Located within the heart of the city, prisoners have spoken of being able to watch the legs of pedestrians passing outside, and those outside later admitted to hearing the screams of tortured inmates. The proximity between detention center and city was exaggerated by the constant threat of detention and torture. Some have spoken of how the city beyond the detention center was transformed after the arrest and/or disappearance of their family or friends: "I could be in a very familiar place, like the corner of my street, and suddenly not recognize where I was" (cited in Di Tella, 1999, p. 103); "I had a friend who was detained in the street because they wanted to know who she was looking at and why. After that, I didn't have the courage to look at people in the street" (cited in Di Tella, 1999, p. 104). The transformation of the city was further intensified by the military's project to make domestic life part of their wider national, public project. Positing the family as the basic unit of the nation and the principal site of moral education (Filc, 1997), the regime presented itself as the upstanding father to a wayward, childlike citizenship. The family thus became an entity entirely subject to the public sphere, a point reinforced by the frequent raids on private residences in the name of antisubversion. Such instances of forced entry might be considered highly private events (Robben, 2000, p. 70), but it is worth remembering that even if 64 percent of arrests resulting in disappearance took place in the home (CONADEP, 2003, p. 17), such arrests were frequently highly "public." In extreme cases, megaphones, grenades, and firearm discharges were used, but even the forced removal of victims into cars parked on the street meant that, as Marguerite Feitlowitz puts it, "lots of Argentines saw kidnappings and knew perfectly well what they were witnessing" (1998, p. 151). Thus, though it went to great lengths to hide the mechanics, the documentation and the testimony of torture and disappearance, the military often took few pains to hide the moment of arrest and the threat of detention. As Pilar Calveiro argues, the camp was hardly a space of exception but was rather "perfectly installed at the center of society" (1998, p. 86).

That the city was itself a space of exception, subject to martial law and following a similar conceptual framework to the camp (at least in theory if not in practice), supports Agamben's argument that *homo sacer* is the archetypal citizen of a space in which the exception has become all pervasive. As such, he leads us toward the nature of the commons that resulted from the state-of-exception city. In such a city, enemies are internal, not external. They are individuals who are harder to identify than uniformed soldiers. As a result, your neighbors are always potential subversives (just as you are to them). In his discussion of the way that tyrants and pirates have always functioned as disruptive forces *within* modernity, Jon Beasley-Murray has called this figure the "common enemy" (2005, p. 220), and he demonstrates how such enemies threaten to reshape the commons itself by putting forward "a form of countercommonality that is also an adventurous experiment in community" (2005, p. 223). The dictatorship tried to arrest the formation of such potential countercommonality by transforming the commons into a shared site of exclusion. The consequence was a cityscape in which it was no longer clear who was your friend and who your enemy, not just because "the state starts treating its citizens as potential enemies, as outsiders" (Diken & Laustsen, 2005, p. 19), but also because citizens treated other citizens as potential enemies. The attempt to fashion subversives as nonnational outsiders had the effect, in practice, of constructing a commons based on exclusion because individuals were worried about the potential danger of acting in common with others. The dictatorship made the city in common an exclusionary project, characterized by suspicious encounters and estrangement. As a space of exception, therefore, the dictatorship city limited the expansive potential of life in common, preventing the possibility for constructing alternative urban communities. Not so much an anticommons as an example of the aforementioned "exclusionary commons," the dictatorship employed disappearance not to disappear the commons but simply to limit it to a particular vision of national belonging. They turned the exceptional into a common experience and a common site of belonging. Both within and beyond the detention center, by making the extra-ordinary "ordinary," the paradigm of the exception itself became a commons.

The ordinary nature of the dictatorship can also be seen in the way it handled major architectural projects and urban planning. On the one hand, the dictatorship established and sustained the aforementioned "geography of horror," an urban network of detention centers and military substations around which the institutionalization of disappearance could be based. Such a geography was accompanied by other, less brutal but nonetheless militaristic transformations of the city, such as the 1979–1980 redesign of the Plaza Dr. Bernardo H. Houssay in front of the Facultad de Medicina of the Universidad de Buenos Aires. The changes to the Plaza Houssay have often been taken as typifying the dictatorship's architectural vision—the introduction of benches, walls, and raised flowerbeds made the square less conducive for public gatherings and easier for state forces to control from the streets that form its edge.

On the other hand, as Graciela Silvestri has argued, to focus merely on such obvious military projects is to ignore a raft of other, much larger urban redesign projects undertaken during the dictatorship (2000). Thus the "geography of horror" must be seen as merely part of the dictatorship's wider urban vision, which included projects designed to increase the number of green spaces in the city, such as the construction of the park that now makes up the Club de Amigos in Palermo, or the ecological belt running from Tigre in the north to La Plata in the south. Such projects demonstrate the breadth of the dictatorship's urban vision, which went from transforming mansions into torture centers to creating green spaces that encouraged public recreation, exercise, and fresh air. Both, albeit in different ways, were designed to create a "healthy" citizenship, enhancing the physical well-being of a body politic threatened by the cancer of subversion, a central trope in the discourse of the dictatorship (Filc, 1997, p. 39). The dictatorship could lay further claim to the promotion of order and cleanliness since the green belt itself was built using urban waste as landfill. As a result, the dictatorship's overarching urban vision, under the command of Brigadier Osvaldo Cacciatore, the municipal governor of Buenos Aires during the dictatorship, was one of cleanliness and order, what Oscar Oszlak called "la ciudad blanca" (the white city) (1982). Despite their differences, therefore, the redesign of the Plaza Houssay and the creation of a green belt were coherent and complementary projects that attempted to build and protect a citizenship from what it perceived as threatening ideologies. More than that, however, they demonstrate the complex and far-reaching ways in which the city in common was based on the "ordinariness" of the state of exception as much as its extraordinary nature. The resulting transformation of the city created an environment in which, by assimilating the quotidian nature of the exception, urban dwellers were turned against each other, an assimilation captured in Martín Kohan's novel, *Dos veces junio*.

Times Like These

Narrated by an army conscript, *Dos veces junio* relates a young man's experiences of the dictatorship working as a staff driver for a medical officer, Doctor Mesiano, who is involved in the abduction and adoption of a baby born to a prisoner in a clandestine detention center. Set in Buenos Aires, the novel is divided into two parts: the first part takes place during the 1978 World Cup and the second during the 1982 Falklands/Malvinas conflict. Writer and critic Alan Pauls (2008) has suggested that these famous events were the two great "fictions" of the military dictatorship and that their fictional qualities gave them great potential as narratives of the common, tapping into longstanding and shared passions over national identity.[2] The dictatorship was confronted with the impossible task of reconciling a discourse of national unity with an ideology of exclusion and institutionalized disappearance (Scorer, 2008). The military saw staging national events of football and war as offering the potential to sit beyond entrenched and divisive ideologies, providing them with the means to promote themselves as guarantors of security, order, progress, and national pride. In contrast to the insurrectional gatherings of the

1960s and 1970s, for example, the crowds cheering Argentina's World Cup victory in 1978 could be presented as a symbol of a unified nation, as the words spoken by historian Félix Luna in Sergio Renán's celebratory 1979 film *La fiesta de todos* (A Celebration for All) demonstrate: "These delirious, clean and united crowds are the closest thing I've seen in my life to a mature, formed people, pulsating with a common feeling without anyone feeling defeated or marginalized and, perhaps for the first time in this country, without the happiness of some meaning the sadness of others." The quote is chilling not only because of the disparity between such euphoria and the reality of what was also taking place in Argentina, but also in the way the language of cleanliness and uniformity is used to sanction these public gatherings.

In *Dos veces junio* one urban and architectural focal point that inscribed such a sense of unity is El Monumental, the tournament's centerpiece stadium, the light of which, the novel ominously reminds us, illuminates the adjacent Federal Firing Range (Kohan, 2002, p. 59). El Monumental itself mirrored the dictatorship's urban vision, not just because its capacity of 80,000 highlighted the power of technological construction and engineering but also because it was designed to play a role in the development of a healthy citizenry—the empty spaces beneath the huge columns that supported the bowl-style seating area were transformed into basketball courts and gymnasiums. The stadium was just one way in which the dictatorship promoted a particular urban vision via the World Cup; innovations in design (evident in the official World Cup logo and poster) and virtual networks of communication (the introduction of color television and the creation of Argentina Televisora Color [ATC]), for example, both contributed to the progressive and modernizing image of Argentina (Silvestri, 2000, pp. 40–41). Technological progress, order, and urban health were, of course, the face of a highly selective urban geography: Stadiums for the tournament were located in only five of the 23 Argentine provinces, and the only two chosen in Buenos Aires, El Monumental and Vélez Sársfield, were located in affluent neighborhoods. The regime also took pains to hide urban poverty near the stadiums, building a wall painted with a façade of houses along the main road to Rosario to hide informal dwellings from the visiting public and bulldozing a shantytown in the neighborhood of Belgrano near El Monumental.[3]

Kohan's careful choice of World Cup matches, furthermore, is a reminder of the precariousness and ultimate failure of the tournament in terms of national unity. In the epilogue, the references to Argentina's 1–2 loss to Italy in the 1982 World Cup fly in the face of the claim by the foreign correspondent in Spain that "we are now more united than ever" (p. 187), instead highlighting how the dictatorship's national project collapsed in the wake of the defeat in the Malvinas war. In the first part of the novel, the narrator is sent to El Monumental to look for Doctor Mesiano during Argentina's 0–1 loss to Italy in 1978. The celebratory streets full of fans prior to the game contrast with the funereal march of those returning home after the defeat. The city returns to a state of silent hostility as those leaving the stadium are marshaled by the military and instructed about where they can and cannot walk as they head home.

What makes the novel so striking, however, is the way the characters move effortlessly between the semblance of national togetherness and the concurrent acts of torture. Football and torture are depicted as intertwined elements of an entire vision. When Mesiano puts his nefarious work to one side for a moment to argue passionately that leaving Maradona out of the squad was a grave mistake (p. 82), he demonstrates how the everyday sits alongside rather than in contrast to the exceptional. Likewise, when the narrator waits outside the stadium for the shouts that would greet an Argentine goal, his use of the word "grito" (cry) (p. 60) is simultaneously suggestive of both shouts of joy and of screams of pain resulting from torture. Likewise, the narrator's discussion of the relative merits and disadvantages of the Ford Falcon he chauffeurs is entirely disconnected from its role within the dictatorship (p. 29). For him, the Ford Falcon is a functional element in his job, a car that he must keep clean and drive efficiently. In the epilogue, set during 1982, the narrator visits Doctor Mesiano to pay his respects after he learns that the doctor's son was killed in the war.[4] Once again the narrator turns to the Ford Falcon, making no mention of the fact that this was the military's car of choice when carrying out kidnappings, a role that has made it almost shorthand for the dictatorship. Instead, he simply admires how the old car is still going strong before sharing a joke with the doctor about how he used to struggle to find first gear.[5]

Kohan's choice of a civilian conscript as the protagonist of the novel, one who joins the armed forces for a fixed term as a result of the state lottery and not because of political ideology or military careerism, exaggerates his ordinariness as a citizen. That he is never named in the novel only emphasizes his lack of individuality, and this anonymity is one difference Kohan's novel has with Luis Gusmán's novel *Villa* (2006), first published in 1995, a work with which *Dos veces junio* otherwise has much in common. Perhaps the first cultural vision to portray the ordinary horror of the 1970s in Argentina, *Villa* relates the experience of a medic who becomes complicit with the illicit practices of the Triple A during the government of Isabel Perón (1974–1976). Despite his collusion with practices of disappearance and torture, the protagonist Villa never acknowledges to himself either what is happening or that he is involved, focusing instead on his desire to act as a "mosca" (fly), a man with no more ambition than to serve someone. Both novels narrate the ordinariness of evil without narrative judgment, and Kohan stated that while writing he was handed a copy of Hannah Arendt's *Eichmann in Jerusalem* and that he wanted to think particularly about a character who "has no weight on his conscience, who doesn't have the responsibility of being a torturer, doesn't feel himself a torturer, and at the same time doesn't form an organic part of the repressive forces and doesn't have an ideological formation" (Costa, 2004).

While he acknowledged his debt to Arendt, whose work was subtitled "A Report on the Banality of Evil," Kohan also stated in an interview held after the publication of his novel that, while writing *Dos veces junio*, he had not allowed himself to read any literature written in Spanish, "above all Argentine literature, for reasons to do with contagious forms of language" (Costa, 2004). Though Kohan's own citation of *Villa* in *Dos veces junio* is enough to call into question his claim, the observation is a reminder of the importance Kohan gave to language when writing the novel. The shocking question with which *Dos veces junio* begins—"from what age can you start to torture a child?" (p. 11), a real question cited by a former inmate during the post-dictatorship trial of the military—is horrific both because of the matter-of-fact manner in which the military accept the normality of the question and because, when the narrator first sees the question jotted in a desk notebook, he is bothered not by the question itself but rather by a spelling mistake made by the desk sergeant ("empesar" for "empezar"). The narrator is so disturbed by the breakdown of literacy that he takes the trouble—and the risk, since the sergeant is a superior officer—of correcting the offending letter. From the very beginning of the novel, therefore, Kohan places language center stage by using a genuine question drawn from trial testimony and then rewriting (and then correcting that rewritten question) to emphasize the layered nature of fictional language in an historical novel.

Kohan's choice of a narrator who is complicit in the mechanics of the dictatorship and his interest in the fictional, linguistic nature of relating the dictatorship distances *Dos veces junio* from most other texts that were being published about the dictatorship during the 1990s and the turn of the new millennium. Writing after a decade of intense testimonial production, Kohan indicated that he could not write from the point of view of a victim because that "takes place necessarily through the testimonial register," which he could not offer because "I didn't live that period and I don't have anything to provide testimony about" (Costa, 2004). Instead of relying on testimony, Kohan was writing a kind of "prosthetic memory" (Landsberg, 2004), by which memories from the sociocultural sphere are appropriated and deployed by those who did not live the original experience.[6] That use of fiction itself creates a kind of memory commons, in the sense that memories of the dictatorship are here moved beyond their immediate possessors and become a means of exploring not just the traumatic past but also the nature of silent collusion within any overarching power structure.

Even before the publication of *Dos veces junio* Kohan had argued that literature does not approach history to build "a more immediate representation of the real but, on the contrary, as a means of accentuating the mediation" (2000, p. 245). Kohan's comments on fiction have a great deal in common with Juan José Saer's 1995 affirmation that testimony had little place in his understanding of fiction, which is located between history and myth: "The objective [of fiction] is not to reinstate or interpret history but rather to create a mythic dimension that has value in all times and places" (quoted in Corbatta, 1999, p. 69). Indeed, and despite Kohan's supposed precautions about not reading literature in Spanish, *Dos veces junio* clearly echoes Saer's 1993 novel *Lo imborrable* (The Indelible), not just in its shared concern with narrative realism and the relationship between fiction, history, and politics, but also linguistically, specifically via the language of euphemism. Set in the city of Santa Fé under military rule, *Lo imborrable* relates Carlos Tomatis's attempts to overcome the repressive regime, his collapsed marriage, and his alcoholism. Though *Lo imborrable* "works against the naturalized perception of political history," that does not mean that it does not also "decide the sense of what is narrated according to a social interpretation of the effects of state terrorism on the itineraries of individual subjectivity" (Dalmaroni & Merbilhaá, 2000, p. 340). In that sense, *Lo imborrable* demonstrates how the dictatorship affects Tomatis's personal life. His marriage collapses after the disappearance of Tacuara, a girl from his neighborhood who takes refuge in their house; when his wife asks her to leave, Tacuara is promptly disappeared from the street outside.[7] The brutality, as Miguel Dalmaroni and Margarita Merbilhaá suggest, is not just that the girl is disappeared but also that Tomatis is so enraged that he throws a glass at his wife (2000, p. 340). The exceptionality of Tacuara's kidnapping seeps into the private life of

Tomatis's marriage and, subsequently, his entire urban landscape. He feels, for example, that the neon figure advertising the Hotel Conquistador is watching him (p. 187), illustrative of how the city has become a space of oppression and vigilance, in which guilt precedes the crime. Noting the city's empty streets, Tomatis highlights how the city has become ghostly (p. 236), a memory of itself even as it is experienced, transformed into an old photograph discovered at the back of a drawer (p. 224). The city is thus made strange—it is a disappeared city. The fear engendered by that city leads Tomatis to reflect on the dangers of "the common man":

> The neighbor that gets us out of a tight spot when we're out of garlic or flour at dinner time, is perhaps the very same that insults us anonymously over the telephone in the small hours, and the shopkeeper who gives us a special deal because our children go to the same school might be a police informer. It's precisely what is common about the common man that one has to distrust. (p. 26)

Thus in this dictatorship city, which has become a space emptied of trust, it is precisely the common that has been transformed, turned into a sphere of uncertainty and mistrust. Not just using the rhetoric of realism to undo our confidence in being able to represent the real (Prieto, 2006, p. 415), Saer uses the normality of the unreal to exaggerate its very palpable impact on the city. The city cannot erase the disappearance that haunts it; neither, in a conclusion that highlights how the dictatorship affects everyday life, can Tomatis persist with abstaining from alcohol, to which he returns on the novel's final page as both a metaphor for and a material consequence of the "dark times" in which he lives.

Saer's novel self-consciously explores such metaphorical, euphemistic language from the very start of the book: ". . . of someone who, for example, in some wasteland, one morning, they find castrated, with his own testicles in his mouth, his body riddled with bullets, showing evident signs of torture, they say with sublime discretion that he had problems" (pp. 17–18). The normalization of the abnormal via euphemism highlights how language as a commons was transformed during the dictatorship, and several scholars have demonstrated how the dictatorship introduced an entirely new set of language, from the euphemisms of the world of the detention center to public speeches and national discourse (Calveiro, 1998; Feitlowitz, 1998). The internalization of this discourse is both a transformation of the language commons and, subsequently, of the commons built through language. In *Lo imborrable*, however, euphemism is also resisted via a kind of dysphemistic euphemism, such that overly dramatic words are used for ordinary situations: When Tomatis's ex-wife prevents him from seeing their daughter, he calls it "a kidnapping" (p. 51), and his friend Alfonso offers him a lift with the words "get in, get in, we're kidnapping you" (p. 192). These instances of irony and humor on the part of Tomatis and Alfonso act as a form of resistance to that dominant appropriation of language, a reappropriation that dismantles the mechanics of the dictatorship's urban commons.

Similar explorations of euphemism in *Dos veces junio*, therefore, mean that Kohan's novel cannot be so simply categorized as being "far from obliqueness, fragmentation or allegorical encoding" and an attempt "to open the possibility of narrating with *complete*, and *direct*, reference to the most atrocious or un-narratable events" (Dalmaroni, 2003, p. 34). It also has some commonalities with pre-1995 work by writers such as Ricardo Piglia and Saer, who precisely explore ways of narrating the dictatorship via "strategies of rewriting (quotation, montage, parody, etc.), of (to a greater or lesser extent) allegorical encoding, or through textual work with the unspoken (voids, silence, incompletion or dismantling the meaning of representation)" (Dalmaroni, 2003, pp. 30–31). Not only does *Dos veces junio* begin with an example of rewriting it also intertwines military euphemism with direct, realist narrative language.

Nevertheless, although both novels use language to illustrate how the characters assimilate the exceptional into everyday life, highlighting how the city is turned into a space of exceptionality and exclusion, euphemism in *Dos veces junio* is never humorous or a means of resistance but part of the state machine. It is apt, then, that Kohan should also use the same phrase that Tomatis so often uses when referring to the dictatorship in *Lo imborrable*: "los días que corren" (times like these). As the narrator of *Dos veces junio* states, "en *los días que corrían* los errores se pagaban muy caro" (in times like those you paid dearly for your mistakes) (p. 35; emphasis added). Ambiguous language in Kohan's novel, therefore, sustains the dictatorship, whether in the advice given to the narrator by his father that "your superior is always right, particularly when he's not" (p. 16) or in Mesiano's reference to rape as "no-one should make use of the detainee" (p. 28).

The simultaneous levels of meaning that language carries in *Dos veces junio* means that the question about the age from which you can torture a child is not just a question about whether the military can torture a baby in front of its mother to force the latter to divulge information, but also, in the scheme of the novel, a question that hides whether, instead of torturing the baby, they can add it to the clandestine list of children put forward for illegal adoption. Certainly the sergeant's subsequent euphemistic rephrasing of the question—"from what age can you first proceed with a child?" (p. 25)—indicates unease with the brutality of the phrase (though not the torture), but it is the narrator himself who emphasizes that the whole dilemma should be treated as "a technical question" (p. 21), before the soldiers embark on a process of reasoned discussion over the correct answer. Just as the description of soldiers cold-bloodedly discarding the placenta of the inmate who has given birth is immediately followed by an anecdote about hair growing on the palms of someone who masturbates too much, it is the ordinariness with which suffering is dealt with and talked of that makes it so shocking. In particular, the structure of the text—short, numbered sections divided up within chapters that frequently alternate between different narrative elements—juxtaposes the horrific nature of the dictatorship (the prisoner's birth) with cold military reason (the obsession with the grammatical mistake). Doctor Mesiano's resolution to the question is particularly ruthless. Age is irrelevant, he says; as every medical student should know, what is important is the child's weight.

The cold, rational answer provided by Mesiano depersonalizes the brutality and emphasizes the importance of numbers to the dictatorship's desired order and hierarchy. The novel's two sections are dates expressed as numbers, and all the chapters except one are numbers, each referring to a fact included in the story, such as 25 million (the approximate population of Argentina in 1978) or 128 (a reference to the car driven by the narrator's father—a Fiat 128). The chapter entitled "Mil novecientos setenta y ocho" (Nineteen Seventy Eight) alternates between the narrative and various lists based on the Argentine World Cup football team noting, in turn, the surnames, names, positions, club, shirt number, date of birth, and height and weight of the players one by one. These purposeless listings highlight a need for order that goes no further than the act of ordering itself. Numbers can be of great significance, such as the raffle number that dictates where the narrator will do his military service, but they can also be beyond meaning. Thus, the one number always associated with the dictatorship, 30,000, is tellingly absent, as if the number itself did no justice to the disappeared and is, therefore, senseless. The tension between order and the meaningless of numerical chaos mirrors the wider conflict in the novel between order and disorder, expressed by Doctor Mesiano's belief that "two forces collided in the formation of Argentina: one chaotic, irregular, disordered, that of the Montoneras; the other systematic, regular, planned, that of the army" (pp. 37–38).[8] Thus, the military's desire for rules and an unquestioning hierarchy creates a machine in which each figure works as an unthinking cog that collectively renders numbers meaningless—the only chapter that does not carry a number for its title is called "S/N" (No number) and is set in the detention center where a militant and her baby are being held prior to the latter being smuggled out and given new parents, stripped of its past life.

The military's concern with order is also evident in urban terms, particularly in the chapter entitled "Cinco" (Five), in which the narrator drives Mesiano to the detention center in Quilmes. Though all the neighborhoods appear to belong to the same city, inhabitants from each individual neighborhood know that "being born this side of the avenue is not the same as being born on that side" (p. 98). But the importance of boundaries, frontiers, and distinctions for the military has little to do with urban identities but rather with an imposed, jurisdictional authority (p. 99). Going through the city becomes a jurisdictional question: Mesiano deliberately uses cars because cars manage boundaries better than trains. Crossing borders is the prerogative of those privileged few who are "authorized to move from one side to another, because they can travel and make transfers" (p. 102). The euphemism "transfer" (traslado) refers to the unlawful killing of detainees during the dictatorship and is a reminder of the geographical dimension of disappearance.

The sociospatial order that is imposed on urban life by the military is reflected in the novel's exploration of gender politics under dictatorship. Women in *Dos veces junio* predominantly fulfill the role of mothers and wives or serve to reinforce the narratives men tell about themselves. Following the defeat that takes place during the first part of the novel, Mesiano takes the narrator and his son to a brothel. The prostitute who sleeps with the narrator tells him, when he insists on knowing her real name, that she does not have one, a symbol for the manner in which she has no identity of her own in this encounter but simply helps him to fulfill his own fantasy. The two of them watch pornographic films, one in which a husband and his friend punish a woman for sleeping with the latter (p. 98), and another in which a group of soldiers rape a woman after she flags them down to help with a punctured bicycle tire (p. 104). With their emphasis on marking the body (the husband's friend in the first film states the wife's body will remind her of her "punishment" even if she wants to forget) and sexual violence, the films encourage the narrator to act out his own fantasy of power with the prostitute. Even though he states that almost everything in the brothel is "pure artifice," he notes that the naked body of the prostitute remains very real (p. 99), and he ties her up so that she genuinely cannot escape, enabling him to act out a rape scene that results in him having his "best night" (p. 107). The chapter is partly a critique, therefore, of how the narrator is blind to the gender inequalities on which the dictatorship is based and which he reproduces. But it is also, since the entire encounter with the prostitute is interspersed with the reflections over mapping and geographical jurisdictions, a reminder of how those gender inequalities are reproduced in spatial terms: Following the description of the narrator's climax, the chapter ends with Mesiano's reflection on the hierarchy of Argentine politics—Quilmes is governed by La Plata, and La Plata by Capital Federal.

It is no accident, therefore, that the detainee around which the plot revolves is a woman, since it is the trope of the tortured mother, stripped of a child who is also nearly tortured and who is eventually illegally adopted, that highlights the twisted nature of the dictatorship's narrative of the family as commons. There are hints of resistance to the dictatorship in *Dos veces junio*; during the first football match, for example, one man pretends to listen to the game on his radio headphones while in fact he listens to classical music. But such minor signs of resistance are never enacted by the narrator himself, who continues to assimilate the extraordinary commons of the dictatorship. In the epilogue, during which the reader learns that Doctor Mesiano stole the tortured prisoner's baby to give it to his sister for adoption, the narrator uses both the name given to the kidnapped boy by his birth mother (which he learns from her in the detention center) and the name given to him by his adopted mother: "She waits a bit and calls again, this time almost with a shout: 'Antonio!' A boy with brown hair, whose name is Guillermo, pops out and asks what the matter is" (p. 178). No expression of judgment or remorse accompanies this blatant acknowledgment of what took place—he simply reflects that when "Antonio" does not respond to his name being called it was "as if they weren't calling him" (p. 185). The only memory of that night that returns to him comes in the form of a dream about the prostitute he slept with 4 years earlier, a dream that simply expresses his desire for this fantasy to be real (p. 188). Stripped of remorse, the epilogue demonstrates the narrator's ability to naturalize the extraordinary, namely his refusal to help the woman in the clandestine detention center when she gives him the telephone number of a lawyer and asks him to let her family know where she is being held. In the only moment in the novel when the narrator loses his dispassionate calm, reflecting precisely his recent desire for violence in the simulated rape with the prostitute, he swears at her angrily and tells her, "I'm going to shut your mouth with my fist, you bitch," before adding finally, "can't you see you're already dead." In the epilogue, that moment of furious panic is replaced by the return to the narrator's passive voice. He says farewell to Mesiano, embracing him and offering his support for the difficult times ahead, tragically accepting the dictatorship in the same fashion that had previously enabled him to state with careful consideration 4 years earlier, that the age when you can begin to torture a child is simply "from the moment when the Fatherland requires it" (p. 26).

Dos veces junio is an ominous reading of the dictatorship, one that uses fiction to turn what is well known and make it strange. In that sense, Kohan undoes the dictatorship's treatment of the commons: If the military made of the exceptional and the exclusionary the basis of common life, Kohan takes the common, shared narrative of the dictatorship and makes it strange precisely by using an exaggeratedly ordinary narrator and matter-of-fact style, unsettling established narratives. For that reason, *Dos veces junio* is almost clichéd in the subject matter it addresses, using two major national events and infamous symbols of the dictatorship such as kidnapping babies and Ford Falcons. Far from addressing anything new, Kohan takes what we already know and makes it strange to highlight how the exceptional and the commonplace are intertwined. In a more recent study of Walter Benjamin's urban imaginary, Kohan describes how the German philosopher makes Berlin—the city Benjamin knows best— strange precisely so that he can lose himself within that city and therefore get to know it better (2007, pp. 29–30). Kohan takes a similar approach in *Dos veces junio*: The more specific the descriptions and directions become, the more unfamiliar and strange Buenos Aires becomes. Buenos Aires thus becomes uncanny, a city caught between the exceptional and the ordinary, between the exclusionary and the inclusive.

Remembering in Common

Kohan's treatment of Buenos Aires under dictatorship emphasizes how the city was made strange by the transformation of the commons. Memory politics in the post-dictatorship era continued the work of resisting the transformation that had begun during the dictatorship itself. Building on the way the Madres de la Plaza de Mayo put bodies in spaces as a marker of presence in the urban landscape, cultural memory practices in the

1980s and 1990s further demonstrated how participants in urban protest could use the city to remember in common. A productive memory politics is crucial to any attempt to aggregate a society in the wake of a social conflict, a means of avoiding Nietzsche's "festering wound" that emerges when collective trauma is not processed in the public sphere (Wood, 1999, p. 199). When this process of "working through" is solely appropriated by official state memory, the difficulty of establishing state responsibility for previous regimes is clear, since the state exists as both a continuous entity and a series of separate administrations (Jelin, 2003, p. 103).[9] As a result, during the post-dictatorship period it was non-state bodies and practices that refashioned the city via processes of remembering in common since, unlike the state, they were not reliant on collective memory, which has a tendency to drift toward sameness.

Memories are always impossible to separate from their social and cultural context, but they are also inseparable from individual subjectivities. Elizabeth Jelin suggests that the ever-present antagonism between the individual and the collective, when understood "in institutional and citizenship terms . . . can be expressed as one between a broad notion of open universal citizenship and the persistence of a community of remembrance, one that is exclusive and closed onto itself" (2003, p. 104). That notion of a community of remembrance being "exclusive and closed onto itself" runs the risk of producing exclusive and exclusionary collective memories. An alternative to the choice between universal citizenship and enclosed communities of remembrance, therefore, might be found in the idea of a memory in common, individual memories that work together to construct a community of remembrance that is never enclosed or finite or even consensual but that creates a shared sphere of remembering. Taking memory itself as a commons, a means of accessing, interpreting, and reshaping a set of narratives about the past, the focus is turned away from a commons based on objects of memory around which collective identity can be constructed, and toward the action of *remembering*. That is to say, the objective of memory processes should not be what Andreas Huyssen terms "collective consensual memory" (2003, p. 17) but rather the process of remembering in common with other members of a community. Working through conflicting views of the past can, in this sense, also bring citizens together even in their disagreement, a reminder of Jan Assmann's argument that "socialization is not just a foundation, but also a function of memory" (2006, p. 4).

Placed within the real context of remembering in post-dictatorship Argentina and the need for justice, whether institutional or otherwise, the tensions between the demands of very different parties with a vested interest in memory politics highlight the difficulties of calling for a consensual remembering. As a result, the debate over individual and collective memories links directly to post-dictatorship debates in Argentina over the "ownership" of the disappeared and the way their narratives can and should be mobilized. If for the military the disappeared did not belong to anyone because they perceived that following questionable ideologies meant forfeiting your right to be considered Argentine, then the Comisión Nacional para la Desaparición de Personas (CONADEP), which documented crimes perpetrated during the dictatorship and which published its findings in the 1984 work *Nunca más*, presented the disappeared as equivalent to wider Argentine society, victims of "a terror that came as much from the extreme right as from the extreme left" (2003, p. 7). In what came to be known as "la teoría de los dos demonios" (the theory of the two demons), *Nunca más* placed responsibility for disappearance with the military and the left-wing guerrillas, locating Argentine civil society as suffering bystanders and the disappeared as the silent victims of that civil society. As a result of constructing the disappeared as silent victims, *Nunca más*, much like the trial of the Junta Militar in 1985, focused on factual testimony, steering survivors away from any attempt to introduce narrative interpretations, impressions, and ideologies (Blejmar, 2012, pp. 22–23). As such, disappearance and the disappeared became fixed ciphers of an attempt to construct a collective memory that would allow the past to be left behind.

The wealth of testimonial accounts and cultural productions relating to the dictatorship that emerged over the course of the 1990s and the new millennium resulted in a more complex understanding of the disappeared. One key debate, which did not refer specifically to the disappeared but that informed debates about them, was the 2005 polemic sparked off by a letter written by Oscar del Barco for the magazine *La intemperie*. In response to a testimony by Hector Jouvé, in which the latter described the execution of one of his companions by fellow guerrillas in the 1960s, Del Barco affirmed that he felt partially responsible for the man's death. As an intellectual involved in militant networks, Del Barco argued that he had failed to uphold the maxim "you shall not kill," a position that garnered a number of vehement responses (*Journal of Latin American Cultural Studies*, 2007). The debate over Del Barco's statements not only brought the notion of a passive victimized public under serious scrutiny, highlighting the moral choices made by left-wing militants, but it also tapped into the "socialization" of the disappeared, since he assumed responsibility for the death of someone he had never met. This debate highlighted how the disappeared were not just victims but fellow partici- pants in a wider struggle.

More recently, cultural memory production in Argentina, much of it created by children of the disappeared, has been increasingly innovative, both in terms of content and form, and in the way it expresses the more active agency given to the disappeared within Argentine society (Blejmar, 2012; Blejmar, Fortuny, & García, 2013; Feld & Stites Mor, 2009). The visual forms of film and photography in particular have been central to these cultural struggles, not least because the photographic image embod- ies the ongoing presence of absence, a metaphor for the condition of the disappeared. Long used in public demonstrations, art exhibits, newspaper advertisements, and on the Internet, photographs of the disappeared from both family albums and identity cards symbolize the tension between the individual and collective nature of memory. Children of the disap- peared who work with images are often caught between representing their personal, familial memories and acknowledging the broader, social implications of their parents' lives. Whereas the family photograph can, as Marianne Hirsch points out, draw "borders around a circumscribed group . . . strengthening its power to include and thus also to exclude" (1997, p. 47), some artists have taken a different stance by problematizing the political vision of the family held by their parents, which dismantled any semblance of a private sphere by making children part of the revo- lutionary struggle. At the same time, the decision to share these artworks in the public sphere is itself a gesture that makes the private quest part of a wider community of remembering.

Debates over the "socialization" of the disappeared are key to many sites of memory and remembering in Buenos Aires. The Parque de la Memoria, for example, intended to commemorate those killed or disap- peared during the dictatorship, was originally to be located behind the Escuela Mecánica de la Armada (ESMA), the most well-known detention center run by the navy, and the Club de la Policía. Due to problems raised by the ESMA over access, the space eventually became a children's park, accessed by a road that the ESMA named Tamborcito de Tacuarí. This reference to the Battle of Tacuarí, which took place during the Argentine struggle for independence and in which a boy drummer roused the troops to an improbable victory, was, according to Graciela Silvestri, akin to "marrying children to the military" (1999, p. 44). Taking advantage of alterations being made to the nearby campus of Ciudad Universitaria, the municipal government decided to relocate the memory park, a move that indicated how the military still wielded significant authority over urban planning. Despite the park's removal to the edge of the city, such that the vast majority of visitors have to go out of their way to visit it, locating the site alongside the River Plate lent symbolic weight to the space because many of the disappeared found their final resting place in the river.

One of the most controversial aspects of the park when it was built was the proposed central avenue, which now cuts a zigzag through the center of the space. The suggestion of the scar and the void had similarities with Daniel Libeskind's Jewish Museum in Berlin, which incorporates both "slashes" in its external walls and inaccessible empty spaces within, the latter a metaphorical representation of the gap in Jewish history created by the Holocaust (Huyssen, 2003, pp. 105–106). Hebe de Bonafini, head of the Asociación Madres de Plaza de Mayo, protested strongly against the decision to engrave the walls of the submerged path with the names of the disappeared (Tappatá de Valdez, 2003, p. 107).[10] Arguing that engraving the names would draw attention away from the demand for justice and the search for those responsible for the crimes by memorializing and fixing the past (setting it in stone), the rejection typified the differing positions that had resulted in the 1986 split in the Madres de Plaza de Mayo into the Asociación Madres de Plaza de Mayo and the Madres de Plaza de Mayo Línea Fundadora. The core of the disagreement within the Madres was based on a difference in opinion over their task: whether to promote the claim "aparición con vida" (appearance with life) or to dedicate themselves to finding and identifying bodies. The Asociación Madres de Plaza de Mayo, demanding "aparición con vida," placed greater emphasis on bringing the perpetrators of the crimes to justice, arguing for the "socialization" of the disappeared, in which all the disappeared would be seen as children of the Madres beyond biological or familial ties. Emphasizing the commonality of the disappeared, the Asociación Madres de Plaza de Mayo highlighted that the disappeared are absent as much for the collective social body as the familial body. Cecilia Sosa (2014) has drawn attention to this tension between what she calls "bloodline normativity" and "the affective transmission of trauma," highlighting how memories can be produced, transmitted, and contested by protagonists who have no blood ties to direct victims of the military regime, similar to the way Kohan writes an assumed memory of the dictatorship in Dos veces junio. Memory practices in the post-dictatorship, therefore, highlighted the difficulty of constructing an inclusive commons around disappearance that would combat the legacy of the exclusionary commons and divisive mistrust established by the dictatorship.

That difficulty was only intensified by the fact that disappearance was not only evident in terms of absent bodies but also in the cityscape itself. During the dictatorship, for example, the famous Montevideo market located between Avenida Corrientes and Calle Sarmiento was leveled, an act that symbolized the regime's disregard for historical patrimony. Better known was the military's decision to proceed with the expansion of the city's motorway network to improve urban traffic flow, a move criticized for enforcing the relocation of those living where new flyovers were to be constructed. Intensifying the ties between these urban erasures and the geography of repression, in April 2002 excavations on Paseo Colón under the 25 de Mayo flyover uncovered the foundations of the detention center El Atlético, in operation in 1977 and knocked down in 1979 during the construction of the motorway. The excavation encapsulated the way that the dictatorship dealt with its own practice of disappearance, erasing the very traces of its criminal acts within the urban landscape. As Silvestri and Gorelik argue, "Cacciatore's 'modernity' destroyed memory, it made it *disappear*: this became a clear metaphor for the dictatorship's crimes" (2000, p. 469).[11]

Given these practices of erasure, it is unsurprising that with the return to democracy the city would be a key site for memory practices and discourses. Sites of disappearance were often the focus for conflicts between groups with very different approaches to the past. In 1995 the Federal Police Chief threatened to resign over the proposal to create a mural on the walls of El Olimpo, a clandestine detention center operating between 1978 and 1979 (Jelin and Kaufman, 2000, p. 97). In August 1997 human rights organizations organized a day of remembrance at the site of El Atlético, but a plaque engraved with the names of the repressors who had worked in the center was covertly destroyed and the names painted over. Finally, in 2007, the Espacio para la Memoria was opened to the public in the former ESMA complex, a clear statement by Néstor Kirchner's government of its desire to wrest symbolic spaces away from the military.

The close ties between city and memory are usually seen in terms of the architectural palimpsest (Crinson, 2005, p. xii). But the memory commons can also be understood as an act, that is, as remembering. As such, as well as thinking in terms of landscapes *of* memory, we can also speak of landscape *as* memory, such that it is "neither inert nor a stage, but a specific configuration that exists precisely because people with different trajectories dwell in a particular field of remembrance and forgetting" (Curtoni, Lazzari, & Lazzari, 2003, p. 72). Even though they are subjective processes that demand historicization, memories are nonetheless not anchored in symbolic and material markers. Such an understanding moves us away from understanding memory sites to be "incarnations of time in stone" (Huyssen, 2003, p. 101), fixed locations that allow citizens to construct identities in the face of neoliberal processes that are often desirous of stripping away history and memory in favor of an eternal present. Holding on to notions of collective memory expressed only in monuments and buildings can offer a means of combating the practice of forgetting, but it also runs the risk of fixing the past around a commons that distances the visitor by creating a spectacle of horror. Remembering Massey's understanding of place as "stories-so-far" and "meeting place," an approach that dismantles the reproduction of difference and otherness (2005, p. 64), more productive sites of memory are those in which remembering creates multiple memories that allow for difference and that can change over time. In that sense, they would be more in tune with the notion of multidirectional memory set out by Michael Rothberg (2009), who refers to memories that can be mobilized at a transnational, transhistorical level. Here a similarly transferrable, nomadic set of memories can be produced as a result of a remembering that goes beyond blood ties and exclusionary discourses of the nation to create memoryscapes that are fashioned in common.

Silhouettes and Erasures

The two organizations around which debates over the socialization of the disappeared have been focused are the Asociación Madres de Plaza de Mayo and HIJOS (Hijos por la Identidad y la Justicia contra el Olvido y el Silencio). Often, these organizations have been critiqued, with some justification, for creating what, in the context of this book, would be classified as an exclusionary approach to the memory commons by emphasizing their "right" to dictate the ways and means to deal with the legacy of the disappeared. Thus it is often true that for "the Madres and the Children, the subject of the memory of these decades is an essential youth, frozen in photographs and death" (Sarlo, 2005, p. 76), and that their claims to justice have sometimes been "based on biological identity and family ties, for the conservation of memory, and against the silencing and covering up of a criminal past" (Nouzeilles, 2005, p. 265). Likewise, HIJOS do frequently construct themselves around "the juridical uniqueness of the children of the disappeared as the rightful and only legitimate witnesses of their parents" (Nouzeilles, 2005, p. 274). Such positions are expressed by these organizations, understandable attempts to negotiate the legacy of the disappeared and to deal with a long history of impunity. In the Kirchner era both organizations have undergone significant changes, with the Madres notably striking an alliance with the government. And more recently the works of children of the disappeared—whether members of HIJOS or not—have often created more nuanced readings of biological and social ties within the context of the disappeared. Nonetheless, the history of these two organizations prior to more recent shifts in Argentine memory politics should not be oversimplified. Two artistic-political actions—the *siluetazo* and the *escraches*, which date from the early 1980s and the 1990s, respectively—are demonstrative of early examples in which both Madres and HIJOS built more open practices based on remembering in common. Using a palimpsest of bodies acting in and through space, these actions constructed anti-monuments, unfixed experiences and situations that offered "an alternative to the fetish of location and the fetish of representations of power" (Perron, 2003). These acts did not "socialize" the disappeared, taking them to be a shared but less mutable entity, so much as position them as being in common, open to different political groups, some of which have no explicit link to the dictatorship and its legacy.

Memory work in Argentina has often employed the present silhouette of the absent body in an attempt to build an inclusive city in common. Silhouettes have become ubiquitous to the city of disappearance, evident in marches, outside former detention centers, and on the walls of faculty buildings at the Universidad de Buenos Aires. The use of silhouettes to refer to the disappeared originates with what has come to be known as the *siluetazo*, a series of art interventions dating from the early 1980s. The first *siluetazo*, which took place on 21 September 1983, just before the end of the dictatorship, was conceptualized by Rodolfo Aguerreberry, Julio Flores, and Guillermo Kexel and put together in conjunction with the Madres de Plaza de Mayo on the occasion of the Tercera Marcha de la Resistencia, the third of a series of human rights marches first organized by the Madres in 1981. The initial intention, influenced by an artwork that used silhouettes to reflect the total number of those killed in Auschwitz by the Polish artist Jerzy Skapski, was to emphasize the number of bodies disappeared by the dictatorship. The artists decided that the sheer magnitude of the number would be best expressed spatially, calculating the distance that would be covered by 30,000 silhouettes (approximately 52.5 km if laid down head to toe) (Flores, 2008, p. 92). As urban interventions, the silhouettes overturned the exclusionary urban practices of the dictatorship into a politics of urban inclusivity by putting back into iconic, busy places bodies that had been absented from the city, sometimes even from those very same places.[12] The material inscription of the urban onto both participants and silhouettes was exaggerated by the particularity of the surface on which some of the figures were drawn: In some of the photographs of the art intervention the blacked-in outlines clearly show the patterns of tiles widely used on pavements in Buenos Aires.

That specifically urban dimension of the *siluetazo* is crucial to the manner in which it was created through a spatial process of remembering that materialized in common. In that sense, the act of memory, the way in which the city is suffused with bodies re-membering in the present, became just as important as what was being remembered—or rather, that the two moments, as if they too were working in common, lent each other an inseparable significance and weight. The watchwords *poner el cuerpo* (put the body), which run throughout the *siluetazo* and its analysis, place emphasis on the body participating in the act as much as the absent body being represented. The process of creating silhouettes, the act of lying down to have one's silhouette drawn, both stressed the collaborative nature of the artwork and served as a reminder of the way all those participating might have been disappeared. Above all, the act of *poner el cuerpo* created a series of affective ties between disappeared bodies and those that survived, giving back an ephemeral corporeality to the absent body but without laying any claim to be completely replacing the absent body, which, since it was disappeared, could not be re-presented. In so doing, it generated a memory of the presence of absence, of absence through presence, and presence through absence. Thus the body of the one remembering became as important as the body of the one disappeared.

The collective, expansive nature of the *siluetazo* also had a significant impact on the treatment of disappearance within urban space. Initially, the Madres placed certain conditions on the silhouettes' form, not wanting them to have faces, names, or details of clothing: "they should only be inscribed with 'aparición con vida' and be erected upright, because the disappeared should be considered as alive" (Flores, 2008, p. 96).[13] Here the Madres clearly wanted to use the metonymic nature of the silhouette to present the disappeared as socialized figures that stood in for each and every absent body.[14] When the artists invited others to join them in the act of making the vast number of figures, however, both the event and the treatment of the disappeared was transformed by the participants, some of whom began to write names of the disappeared on the silhouettes along with the dates of their disappearance. Even the Madres began adding the

names and dates of disappearance of their children, thus veering away
from the limitations they had originally imposed and highlighting how the
process of production itself undermined any attempt at a homogeneous
politics of memory. In that sense, as Eduardo Grüner argues, "each abstract
figure of a silhouette, formally equivalent to all the others, represents *one*
disappeared and *all* disappeared; neither singularity nor universality, even
if superimposed one on the other, can be mutually *reduced*; both over-
flow their meaning leaving an unspeakable leftover of sense that must be
constructed by the spectator" (2008, p. 297). The *siluetazo* was, therefore,
a powerful example of how memory could be created in common: Each
silhouette's unique qualities (whether in terms of size, outline, inscriptions,
etc.) sat alongside what they had in common, and it is that commonality
of form and the way they were produced in and through the city that gave
the interventions their political and social impact.

The common nature of the *siluetazo* is made clear by a similar
intervention entitled "Los niños" (The children) organized by the group
Urbomaquía in several Argentine cities between 2001 and 2004. The group
placed 80 identical standing figures carrying the same image of a child in
central pedestrianized spaces in the city, leaving pieces of chalk next to
the figures, which passersby could use to write messages on the back of
the figures as if they were blackboards. The artists were protesting child
poverty, and used the figure of a girl living on the streets, a symbol, in
the words of Ana Longoni, of "the new disappeared, the new outcasts
of neoliberalism" (2010, p. 18). Two inscriptions written on two of the
figures went beyond the initial conceptualization of the intervention and
highlighted the expansive power of the silhouette in the Argentine context.
One figure was inscribed with the name of a disappeared person and the
date of their abduction, an act, given that here all the figures on the street
were identical to each other, that highlighted the simultaneously personal
and social nature of that disappeared person. The inscription highlighted
how the disappeared have themselves become a commons, a memory site
around which individual and community can position themselves, a point
exaggerated by the fact that a second figure was inscribed with the slogan
"¡que se vayan todos!" (get them all out!), the phrase used during the
protests of 2001 and 2002 to express outrage at Argentine politicians. The
inscriptions highlight how the figure of disappearance can refer both to the
dictatorship and also to all victims of political, social, and economic repression. Disappearance is thus turned into a broader commons that facili-
tates the expression of political discontent and rebellion. The disappeared
body becomes more than itself, more than absence, and a springboard for

a variety of different political practices: "The silhouette is universalized and remade in relation to other crimes, injustices or absences" (Longoni & Bruzzone, 2008, p. 23). The body thus functions as both a reminder of the repressive state and its practices of torture and also as a means of resistance: "The body as the stage of politics and site of conversation between sadness and happiness: target of violence and source of aggressive resistance" (Grupo de Arte Callejero, 2008, p. 431). As a collective art act, the *siluetazo* transforms the body from working as part of a political act of urban art to functioning as an urban act of artistic politics: "Instead of dissolving art in politics, the *siluetazo* makes evident that the dimension of aesthetics is inseparable from the politics that accompanies it" (García Navarro, 2008, p. 343). The city is transformed by acts of artistic politics created by bodies acting in common.

That artistic politics is also evident in another form of urban intervention that began in the mid- to late 1990s: *escraches*. In *lunfardo*, *escrachar* means both to photograph and to denounce, to make public a hidden past. *Escrache*, therefore, means a photograph for an identity file (hence *escracho*, a face or ugly person; *escrachador*, photographer; and *escrachería*, photographic studio) and a public act of denunciation. The relationship is a reminder of how official photographs can be transformed into public condemnation and taps into the way state identity photographs have often been used within memory practices to protest state violence. Originally instigated by HIJOS, the *escrache* culminates with a public gathering outside the house of a figure complicit with the military dictatorship but who escaped state justice. The act flags up the residences of those who have managed to perform their own act of disappearance by integrating themselves into the city without their past being punished or even acknowledged.

The *escrache* is based on the figure of the neighbor, a reminder of the way that common law has traditionally been grounded in the neighborhood (Linebaugh 2008, p. 275). Like the *asambleas barriales*, neighborhood-based assemblies that also re-appropriate public space and act as a "site of conjunction" (Dinerstein, 2003, p. 196), the *escrache* is inseparable from the *barrio* within which it takes place and in so doing it enacts a shift in memory politics away from the Plaza de Mayo (Longoni, 2010, p. 14). By creating a network of affective ties between all participants, it is, as Colectivo Situaciones write, "produced within the logic of encounter according to a modality that makes *something in common* emerge between the 'Mesa de escrache Popular,' the neighbors and the other eventual participants" (2002b). Drawing bodies together, the *escrache* creates a new network of sociopolitical ties through which the city of impunity and erasure is turned into a city of remembering in common.

The *escrache* is simultaneously an aesthetic intervention, not least as a result of its close ties to the art collectives Grupo de Arte Callejero (GAC) and Etcétera. As a result, *escraches* incorporate flyers, signs, maps, and performance as part of the process of involving local participants. On the occasion of the anniversary of the military coup in 2001, for example, GAC created a poster entitled "War criminals live here," a map that included the location of clandestine detention centers and the residences of those who had been *escrachados* (Grupo de Arte Callejero, 2001). It was symbolic of how the *escrache* attempts to transform what Vezzetti called the dictatorship's "geography of horror" (2002, p. 175) into a geography of memory and resistance created in common. Such aesthetic elements are integral to the very meaning and nature of the *escrache*; without the use of *murga*, for example, a combination of music and performance similar to carnival and with a long history in Argentina, HIJOS argue that "the *escrache* fails in some sense," becoming "something else, a procession" (cited in Colectivo Situaciones, 2002b). Thus, if traditionally there is a clear separation in politics between "celebration and protest," between content and form, and between oratory and recreation, then *escraches* dismantle that division (Zibechi, 2003, p. 55).

At the heart of the *escrache* lies the motto "if there's no justice, there's *escrache*." Working against state injustice during the dictatorship and after, the *escrache* is built around a form of "common" law, a form of justice built in common beyond absolute sovereign authority. As an act in common, it puts bodies in spaces to achieve justice and, in so doing, moves beyond representation toward the acting out of fraternity, since the affective presence of bodies acting in common can never be anything but here and now. It neither purports to represent the disappeared nor asks for justice to be done on its behalf: It is in itself an autonomous act of justice that constructs the city in common. Hence, "no one goes to *escraches* because they think that there will be justice but because it is already there," an enactment that "has no room for pity but for self-affirmation: the production . . . of forms of justice founded in social condemnation" (Colectivo Situaciones, 2002b). *Escraches*, therefore, are clearly not examples of practices in which the disappeared are appropriated by human rights organizations. They are not a form of representation. They are not retrospective, and they do not pay homage to the disappeared. They neither look back to the past nor toward a future justice but transform the figure of disappearance into an act of justice in the here and now through the city in common.

The expansive nature of memory practices in Argentina was already clear by the start of the new millennium. Gay and lesbian protest groups, victims of police violence, and the unemployed, for example, all began to participate in the street marches and demonstrations for 24 March, the anniversary of the start of the dictatorship (Lorenz, 2002, p. 87). Likewise, the *escrache* began to be employed against corrupt officials who had no connection to the dictatorship. As with the figure of the silhouette, the understanding of disappearance is here broadened to situate it both within and beyond the dictatorship, and within and beyond human rights organizations. As a result, the *escrache* "in some sense, stops being an activity 'of' HIJOS, to bring about a practice that is truly autonomous, even from its very practitioners" (Colectivo Situaciones, 2002b). The political impact of the *escrache* is further intensified during the neoliberal era, one in which deregulation and privatization have fomented popular forms of justice, ones that, as Atreyee Sen and David Pratten argue, carry "different kinds of imaginaries from those available in the official sites and representations of justice and law" (2007, p. 7). Of course, as Colectivo Situaciones (2002b) have suggested, "it is possible to do *other escraches*, but not to generalize the *escraches* of H.I.J.O.S.," a point emphasized by Longoni, who notes that the *escrache* cannot simply be reproduced under the same conditions ad infinitum (2010, p. 20)—one reason why the number of *escraches* performed in recent years has declined. Indeed, GAC have themselves wrestled with the way that the memory practices in which they have participated have been institutionalized and incorporated into museums (GAC, 2009).

Practices of memory in Argentina are understandably conflictual and revolve around deep-seated, emotional torment. No society that has experienced the kind of widespread trauma brought about by the disappearance of 30,000 people will find resolutions to satisfy all. Indeed, the *siluetazo* and *escraches* are, in many ways, very different practices—if the former is based on expansive inclusivity, the latter retain an undeniably exclusionary demand for justice via the call for outing repressors from physical spaces. And yet both forms of urban intervention demonstrate the political potency of commoning by putting bodies into spaces as a means of re-appropriating and rewriting the urban text. They highlight the transformative potential of the city itself within the demand for justice, illustrating how remembering in common can sustain both singular and community memories around the trope of disappearance without collapsing them into the exclusionary and homogenizing tendencies of collective memory.

Chapter 3

Surviving the City in
Post-Dictatorship Argentine Comics

In 1986 Raúl Alfonsín, the man elected to take over the presidency when
the dictatorship came to an end in 1983, proposed moving the Argentine
capital to the urban conglomeration formed by Carmen de Patagones,
the southern-most town of the Province of Buenos Aires, and Viedma,
the capital of Río Negro Province in Patagonia. The project, a symbolic
union of Patagonia with the political heartland to the north, was part of
Alfonsín's overall political strategy to counteract the power of the capital
by decentralizing government and bolstering provincial autonomy and
development (Estrade, 2007). The President stated publicly that "oceanic
Argentina begins a lot further south than that maternal waterway that is
the River Plate," making it essential to grow, in his famous phrase, "hacia
el sur, hacia el mar y hacia el frío" (toward the south, toward the sea and
toward the cold).

The proposed relocation of the Argentine capital is part of a long
national tradition: Bahía Blanca in 1900, La Plata in 1912, a vague "interior" following in the footsteps of Brasilia in the 1950s, Córdoba in 1964,
and Santiago del Estero in 1973 and again in 2014 have all been discussed
by various parties as alternative capitals to Buenos Aires. In addition, the
1982 Malvinas/Falklands War had reminded *porteños* of the significance
of Patagonia to national politics, history, and geography. Nevertheless, the
Proyecto Patagonia elided an equally important national history. There
was no mention of Viedma's political history, its foundation as an outpost
of the Spanish Crown to counter possible British expansionism, or its role
in the so-called Conquista del Desierto (the Conquest of the Desert) and
the destruction of the Tehuelche. On the one hand, the project attempted to reconfigure the political geography of the country by creating a
more representative national capital; on the other hand, it washed over
the dark heart of that nation's very foundation. Though the Argentine

Congress approved the proposal, by the end of 1989 the project had foundered, before being discarded entirely by the incoming president, Carlos Menem. Chronic hyperinflation and economic woes had scuppered not only Alfonsín's presidency but also the relocation of the capital, the cost flying in the face of a seriously indebted government. Equally important, however, was the counter-discourse of vocal politicians and the Buenos Aires–based national media, who argued against the move on the basis of Viedma's lack of infrastructure, its apparent inability to provide rigorous jurisprudence, and, tellingly, historical precedent. There were, quite simply, too many parties interested in keeping the capital where it was.

The failure of the Proyecto Patagonia, what Silvestri and Gorelik called the last great urban planning project headed by the Argentine state (2000, p. 481), demonstrated the difficulties of revamping a shared national narrative that had been so systematically destroyed during military rule. As part of Argentina's ceaseless struggle between federalism and centralism that runs from Rosas to Cobos and which James Scobie captured so aptly in the title of his work *Argentina: A City and a Nation* (1964), the project's failure also highlighted the ongoing difficulty of positioning Buenos Aires within the nation.[1] The plan to relocate the capital highlighted a desire to rebalance the national status of Buenos Aires; that it came to nothing emphasized the fractious nature of Argentina's national identity post-dictatorship. As a consequence of the splintering of national identity through torture, disappearance, and the militarization of everyday life, and as a result of the failure of the 1982 war, which tarnished the one untainted symbol of Argentine nationhood, the nation was losing its grip as the privileged form of collective identity (Guber, 2001, p. 168). Under military rule the imagined community of the nation was revealed to be an exclusive commons built around a set of clear boundaries (whether geographical, biological, or cultural) that constructed fixed groups of friends and (internal) enemies. At the same time, the inability to think beyond the nation as the principal site of belonging or beyond Buenos Aires as that nation's capital meant that it was also impossible to find a way out of Buenos Aires—no doubt why Alfonsín, speaking in 2007, stated that his greatest political regret was failing to move the capital southward, adding "I should have gone even if I'd gone with a tent" (*Perfil*, 2006).

The notion of a displaced Buenos Aires was taken up regularly in one of the most productive and vibrant Argentine cultural products of the 1980s: *historietas* (comics). The most important comics publication of the decade, *Fierro a fierro: historietas para sobrevivientes*, also known as *Fierro*, was a self-conscious and regular participant in the attempt to reconstruct a national commons damaged by the dictatorship and, as often as not, it explored that national commons through and in the city. If in 1980 Juan Sasturain, who would later become the editor of *Fierro*, could suggest that, together with tango and folklore music, the marginality of comics best demonstrated "the possibilities Argentines had to create their own mode of expression, authentically creative and not dependent on Eurocentric or North American models" (1980, p. 185), then *historietas* over the course of the 1980s also displayed an unease with the very notion of a national culture. With nationhood a problematic form of identity, *historietas* expressed a desire to move beyond the nation at the same time as an inability to move beyond its iconography and symbolism. The inescapable, dystopian, and displaced cities that they depicted only reinforced that entrapment. As much as any other cultural medium, *historietas* and their readers highlighted irreconcilable tensions in the vision of nation and city post-dictatorship, challenging those readings that see the return to democracy, the so-called "primavera democrática" (democratic Spring), as a period of national unity. Comics illustrated that the city in common did not sit well with the nation.

Debates over national identity in the 1980s were coming on the back of the Cold War struggle between national security and national liberation, almost a decade of institutionalized disappearance at the hands of a national state that constructed itself around a discourse of the subversive-next-door, and a period of neoliberal reform that encouraged foreign investment and imported products. Already an estranged site of belonging, Argentine national identity was further eroded by the disastrous 1982 Malvinas/Falklands War, which tarnished the foremost symbol of Argentine nationhood. As Virginia Osuna suggests, "the common after Malvinas" underwent a series of reconfigurations, not least in terms of the national itself (2007, p. 70).[2] When Alfonsín came to power at the end of 1983 he was confronted with having to piece together this disjointed national identity, and his successful election was partly due to the perception that he was the most likely candidate to generate the desired national cohesion. Alfonsín had been heavily involved in human rights activities prior to and during the dictatorship: In 1973 in his capacity as a lawyer he had represented Mario Santucho, head of the left-wing guerrilla organization Ejército Revolucionario del Pueblo (ERP); he stood out for the number of habeas corpus writs he had signed; and in 1977 he met with a team from Amnesty International during their visit to investigate human rights abuses. Crucial to his election success, furthermore, was the fact that Alfonsín was not a Peronist (the 1983 election was the first in which a Peronist had run and lost), a symbol of the post-dictatorship desire to move on from pre-dictatorship politics. The two main aims of Alfonsín's presidency (1983–1989) were stabilizing a wildly unsettled economy and coming to terms with the recent past. The military dictatorship had left Argentina in arrears with their foreign debt and subject to dangerously high levels of inflation. The latter, which reached a staggering 5,000 percent in 1989, would ultimately bring about Alfonsín's demise, forcing him to hand power over early to Carlos Menem in the same year. Alfonsín was also criticized for the measures he had instigated to deal with the recent past. Following the formation of the Comisión Nacional de la Desaparición de Personas (CONADEP), which published its findings as the document *Nunca más* in 1984, and the 1985 trials of the military and guerrillas, came the highly contentious laws of Punto Final (1986), which placed a final date after which no new cases could be brought against the military, and Obediencia Debida (1987), which exempted those who could prove their acts were being carried out under orders of superior officials. With the ongoing threat of military revolt, encapsulated by the barracks uprisings carried out by the so-called "carapintadas" (painted faces) in 1987, the period was marked by a lack of consensus over how to shape a shared narrative of the past.

Argentine cultural practice during the 1980s reflected this fragmentation. Unlike during the 1960s and 1970s, when debates over the role of culture, politics, and armed struggle created a charged intellectual sphere, the legacy of censorship, enforced exile, and disappearance meant that everyday cultural activity had become an increasingly isolated practice. Many of the period's most famous writers, for example, had gone into exile either before, during, or soon after the dictatorship (Juan José Saer, Manuel Puig, Antonio di Benedetto, Osvaldo Soriano, Ricardo Piglia, Luisa Valenzuela); others were marginalized by the Argentine intelligentsia either for their populism (Antonio Dal Masetto and Soriano) or because of their commercial success during the dictatorship (Jorge Asís); others returned from exile but remained disconnected from Buenos Aires by living in other provinces (Hector Tizón); and still others were decidedly not part of any literary establishment or movement (Fogwill). Equally, the number of film productions between 1983 and 1989 remained low. Those directors who did have some success—such as Héctor Olivera, María Luisa Bemberg, Bebe Kamín, Luis Puenzo, Fernando Solanas, and Eliseo Subiela—were not part of a shared cinematic project, whether thematic or aesthetic, in the way that filmmakers of the 1950s, 1960s, and early 1970s had been. In general, then, cultural productions appeared to be underwater, much like the city in Solanas's film *El viaje* (1992), in which Buenos Aires rots amidst human excrement, corruption, and land privatization.

Not all cultural forms experienced such stagnation during the 1980s, however. Cultural magazines (*Punto de vista,* in particular), rock music, and comics (especially those published in *Fierro*), would emerge as vibrant sites for exploring the political, social, and cultural nature of post-dictatorship Argentine identity. There are various reasons for the success of these cultural forms during this period. First, rock concerts, music, and magazines were relatively cheap to produce, and also easily shared and distributed, crucial in times of economic uncertainty. Second, they were all self-consciously oppositional. Third, they had either opposed, in one sense or another, the military dictatorship or were young enough or marginal enough not to have been "politically compromised." Fourth, they generated an open format that encouraged widespread participation, particularly from the burgeoning "post-dictatorship" generation. And, finally, those activities that publicly outlasted the dictatorship could play on their success as survivors (Wortman, 2002, p. 330).

Cultural magazines, both those published within Argentina and in exile, formed one of the principal areas of intellectual debate during the waning of the dictatorship and the return to democracy. During the 1980s, *Punto de vista*, founded on the principals of anti-institutional marginality and opposition, particularly in the face of military censorship, began to expand on its early focus on literary criticism to include essays on aesthetics and politics, intellectuals and democracy, and psychoanalysis. Reveling in the wake of the Peronist election failure, the magazine attempted to construct an intellectual practice of the left that was both post-Peronist and that moved beyond the debates over the militant basis of culture during the 1960s and 1970s (Patiño, 2006). By the end of the 1990s, *Punto de vista* had also become one of the first cultural magazines in Argentina to discuss urban theory and the city with some frequency, publishing articles by Anahí Ballent, Adrián Gorelik, and Graciela Silvestri on urban theory and architecture (No. 32, 1988); by Celeste Olalquiaga on urban culture (No. 35, 1989); and by Silvestri and Gorelik on shopping and shopping centers in Buenos Aires (No. 37, 1990) and on the dying of Buenos Aires as a port city (No. 39, 1990). Many of these contributions to *Punto de vista*, not least those written by the magazine's chief editor, Beatriz Sarlo, as can be seen in her contemporaneous work *La modernidad periférica: Buenos Aires 1920 y 1930* (1988), marked a shift in writing about the city, influenced by the political, sociocultural approaches to the urban taken by Marshall Berman, Carl Schorske, and Raymond Williams.[3] Toward the end of the 1980s, another magazine, *Babel*, receiving contributions from writers including Daniel Guebel, Alan Pauls, Sergio Chejfec, Horacio González, César Aira, Nicolás Casullo, Ricardo Forster, Daniel Link, Graciela Montaldo, Daniel Samoilovich, Matilde Sánchez, and Héctor Schmucler, marked a notable shift in cultural-intellectual terms to a younger generation, the majority of whom would only become established names in the 1990s. In addition, as Roxana Patiño suggests (2006), while *Punto de vista* attempted to reaffirm an Argentine literary tradition based on the modern intellectual, *Babel* rather asserted the universal autonomy of literature and included a considerable quantity of foreign literature, a further indication of increasing uncertainty over the boundaries of national cultural traditions.

Punto de vista, however, was also pioneering in the space it gave to popular culture and its theorization. One such sphere was *rock nacional*. Issue number 30, for example, included an article debating whether *rock nacional* could be seen as part of the Argentine popular music tradition, a debate that demonstrated both the impact that musical form was having during the 1980s and also the way the publication was incorporating the growth in cultural studies. Though rock had a strong tradition stretching back to the 1960s, in the words of Cecilia Flachsland, it "did not get on very well with what is called 'national and popular'" (2006, p. 60). With the Malvinas War and the ban on music sung in English on the radio, rock received unprecedented time on the airwaves and became *rock nacional*. Though its national tag is indicative of the way rock was constructing a musical identity beyond U.K. and U.S. imports, rock was hardly involved in a project to reconfigure national identity. Rock musicians were notably countercultural in terms of music, lyrics, dress and makeup, drugs and alcohol, and, whilst countercultural is not necessarily counternational, this period saw the beginnings of a transition to more urban, localized, and neighborhood-focused musical forms. Invigorated by the return to the democracy and the concurrent freedom of expression, intellectual magazines and rock music provided a crucial cultural commons for post-dictatorship Argentine society, one that offered an alternative to a culture dominated by national figures and intellectuals. They fomented grassroots debate about the state of the nation and the role of culture within the construction of national identity. As much as in any other cultural medium, that debate would also ignite the world of comics.

Comics for Survivors

The history of comics in Argentine culture goes back to the 19th century, though its so-called golden age began with the appearance of the magazine *Patoruzito* in 1945, run by Dante Quinterno, and it lasted until around 1960. Argentines worked alongside many Italian scriptwriters and artists who had been brought to the country by the publishing house Abril to contribute to the magazine *Misterix*, perhaps the most famous example being Hugo Pratt, creator of *Corto Maltese* (Gociol & Rosemberg, 2003, p. 34). The late 1950s saw the birth of several major publications, namely *D'Artagnan*, *Tía Vicenta*, *Hora Cero*, and *Frontera*, the last two founded by Héctor German Oesterheld, the most famous Argentine comic book writer. During the 1960s, not least as a result of the success of both comic strips (notably *Mafalda*, created in 1964 by Quino) and graphic novels such as *Mort Cinder* (written by Oesterheld and drawn by Alberto Breccia), comics gained a certain presence in the art world through the figure of Oscar Masotta who co-organized the 1968 Primera Bienal Mundial de la Historieta at the Instituto Di Tella, then the foremost Argentine art institute, and who co-edited the three editions of the magazine *L.D. Literatura dibujada* (1968–1969). Despite these advances in national production and recognition, however, the Argentine comics industry declined steadily over the 1960s, suffering in the face of expansion in other cultural forms, particularly television.

During the late 1960s and 1970s comics mirrored the general politicization of culture, with writers and artists turning to increasingly national, localized questions. In 1969, Oesterheld rewrote his classic *El eternauta* (Oesterheld & Solano López, 2008), originally published between 1957 and 1959, for the magazine *Gente* (Oesterheld & Breccia, 2006). Following the 1968 graphic biography of "Che" Guevara, *Vida del Che*, a collaboration with Alberto Breccia and his son Enrique Breccia, published barely 3 months after the guerrilla's death, Oesterheld's increasing affiliation with the political left was also evident in this revised version of *El eternauta*: The alien invasion of South America was turned into a direct result of a deal struck between the extraterrestrials and the Western superpowers. Alarmed by the new direction the story was taking, the society publication *Gente* pulled the story. Living clandestinely, Oesterheld participated in a series of publications that utilized comics to express political ideas, including *El Descamisado* and *Evita Montonera*, both created by the guerrilla organization Montoneros. Based on revisionist historicism, the magazines offered alternative readings of what they saw as 500 years of exploitation and colonialism in much the same vein as the 1968 film *La hora de los hornos*, Eduardo Galeano's 1971 *Las venas abiertas de América Latina*, and Ariel Dorfman and Armand Mattelart's 1972 analysis of Disney's imperialist ideology, *Para leer al Pato Donald*. This national-political turn in comics was abruptly broken by the 1976–1983 military dictatorship. National comics production, the sales of which were down 40 percent as a result of a dramatic increase in imported Mexican comics and the economic crisis (Gociol & Rosemberg, 2003, p. 45), was further hampered by censorship; the exile of key comics producers, including Ricardo Barreiro, Juan Giménez, Carlos Sampayo, and Francisco Solano López; and the arrest and subsequent disappearance of Oesterheld in 1977. Nevertheless, one of the most well-known sites of cultural resistance to the dictatorship was a comics publication, the satirical magazine *Hum®*, which first appeared in 1978 and which flourished despite the political climate, selling some 350,000 copies every fortnight (Ostuni et al., n.d., pp. 5–6).

Following the end of dictatorship, *Fierro* quickly became the most significant comics publication in Argentina, reaching a circulation of around 25,000 copies at its height (Sasturain, 1995, p. 41). Drawing on the short-lived publication *Tiras de cuero* (also known as *Cuero*) from 1983, itself influenced by the French science fiction and horror magazine *Métal Hurlant*, the novelty of *Fierro* was broadly a result of its inclusion of work by three marginalized groups of comics producers: Europeans (including Moebius, Mino Manara, and Hugo Pratt, among others), those in exile, and an underground "younger generation" (Reggiani, n.d., p. 14). *Fierro* was also often sexually explicit. Naked women, usually in the grasp of some evil creature or metallic monster, a symbol, perhaps, of the female *patria* threatened by the dictatorship machine, dominated cover art from the very first issue. The nudity not only reflects the magazine's overt masculinity, both in terms of content, readership, and contributors (Patricia Breccia was the only regular contributor who was a woman), but also highlights the sense of release from the dictatorship's clampdown on public sexuality. All the same, such sexual liberation is nearly always filtered through the prism of male fantasy, sometimes, as in the case of "El instituto," written by Ricardo Barreiro and drawn by Solano López, in stories that border on the pornographic.

Fierro's emphasis on innovation was placed alongside strong traits of history and tradition, illustrative of its desire to think through post-dictatorship Argentine national identity, even though this approach created an ongoing tension in the magazine between established conventions and avant-garde transformation (Vazquez, 2010, p. 294). Thus, the title of the magazine referenced both *Métal Hurlant* and Raúl Roux's gaucho series *Fierro a Fierro*, which had been published in *Patoruzito*; José Hernández's founding epic poem *Martín Fierro*; and the slang word for firearms used by guerrillas (Ostuni el al., n.d., p. 10). Indeed, *Fierro* constantly referred back to the national past, both reaffirming and, at the same time, reconstructing and revising that past. Thus, there was a story about the 1982 war, *La batalla de Malvinas* (Ricardo Barreiro, Alberto Macagno, Carlos Pedrazzini, & Marcelo Pérez, 1984, no. 1 and no. 2), a biography of Argentina's most famous anarchist "Severino Di Giovanni" (Carlos Albiac and Alfredo Flores, 1985, no.14), and a story about a Bolivian shepherd and the death of "Che" Guevara by Horacio Altuna called *Pastores*, which links two histories with the suggestive final line, "the military have fucked us over" (1986, no. 21, p. 31).

Debates over national identity and the formation of a "national comics" played a key role in *Fierro* from the very start. The magazine attempted to highlight the role that comics had played—and, therefore, could continue to play—in popular culture and, by extension, Argentine national identity. For all its innovations, therefore, *Fierro*'s approach to reinvigorating a national audience was precisely to return to Argentine traditions, history, and culture, and to a particular tradition of Argentine comics (a tradition that reinserts popular culture as the true marker of Argentine identity). At times, the magazine was unable to escape the established canonical approach to Argentine comics history, basing its vision of a "new Argentine comic" on an unsurprising group of comics protagonists and publications (Vazquez, 2010, pp. 300–304). Nevertheless, the magazine also sometimes approached Argentine national history and traditions with a certain revisionist perspective.

The series edited by Ricardo Piglia, *La Argentina en pedazos* (Piglia, 1993), a number of comic versions of famous Argentine literary works, was key to this historical-cultural revisionism. Piglia's series, which was published in *Fierro* between 1984 and 1992 and included, among other works, versions of Esteban Echeverría's *El matadero*, Germán Rozenmacher's *Cabecita negra*, and Borges's *Historia del guerrero y de la cautiva*, revamped the Argentine literary canon by prioritizing the works' visual rather than literary impact and transforming a supposedly high-cultural format into popular culture. Piglia's choice of *historieta* to engage with history and literature was a markedly anti-academic decision as well as a shrewd means of dismantling homogenous national narratives post-dictatorship, a project he would continue with his antagonistic suggestion toward the end of the 1980s that the Polish writer Witold Gombrowicz, who was exiled in Argentina in the 1940s and 1950s, was the greatest Argentine writer of the 20th century. As Jean Franco has suggested, "Piglia's comic-stripping of Argentine literature seems to underscore the fact that 'the immense book' (whether of the nation or of Latin America as a whole) can no longer be bodied forth from high culture" (1999, p. 421). *La Argentina en pedazos* hints that any such "immense book" of the nation was altogether impossible since it was, as the title implied, in comic strip fragments. In that sense, if *Fierro* can be seen as expressing the desire to reconstruct national identity by revisiting Argentine history (Vazquez, 2010, p. 303), then Piglia's series reveals the impossibility of that task.

The inherent tensions within *Fierro*'s "national project" are particularly evident in the way that the magazine interpellated a national audience. Not only did the comics themselves draw on national tropes and myths around which its reading public could engage, but the publication's editorial statements referred to a "community of readers" that Laura Vazquez suggests can be understood to mean "national community" (2010, p. 293). If, as she adds, the "presence of the 'the political' within the magazine was founded on a specific conception of 'the national' around which it tried to establish integration so as to neutralize the ideological positions of different social sectors" (2010, pp. 299–300), then what *Fierro* actually highlighted was how stark such political differences still were. Thus, one result of the interpellation of a national public was a debate over what constituted a "national comic" during 1987, at the same moment that the *carapintadas* were threatening another military takeover. Suggesting that Argentine national culture had been mutilated by North American imperialism, one reader argued that Argentine writers, production, and themes defined whether a comic was national (1987, no. 31, p. 21). Another reader disputed these criteria, arguing that a national comic did not necessarily need to be created by Argentines because many foreign authors touched on what he saw as the authentically national issues of authoritarianism, repression, and torture (1987, no. 33, p. 64). The foregrounding of a debate over national culture suggested a commonality based on genuinely shared and reflective considerations over what constituted the national.

In an earlier debate two readers thanked the magazine for helping them to survive in the post-dictatorship period and for "keeping us afloat at a time when the boat was sinking" (1985, no. 8, p. 24). *Fierro*'s subtitle—"historietas para sobrevivientes" (comics for survivors)—implied both victorious longevity and exhaustion in the wake of a shipwreck, the shared experience of survival suggestive of a community constructed around the collective sigh of "we made it." The problem was, however, that interpretations of the process of surviving were increasingly conflictive. In the very same issue, another reader lambasted *Fierro* for failing to recoup the combative nature of old heroes and the way they encapsulated "the eternal and tireless UTOPIAN WORKER" (1985, no. 8, p. 25). *Fierro*, the author lamented, displayed a "defeatist, surrendered and weakened perspective," populated by "tormented puppets" who lacked self-determination and promoted passivity. The criticisms indicate that the radical political discourse of certain sectors of the left in the 1970s had hardly disappeared in the wake of collective suffering. Such tensions continued in discussions over the aforementioned story about the anarchist Di Giovanni. In an article accompanying the story, Alvaro Abós criticized the violence of anarchism, comparing Di Giovanni to the armed left of the 1970s, both of whom, in his words, "tried to pave the way to an improbable paradise with gunpowder," such that the grandchildren of the anarchist only managed to release on the Argentine people "a nightmare of suffering and mourning from which it will take us a long time to recover" (1985, no. 14, p. 17). Whilst one reader responded with typical reference to the old-time enemy, accusing Abós of failing to recognize the only true enemy, Yankee imperialism (1986, no. 17, p. 46), another letter from the Grupo Editor de la Revista Utopía warned that such comparisons were dangerous and subsumed very different historical contexts and violences (1986, no. 17, p. 28). These debates demonstrated the difficulty of shaping a commons around the nation and its mythic past, precisely because of the highly divisive political legacy of the dictatorship and Peronism, a point that would be even clearer in the response to the most polemic story in *Fierro*, Enrique Breccia's *El sueñero*.

A work that plays with and dismantles a whole number of different myths, *El sueñero* is unique in its combination of fantasy, science fiction, and humor, and its transmogrification of Argentine history. Published in *Fierro* between 1985 and 1986, the story relates the journeys of Ñato, otherwise known as "el Sueñero," a caped mercenary who lives in a land plagued by boredom after years of war. The elders and wise men decide that the solution to such ennui is to reinstate the Roman circus, and el Sueñero is employed to journey through time to collect fighting beasts, during which travels he meets Diogenes, Churchill, Jack the Ripper, and the Yeti, encounters that are symbolic of the way the comic plays fast and loose with historical time, geography, and myth via text and image. Breccia's "hero" is markedly unheroic, and the story ends with him working as a shopkeeper, indicative of the demythologizing intentions of the work. When Dr. Jekyll is seen rubbing Aladdin's lamp, for example, someone else on the inside is rubbing another magic lamp, which results in both being magically beholden to each other in the same instant, a metaphor for the way Breccia constantly turns history, legend, and myth inside out. Thus, when Theseus tells el Sueñero that he will continue the eternal struggle between good and evil alone, el Sueñero simply mutters, "Evil smells just like cow dung" (2007, p. 16). In the end, Theseus is killed and it is el Sueñero who ends up taming the Minotaur and fathering Ariadne's children (2007, p. 20). These reworkings, jokes, and subversions also include linguistic displacement. Letters are reversed, names are spelt phonetically ("Irhigo-Yen" for Yrigoyen, for example), and riddles are used for when characters speak in English: "Mailedidi, ¿de rous is red an de pensil is blú???" footnoted as meaning "Señora, ¿podrías decirme cómo puedo hacer para llegar a la casa del Sr. Hyde?" (Madam, could you tell me how I might get to the house of Mr. Hyde?) (2007, p. 31).

The central episodes of the work, however, do not just play with myth but are increasingly political, relating the conflict between "Grhin-Ghó, el gusano de afuera" (Gringo, the foreign worm) (2007, p. 57), a shape-changing creature who strips victims of their origins and identities (2007, p. 82), and Helje-Nerhal, also known as "el viejo" (the old man), a reference to Perón. Grhin-Ghó's troops are the famous "ghori-lhas" (gorillas) (2007, p. 62), who sport badges saying "I.M.F. or death" (2007, p. 71) and flags that are a mix between the Stars and Stripes and the communist hammer and sickle (2007, p. 69), a nod to Perón's "third way."[4] Helje-Nerhal's army, by contrast, carries Argentine flags and one poorly hidden flag of the CGT (2007, p. 64), and it confronts the ghori-lhas with espadrilles and the chant "halpargataszílibrossnhó" (2007, p. 67).[5] Breccia even goes so far as to include *federales* and Rosistas as part of his army of national liberation (2007, p. 65), challenging the post-dictatorship liberal trait of using the 19th-century dictator Rosas as a symbol of the more recent military regime (Reggiani, n.d., p. 12). After the battle, however, the story distances itself from this immediately political content. Though there is a "Perón vuelve" (Perón will return) symbol on a wall (2007, p. 131) and on Ñato's t-shirt (2007, p. 134) and a swipe at Alfonsinistas ("Don't kill worms. They might be Radical diplomats re-incarnated") (2007, p. 140), these appear as humorous asides that barely disrupt the text's return to its former myth-breaking project.

The way the text makes the familiar strange, its emphasis on dreams, and its uncanny nature is a warning against overly literal readings of the text. Nevertheless, the text's displaced signifiers hardly challenge Peronism in the way that they do classical myth. Breccia's perceived failure to critique Peronism, which was hardly surprising for an unapologetic Peronist, stoked furious debates about the work. Such was the response that, in his role as editor, Sasturain created a special section entitled "Piedra libre" in *Fierro* just to field readers' letters. Opening the debate, Sasturain stated that *Fierro's* philosophy was not to defend any particular comic but rather the magazine as a space of discussion fueled by the critical intelligence of its readership. One reader accused Breccia of Peronist "pamphleteering" and "proselytizing through the comic" (2007, p. 22). His accusations indicate both unease with party politics, particularly Peronism, and with comics being a suitable medium for political ideas. The Peronist readership was quick to respond:

> Are you hurt that E. Breccia is a Peronist? I read someone who says: "the Peronist within him came out. . . ." So what? . . . Another reader says that *Fierro* is not the place [for such comments] and I ask: why not? And to a third (no doubt a supporter of "LOSGHO-RHIIIILAS") who accuses him of being a pamphleteer of the Peronist Youth . . . I have to tell him that for many people (very many) being part of the so-called "glorious" Peronist Youth is a point of pride, PRIDE THIS BIG. (1986, no. 21, p. 71)

Evidently, Breccia's vindication of Peronism had struck a chord, and not everyone, least of all the left, was living democracy in quite the same way. The sense of discord over ways of reading the past and of thinking future commonality would come to the fore in the comic book treatment of a series of displaced cities.

Trapped in the Displaced City

The unease evident in the debates over Breccia's *El sueñero*, highlighting the problematic nature of post-dictatorship politics and nationhood, would also be explored in and through the comic book city. If *El sueñero* displaced myth and history precisely to replace Peronist politics and militancy within Argentine history, a number of other comic strips would envision variously displaced, refashioned, and imagined Buenos Aires as a means of expressing discontent with the national city. In the very first issue of *Fierro*, for example, the series entitled *La batalla de Malvinas*, written by Ricardo Barreiro and drawn by Alberto Macagno and Marcelo Pérez, demonstrated graphically the problematic nature of the national commons in a sequence depicting General Galtieri's victory speech in the Plaza de Mayo. Whilst the accompanying narrative critiques Galtieri's discourse of national unity, two photographs of the Casa Rosada were reproduced—the top image was repeated at the bottom of the page, but this time torn into four pieces (1984, no. 1, p. 35). The image symbolized the way that the city would be seen as a fragmented, divisive entity throughout comics produced during the 1980s. Several other stories published in *Fierro* during the 1980s, notably *Evaristo* and *Parque Chas*, as well as series published elsewhere, including *Ciudad*, which was published in *Tiras de cuero*, used strategies of displacement to engage with the antagonistic democracy of the 1980s, creating cities in which urban dwellers struggle to find any shared sites of commonality, least of all through the national.

Between the late 1950s and the start of the dictatorship in 1976, the city found in Argentine comics is increasingly the object of struggle for sociopolitical cultural conflicts, evident in the seminal 1959 work *El eternauta*, for example, which sets out a specific and local geography of resistance. The theme of defending cities from foreign invasion reappeared in the 1969 redrawn version of *El eternauta*, the 1970 and 1974 versions of *La guerra de los Antartes* (Oesterheld & Trigo, 1998), and the second part of *El eternauta*, produced while Oesterheld was living clandestinely in 1976.[6] A rather different approach to the very same struggles over urban space can be found in the famous comic strip *Mafalda*, which Quino ceased drawing in 1973. As David William Foster (1998) has pointed out, *Mafalda* is built around struggles over urban visibility, the power of the gaze, and the tensions between domestic and public spaces, with the latter in particular offering the possibility of strategies of subversion. In post-dictatorship comics cities continued to be depicted as spaces of danger, but the threat was now less foreign invasion than internal urban forces and power structures. Like the "survivors" of the dictatorship, the inhabitants of these cities had to find strategies to endure these internal threats, seeking out ways in which the collapse of a unified national city might be refashioned into an alternative urban future.

Comics have a number of ties to the city and urban life. The combination of words and images in comics is similar to the urban experience of advertisements, signs, and graffiti, and the panels of the comic grid structure are comparable to the organization of the city itself (Jörn Ahrens & Arno Meteling, 2010, pp. 6–7). Jens Balzer notes that the birth of comics "reflects a semiotic shift occurring in the urban living space at the turn of the century," one that he ties, via the fragment, into Walter Benjamin's reflections on the way that the new diverse perceptory experiences of the city de-centered the gaze (2010, pp. 25–26). That de-centered city would be a recurring trope of urban life in Argentine comics during the 1980s, not because of semiotic transformations but rather because the entire locale, not least as a national space, had become estranged. *Fierro* published a number of *historietas* about the city, including Carlos Trillo and Horacio Altuna's *La ciudad muerta* (1985, no. 13), about a dying, castrated city in which people die when sexually aroused; Ricardo Barreiro and Solano López's *Ministerio* (1986), about a city that has become one huge tower in which bureaucracy has become the basis of existence and government; Carlos Trillo and Jordi Bernet's series *Custer* (1986), about a detective plying her trade in a noir, cinematic city; and Ricardo Barreiro and Alberto Dose's *El caso de Rodolfo A.* (1986), about a crime journalist in 1930s Buenos Aires. What marks all of these productions, a trend that characterizes almost all urban landscapes in *Fierro* and comics in the 1980s, is a series of displacements. The city is nearly always its own other, either a generic, post-media-revolution, futuristic city, or a Buenos Aires of yesteryear. Yet the underlying preoccupation is, nonetheless, with post-dictatorship Buenos Aires, a concern expressed through the dominant themes of policing, state control, power, and crime, all themes that came to the fore in the series *Evaristo*.

Evaristo, drawn by Solano López and written by Carlos Sampayo, first appeared in *Superhum®* before switching to *Fierro*, where it ran between 1984 and 1987. The *historieta* relates various cases undertaken by the tough detective Evaristo. Most of the stories are set in Buenos Aires, though some cases involve the protagonist traveling to other destinations, including Cuba at the time of the Revolution. Evaristo's present is the late 1950s and early 1960s, made evident within the images themselves: In "El célebre caso Lubitsch" (The Famous Lubitsch Case), for example, graffiti on a wall states "Viva el tirano prófugo" (Long live the fugitive tyrant) (p. 32), a reference to the exiled Perón; "Villa Cartón" includes graffiti demanding "Vote Frondizi" (p. 68); and in "Fotos de pianista famoso" (Photos of the Famous Pianist), the telephone book is dated 1958.[7] In part, that Sampayo and Solano López decided to set their story in a previous period of Argentine history can be put down to the fact that both were in exile at the time; their own displacement is made evident in the temporal and spatial displacement of Buenos Aires. But the fact that the narrative is also interspersed with flashbacks to the 1920s, 1930s, and 1940s, using temporal icons from that period, including period dress or trams, adds a further layer of complexity to this temporal de-centering.

In his study of Jason Lutes's long-running and still incomplete graph-ic saga *Berlin*, Anthony Enns demonstrates how the comic form allows Lutes to reproduce a sense of fractured time, a dialectics that "disrupts the unified plan or historical narrative of the city" and that is "indelibly linked to the experience of the modern city, where the past constantly collides with the present and the real constantly merges with the mythological" (2010, pp. 48–49). Using the idea of the montage, which captures the way Lutes uses both flashbacks and also blends factual and imaginary images, Enns celebrates the fractured nature of *Berlin* for resisting an urban meta-narrative of the city as a unified whole. As a result, Enns argues, Lutes is able "to restore the lost fragments of the past and thereby rescue the dead," "to construct a fragmented text that challenges linear narratives of historical continuity," and to "[deconstruct] the mythological topography of Berlin and [offer] new possibilities for imagining the future" (2010, pp. 57–58).

The traits of montage and fracture that recur in *Berlin* can also be seen in *Evaristo*, which also blends fiction and reality, includes flashbacks, and uses the graphic form to represent temporal and spatial fracture. In similar fashion to Lutes, Solano López stated that because the Buenos Aires of *Evaristo* was drawn in exile, it is a city created "within an archive, from memory" (cited in Gociol & Rosemberg, 2003, p. 40). But *Evaristo* does not generate any of the same positive resistance to death or affirma-tive imaginaries of the future that Enns sees in *Berlin*. The Buenos Aires of *Evaristo* is a city foundering in its temporal and spatial fracture, one that cannot escape its destiny of partisan conflict, spatial inequalities, and disappearance, a point evident in the characterization of the protagonist himself. Given that the police had been complicit in the detentions and torture that had taken place during the 1976–1983 dictatorship, the post-dictatorship period was hardly an opportune moment to make a police-man a hero. Moreover, as Pablo De Santis asks, "If the ideal figure of the detective story is the private detective or the police, how was it possible to construct a hero in a country where private eyes are either incredible or are mere telltales, and police barbarity cannot be presented as heroism?" (1992, p. 37). The answer, De Santis suggests, was to go back in time to an equally conflictive period but one that would not stir up the same sentiment. Nevertheless, even if some of the crimes depicted in *Evaristo*, particularly in the flashbacks to the earlier decades, which include knife fights and acts of vengeance, appear to hark back to a time of some kind of a moral code and honor, they in fact contain within them acts of severe and lasting brutality, often directed toward women: Evaristo is seen to discard a woman who is pregnant with the son he disowns before he is even born, and in one frame in "Melodrama de desempate," the silhouette of a man beating a woman can be seen in a house in the background, making domestic violence integral to this urban landscape (20).

Indeed, the temporal displacement of the series did not appease all readers of *Fierro*. Though Sasturain thought them misguided in seeing in the protagonist "a praiseworthy repressive cop" (*Fierro a fierro*, 1986, no. 22, p. 20), those concerned about the valorization of Evaristo did, at least in part, have some justification. Part of the appeal ascribed to Evaristo in the comic stems from his links to the archetypal figure of hard-boiled detective fiction, Raymond Chandler's Marlowe. Despite being a salaried policeman, Evaristo is also a detective in Marlowe's mold, his work involving tough punches, plenty of legwork, and the tracing of events to their logical conclusion more than reasoned analysis. Moreover, Evaristo's corrupt qualities, which often allow him to move beyond the parameters of the law to enact justice, mean that he shares some of the qualities of the North American private eye who emerges, as Dennis Porter argues, within a world of capitalist inequality, political corruption, and dystopian cityscapes, appearing as "a disabused, anti-authoritarian, muckraking hero" who could become "the stubbornly democratic hero of a post-heroic age, righting wrongs in a fallen urban world in which the traditional institutions and guardians of the law . . . are no longer up to the task" (2003, pp. 96–97). In the Argentine context, then, Evaristo is the institutional detective who acts both within and outside the law precisely to restore the intent of that law. He becomes, in Piglia's phrase, the "urban manifestation of the cowboy" (2000, p. 70). Sampayo and Solano López thus temper Evaristo's less attractive qualities by making it clear that he only deploys violence or blackmail against criminals, and he purports to maintain some kind of ethics (using an electric prod as a torture instrument is not acceptable, but beating someone up is). That ethics is, at the same time, presented as an outdated, outmoded mode of being and we appear to be invited to feel some sympathy for Evaristo, particularly at the end of the episode about the lion that has escaped from the zoo. When he eventually finds the beast, which turns out to be a lot more docile than the press have been suggesting, Evaristo is aware of his own anachronistic nature when he pats the lion and says, "friend, you and I are lost" (p. 98).

The paralegal nature of Evaristo's activities, however, troubled the post-dictatorship readership. After all, the military dictatorship itself had epitomized the consequences of a state institution acting outside of the law to uphold the law. Like the real-life police commissioner on whom the protagonist is based—Evaristo Meneses, who used to say that his *picana*, the electrical prod that became one of the more infamous symbols of the 1976–1983 dictatorship, "was the pencil" (Velazco, 1965)—Evaristo does spurn such instruments of torture. But his brutal treatment of criminals, particularly when he hits a detainee across the face with the words "this is an extra-official conversation" (p. 35), is an unsettling reminder of the dictatorship's treatment of detainees. Sampayo himself seems to be aware of Evaristo's dubious status from the start, when one character calls him a "son of a bitch repressor" (p. 19), the latter a word almost impossible to detach from state repression during the last military dictatorship. Moreover, the visual reference to the *picana*, which appears in the foreground of one frame in "Cerco de amenazas" (p. 187), only serves to demonstrate how *Evaristo*, despite moving further back in time, cannot escape the political realities of Argentina during the 1960s and 1970s.

The sense of impending crisis in *Evaristo* is fundamentally channeled through the exploration of an increasingly corrupt, questionable state acting within an increasingly divisive urban landscape, a tension that comes to the fore in the episode entitled "Operación Hermann." Based on the arrest of Adolf Eichmann in Buenos Aires in 1960, the story begins (although it does not acknowledge its source) with an anecdote taken from Isser Harel's 1975 account of Eichmann's arrest, *The House on Garibaldi Street*. Harel described the manner in which, unfamiliar with Argentine cafés of the time, he sat down on his own in the family section of a café because it was less crowded than the other section. Far from keeping a low profile, however, Harel's choice of seating only caused the men in the café to stare at him, wondering what he was doing sitting in an area designated for women and children (1975, p. 152). That division is captured in the first frame of the chapter, in which we cannot see the offender but merely the characters looking over the screen at him. This notion of being out of place in the city continues throughout the story.

"Operación Hermann" plays on Eichmann's own placelessness following his arrest, a point highlighted by Hannah Arendt, who pointed out that the Israeli judges at his subsequent trial ruled that no breach of international law could be applied in Eichmann's case because such law "concerned only the states of Argentina and Israel, not the rights of the defendant," and that since both governments had declared the matter resolved, the law was no longer relevant (1994, p. 239). It was, Arendt argued, "Eichmann's de facto statelessness . . . that enabled the Jerusalem court to sit in judgment on him," something that Eichmann should have been able to appreciate since, as she pointed out, "the Jews had had to lose their nationality before they could be exterminated" (1994, p. 240). As if to exaggerate the manner in which Hermann is "out of place," Sampayo and Solano López reproduce the spatial geography of Eichmann's actual arrest. Detained in the northern suburb of Bancalari, now close to San Fernando, Eichmann was living on the "desolate outskirts" of the city (Goñi, 2002, p. 314), a landscape inscribed, at that time at least, by the beginnings of the *pampas*. The detailed visual depiction of the setting in *Evaristo* emphasizes the symbolic nature of the arrest—to be on the periphery of the city is to be on the periphery of urban and state justice, a point reinforced by other actions in *Evaristo* that take place in similar surroundings. Thus, alongside explicit images of Eichmann's brutality, including of him about to shoot a kneeling prisoner in the head, for example, the comic also raises questions about both the state's failure to bring a Nazi war criminal to justice and, subsequently, to the manipulations of legality that allow it to act with impunity. The newspaper editor states that the whole affair highlights "signs of weakness in the government . . . one might almost say there's no state" (p. 57), and a discarded newspaper carries the headline "State in Moral Bankruptcy" (p. 63), before a later edition states, "War Criminal Hermann Kidnapped: Foreign secret services acted with impunity: Last proof of our government's corruption" (p. 64). Though the comic reveals that justice has been done, the moral rights and wrongs are qualified in this episode since the methods of achieving that justice are questionable, a doubt that harks back to Evaristo's own acts. The last page of the Hermann episode is especially effective at reproducing the consequences of these fractious questions and the collapse of a morally strong state. The two frames in the middle of the page are divided by the gutter, but they are designed to work in opposition to each other—in the frame on the left, a tank moves left to right along a downtown street in Buenos Aires; in the one on the right, a jeep pursues a group of protestors moving right to left. The organization of the frames exaggerates the way that the military is converging on the bodies of those in the streets (p. 64). An episode that focuses on state impunity and questions over the legalities of justice, therefore, ends with an image of urban fracture and division.

The same inescapable fracture and growing internal conflict within the Argentine state, divisions that push Evaristo off the case in "Operación Hermann," are evident in two of the later episodes in the *Evaristo* series: "Villa Cartón" and "Cerco de amenazas." Other than Evaristo playing hero to the children from the shantytown by beating up an officer who punched them in search of information (p. 74), the lasting images of the episode are at the beginning and the end. Here the shantytown is positioned simultaneously within and separate from the city. The first frame, a full-page image, depicts the shantytown from a raised position, with the muddy stream drawing the reader's gaze into the image where the shacks eventually become fainter, almost imperceptible because of the rain. The framing simultaneously draws us into the space at the same time as reminding us of our distance from it. That distance is exaggerated in the following frame, in which Evaristo's police car moves down the center of a street that divides the new apartment blocks on the left from the wall that hides the disorder of the shantytown on the right. In the sequence's final image, the shantytown dominates the frame, an inescapable, no-go-out zone of urban poverty that supports Evaristo's comment that the kids who live there will never get out.

In "Cerco de amenazas," a similar sensation of entrapment is created by the rain driving across the frame from left to right and falling on the industrial factories and the port, generating an atmosphere of darkness and oppression. The opening frames of the episode heighten the tension; one reproduces the round sights of a pair of binoculars through which Evaristo and his colleague Maura can be seen at a distance, and a later frame includes the crosshairs of a rifle sight, a reminder of the silent, oppressive force—in this case, the state—that watches at a distance. In this episode, Maura and Evaristo hide from other arms of the state that are hunting them down. In this city the utopian promises of Peronism—evident in the graffitied "Peron o muerte" and "P/V" (for "Perón vuelve" [Perón will return]) on the wall (p. 182) and the shantytown dwelling with a picture of Evita on the wall (p. 183)—have been trampled underfoot by a corrupt military-business pact and the Peronist in-fighting and factions that would eventually result in the 1973 Ezeiza massacre, in which right-wing Peronists opened fire on left-wing Peronists. In one symbolic frame, a unionist who has been released from his detention as a result of a *habeas corpus* request is assassinated. As he is shot in the back, his suitcase falls open and reveals a copy of *La fuerza es el derecho de las bestias* (Force is the prerogative of beasts), a book written by Perón while in exile during the late 1950s. So even if Evaristo cries in this episode that no one in his section tortures anyone, the story ends with the dossier on the coming coup being ripped up. The detective can neither restore confidence in a rational order protecting citizens from urban chaos nor assuage fears over state authority. The sense of impending fear is captured in the frame drawn from the perspective of the underground hiding place in the shantytown where Evaristo and Mauro are holed up and from which they can see the drool dripping from the lolling tongue of the military dog that is hunting for them.

Faced with a crisis of post-dictatorship belonging, therefore, Sampayo and Solano López look back to a past Buenos Aires for some semblance of a moral code that preceded the acts of state impunity and military rule that would eventually destroy the fundamental sites of commonality around which the nation had coalesced. But *Evaristo* can never generate real nostalgia for that former Buenos Aires, despite heading back to the cityscapes of street corners and codes of honor of the 1920s and 1930s, precisely because that city, and the protagonist who represents it, creates an environment in which women are subject to acts of violence and criminals to paralegal detention and torture practices. The pre-dictatorship city only reinforces the divisive and fragmentary nature of the post-dictatorship city. In *Evaristo*, therefore, the fractured nature of the comic form does not valorize the fragment or the urban archive but rather emphasizes the impossibility of deploying Buenos Aires as a site around which to reconstruct national belonging.

Escaping the Post-Dictatorship City

Whereas *Evaristo* looked to the past to highlight the divisive, divided, and isolating nature of the city, several other comic book cities that date from the same period turned to futuristic, science fiction cities to express feelings of displacement and isolation. One such comic was *Ciudad*, written by Ricardo Barreiro and drawn by Juan Giménez. First published abroad at the start of the 1980s, the first three episodes were republished in Argentina in *Tiras de cuero* in 1983, before being restarted in *Hora Cero* in 1990 and then republished in book format in 1991. Despite being less well known than other *historietas*, *Ciudad* marks the direction that many later comics would take when envisioning the city during the 1980s.

Carl Freedman suggests that the science-fictional text "is determined by the *dialectic* between estrangement and cognition" (2000, p. 16) and by "its creation of a new world whose radical novelty estranges the empirical world of the status quo" (2000, p. 69). Freedman's definition is very apt for the science fiction city of *Ciudad*, an uncanny site that is both knowable and yet displaced. To begin with, the story opens in Paris, where Barreiro himself was living in exile, but after the protagonist Jean takes a wrong turn returning home after a night out, he finds himself on El Aleph Street. The name is a nod to Jorge Luis Borges's short story "El Aleph," which recounts how Daneri finds a point in his basement that contains all spaces within the universe, and it is a reminder of the layered nature of Barreiro's city in *Ciudad*, which is simultaneously Paris, Buenos Aires (one subway station is called "Aguero"), and New York (in the episode "Barrio Castillo" we see signs reading "E161st" and the symbolic "Don't Walk"). We can also see English and Spanish graffiti (in "Hamelin" one barricade states both "keep out" and "¡fuera!"). Thus, El Aleph Street becomes a portal to a city known only as "la ciudad" (the city), an infinite, multiple city that contains all other cities.

Such multiplicity is not just spatial and individual—in the first episode Jean appears superimposed over the other frames, a disjointed, fragmented figure who appears twice in the same image—but also temporal. On the one hand we are faced with an urban environment that is futuristic, unworldly, and built around the imaginary of science fiction, but on the other we are confronted with an environment that taps into the Argentine post-dictatorship period and concerns over the Latin American neoliberal city. The connection to the Argentine present is clear in the way that the characters refer on several occasions to the fact that they are "shipwrecked," a common post-dictatorship trope. Karen tells Jean soon after his arrival in La Ciudad that they are in "a monstrous metropolis, infinite and nameless in which all its inhabitants are castaways who've gone mad," a destiny that characters almost live literally in one episode in which the waters of the flooded city recede to reveal Noah's ark as a shipwreck. But the concern over the neoliberal present is perhaps most obvious in "Auto Supermarket," in which the characters get trapped within an automated supermarket. Replacing the neighborhood corner store built around local networks and relations, the supermarket is a symbol of capitalist expansion and the centralization of the shopping experience into large-scale, profit-driven enterprises. The dominant presence of the space of consumption within the urban landscape is emphasized on the opening page of the episode, in which the supermarket block stands as high as the skyscrapers that stretch forever onward under a threatening sky. The lack of personality is exaggerated in this episode in that the supermarket functions by itself, automatically registering purchases, filming the characters via security cameras, and deploying robot guards when Jean and Karen attempt to leave without paying. This city is less abandoned than a space that continues to function around the inescapable logic of the market. As if to exaggerate the fragility of those trying to survive within that logic, in the last frame of the episode the huge lettering of "auto supermarket" is barely visible, stretching beyond the frame. The speech bubble containing the characters' words also comes from beyond the frame, almost as if the comic format itself is unable to reign in the market excesses of this city.

Figure 3.1. Image from the episode "Autosupermarket" in *Ciudad*, written by Ricardo Barreiro and drawn by Juan Giménez.

Though Jean and Karen escape the supermarket with the aid of a rebel living inside, they are otherwise unable to escape the wider urban conglomeration—after all, how could one escape from the place that contains all places? As Jean's companion Karen tells him in the episode entitled "Sin salida" (No Exit): "The city is an infernal labyrinth from which we will never escape." In this inescapable city, in which these wandering castaways also become trapped on a neverending subway ride and are nearly devoured by a city park that turns out to be a carnivorous beast, the only tangible goal is survival. Like the entangled trees and plants of the creature, the very nature of the city is deceitful and labyrinthine. The anthropomorphic city is only one danger, however, as the city is also rife with gangs and individuals intent on survival. In "Hamelin," for example, they come across a wizened former musician in control of the city's rats. Far from welcoming the protection the rats provide him, the old man is distraught because he cannot find the sea in which to drown the rats. Not only is he unable to fulfill his destiny as the pied piper, his rodent companions mean that he is turned away from barricaded protection zones. These internal barriers and no-go-out zones are defenses against the frontier nature of the city evident in "En nombre de la ley" (In the Name of the Law), in which Stetson-wearing, gun-blasting policemen apply a nonexistent law. The most significant of these exclusion zones is "Barrio Castillo" (Castle Neighborhood), an area that has its own state, offering, in the words of the guide, "a little bit of peace, of order, of reference points." The appeal of being able to map oneself (the episode includes an image of a map), however, is quickly dispelled when Jean and Karen discover that the enclosed community, a nod to the gated communities that had started to grow in number in Buenos Aires, is suffering from a highly contagious epidemic: Constructing communities in common such as these, an act that reproduces what Roberto Esposito calls the logic of immunization (2008), turns the act of exclusion back onto itself with fatal consequences. Anticipating a growing tendency in urban representations over the course of the 1980s and 1990s in Argentine culture, *Ciudad* depicts urban survival as being dependent on small, tightly knit groups, urban tribes that rely on mutual need to counter the very real threats of the city. In turn, that city—"la ciudad"—is palpably a generic urban space, stripped of any semblance of community belonging, let alone national identity.

In the final episode, "La salida final" (Final Exit), Jean and Karen meet Juan Salvo, the protagonist of Oesterheld and Solano López's seminal *El eternauta*. The decision to include Juan Salvo, one of the most famous characters in Argentine comic history, exaggerates the manner in which the authors attempt to explore the role of cultural production within a context of urban crisis. Neither is Juan Salvo the only cultural reference in *Ciudad*: Apart from the influence of works such as Ridley Scott's *Blade Runner* (1982), David Lynch's *Dune* (1984), and Moebius's comic *The Long Tomorrow*, which was serialized in *Fierro*, in the episode "En la oscuridad de las cloacas" (In the Darkness of the Drains), Jean and Karen are rescued from sewer beasts by Frankenstein, the Mummy, Dracula, a werewolf, and the alien from Ridley Scott's 1979 film *Alien*. In this episode, Dracula tells Jean that they would never hurt humans precisely because they have been given life by mankind's dreams, legends, and fantasies. The inclusion of post-national figures of global popular culture has similar traits to Alison Landsberg's theory of prosthetic memory, by which a person appropriates and adapts a set of images taken from mass culture and integrates them into their own life narratives. Mass culture, Landsberg argues, provides "shared social frameworks for people who inhabit, literally and figuratively, different social spaces, practices, and beliefs" (2004, p. 8). Within processes of globalization and transnationalism, images can be assimilated by a diverse body of spectators who can "experience a bodily, mimetic encounter with a past that was not actually theirs" (2004, p. 14). Though Landsberg argument refers more specifically to the "mass-mediated experience of a traumatic event of the past" (2004, p. 19), the notion of prosthetic memory is equally useful for thinking through imaginaries of the future that are themselves infused with future prosthetic memories. That is, *Ciudad* imagines how a post-national set of cultural figures can be deployed as a means of combating the city in the crisis. Whereas the non-national figures offer a means of protection, however, the presence of the recognizably Argentine Juan Salvo serves to highlight how difficult it is to escape an internal meta-fictionality of Argentine cultural production. This national prosthesis does not offer a means of liberation through memory but rather a sense of entrapment, illustrated by the frame that depicts a hand holding a comic book page depicting the same page that we are reading in which a hand holds the same page and so on, an infinite series of images that are meaninglessly repeated forever.

Neither can Juan Salvo offer a means of escaping the city itself. Like the other urban inhabitants, he has taken refuge in the city center, a round central plaza symbolic of the modern city, which forms a sort of safe no-man's land. Juan Salvo informs Jean and Karen that the only means of escape from the city is the lift out of the central plaza, which he eventually uses, even though he recognizes that taking the lift could mean death. Before he departs, however, he speculates that the very order and peace of the city center is a trap, a means of controlling citizens—he demonstrates how a mysterious force prevents acts of intended violence by stopping thoughts being turned into action. Juan Salvo's decision to leave the city, even at the risk of losing his life, emphasizes his desperate desire to escape the urban nightmare that "la ciudad" has become. *Ciudad* thus poses the city itself as much as its inhabitants as the real threat to the survival of Jean and Karen. The point is exaggerated by Giménez's artwork and decisions over layout. Though he varies the size of the panels within the confines of the page with some regularity, often using page-wide panels to give a sense of speed, Giménez rarely uses bleeds to move beyond the panels and only sometimes are the edges of the panels trans-gressed. When they are, as when Jean's shadow falls outside the frame in "En nombre de la ley," the transgression is minimal. Nevertheless, many frames include images that emphasize the impossibility of viewing the city as a whole—though the panels mirror the urban grid of the city, therefore, the real sense of the way the city traps its inhabitants is due to its sheer size and endlessness. The foreboding nature of this colossal urban monstrosity is intensified in the first and last panel of nearly every episode, Giménez using almost without fail depersonalized panoramic cityscapes of endless towers and the repetitive façades of skyscrapers. In several episodes, furthermore, including "El jardín de las delicias," "En nombre de la ley," and "La salida final," the threatening effect of the city is heightened by the use of a panning out over several panels, a means of exaggerating the impersonal scale of the urban landscape. In "El jardín de las delicias," the final image of the urban grid is accompanied by the words "la trampa" (the trap), and the last panels of the work in "La salida final" are a series of bird's-eye images of the city that increase in distance, an image that not only mirrors the view from the lift out of the central square but also gives a vertiginous, threatening element to the neverend-ing city. Foreshadowing the way that many would see the city over the course of the coming decade, Barreiro and Giménez make the city into the ominous protagonist of the work, creating a dystopian urban landscape in which national cultural production cannot offer a solution to an urban environment in which death appears to be the only escape and survival the only means of existence.

Barreiro would explore other threatening cities in stories he wrote for *Fierro*, including the 1986 *Ministerio,* a story about a city turned nev-erending dystopian tower in which the modernist ideal of the skyscraper is transformed into a symbol of the nightmare of the bureaucratic state. The refined *Parque Chas*—written by Barreiro and drawn by Eduardo

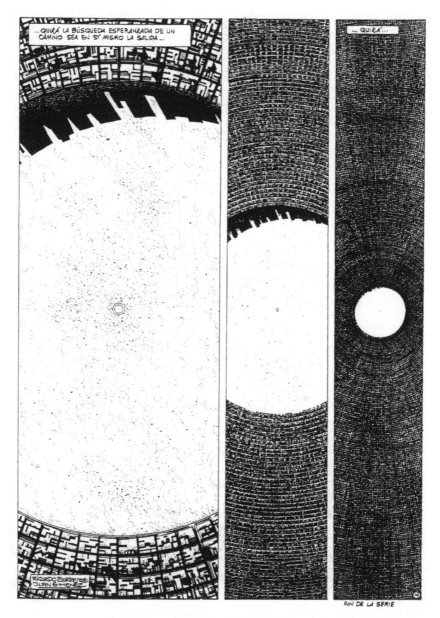

Figure 3.2. Image from the episode "La salida final" in *Ciudad*, written by Ricardo Barreiro and drawn by Juan Giménez.

Figure 3.3. Image from the episode "Dueño alquila un ambiente" in *Parque Chas*, written by Ricardo Barreiro and drawn by Eduardo Risso.

Risso, the first part of which was published in *Fierro* between 1987 and 1988 and which I focus on here—however, is a more powerful reading of the post-dictatorship city. The choice of Parque Chas, a neighborhood located in the northwest of Capital Federal, as the setting for the comic uses an area famous in Buenos Aires precisely for its atypical layout, evident on the very first page, where panels are placed over a map of the city that highlights the contrast between the circular arrangements of streets in Parque Chas, which here appears in a darkened circle, and the grid that dominates the rest of the city. The opening symbolizes the manner in which Parque Chas disrupts the ordered narrative of the city and, moreover, the manner in which the comic book form can explore that disruption, precisely because it works between fragment and order. Frames depicting the narrative are placed over the map, heightening the sense of fracture and rupture and also the way that the story emerges from that fractured urban landscape. Indeed, the narrative itself is depicted in this sequence via a series of frames that indicate disjointed temporal instances: the arrival of a telegram, the protagonist predicting its contents, the telegram itself informing him of the termination of his rental agreement, buying a newspaper, and then reading the classifieds. As in all comics, the reader must piece back together the narrative from the fragments, but here the gutter itself is not blank but full of the city.

Parque Chas was originally envisioned as a means of introducing nonconcentric, European urban design within the traditional grid design of the Argentine capital. It was designed to break the monotony of "the old straight, parallel, interminable streets, in which the gaze never rests" (quoted in Berjman, n.d.). The design makes Parque Chas unique in Buenos Aires for several reasons: It has curved streets, it has several dead ends, and many of its street names are cities. Certainly the experience of walking the neighborhood is unusual in a city normally constructed on a grid. Nevertheless, the actual geographical area of Parque Chas's curved streets is quite small, hardly justifying the apocryphal myths about the neighborhood: that taxi drivers will not go there for fear of being unable to get out; that there is a no. 187 bus full of dead passengers loaded with stolen cash trapped in the area; that a car crashed into itself on a circular street; and even that the neighborhood is a portal to hell. Nonetheless, Parque Chas tells us quite a lot about how *porteños* imagine Buenos Aires and how they rely on its familiar geographic regularity. Any disruption of the grid pattern carries great symbolic and cultural weight, here creating a kind of Bermuda triangle that has found its way into the work of Julio Cortázar, Ernesto Sábato, Tomás Eloy Martínez, and Alejandro Dolina.

The comic *Parque Chas* relates what happens to the protagonist, Barreiro, when he rents an apartment in Parque Chas with the proviso that he not open its one padlocked window.[8] Unable to resist temptation, the protagonist dreams of a woman trapped in a storm on the other side of the window and opens it, setting free Aitana, none other than the alter ego of his landlady, who subsequently throws him out for breach of contract, inspiring him to go in search of other strange stories about the neighborhood. These include "El subte" (The Subway), which relates the construction of a secret subway line connecting the Casa Rosada to a warehouse in Parque Chas, providing an escape route for President Perón; and "Un asesino anda suelto" (A Murderer's on the Loose), in which a woman relates a series of murders that took place in the neighborhood between 1976 and 1983, all of them committed by a driverless green Ford Falcon, connecting the *barrio* to the history of the dictatorship.[9]

The temporal displacements are indicative of the way the comic plays with parallel times and universes: When Barreiro opens the window, his conscious world mixes with that of myth, dreams, and storytelling, which unsettles chronological and spatial certainty. In "El subte," for example, one frame depicts a glass in the foreground being held by the old man who is telling his story about Perón, while his hand is superimposed over the Casa Rosada building in the background, thus drawing past and present together. Likewise, in "Reencuentro," which is set in the 18th century, surveillance cameras monitor Casanova's fancy dress party, creating layers of historical time. Nevertheless, such technological references are a reminder that, for all its historical explorations, *Parque Chas* is very much about Buenos Aires during the 1980s. There are references to the memory politics of the period via the use of the term "nunca más" at the end of "Un asesino anda suelto" or the graffiti "No a la obediencia debida" (No to Obediencia Debida), a reference to the debates over impunity laws under Alfonsín. There are political references, such as an election poster declaring "Gobernador Casella para confiar" (Trust in Governor Casella) and a newspaper referring to the U.S. bombing of Iranian oil rigs in 1987. And the growth of neoliberalism and economic crisis is expressed via references to private education, to public schools saving on lighting bills, and to imported products (a label on the back of a record player is written in English). Indeed, *Parque Chas* begins with an archetypal struggle of the 1980s, one that goes to the heart of urban living during the period: rental prices. If these explicit references were not enough, then the first two episodes also, just as *Ciudad* did, include images of boats in storms, shipwrecks, and castaways, another reference to *Fierro*'s subtitle and the notion that the protagonist is another post-dictatorship survivor.

In addition, and like *Ciudad*, *Parque Chas* incorporates traits of prosthetic memory. In "El libro" (The Book), Barreiro goes in search of the book that holds all the myths and stories about Parque Chas, drawing loosely on Borges's short-story "El Aleph." The protagonist comes across Borges himself in the labyrinthine basement of the local school library, labyrinth and library both further nods to the former librarian. In the library he also comes across Captain Ahab (as drawn by Enrique Breccia in his version of *Moby-Dick*), El Corto Maltese (as created by Hugo Pratt), and, once again, the time traveler Juan Salvo. These myths form a more positive reading of the metafictionality of Argentine culture than that found in *Ciudad*, not least because they are themselves placed in a transnational context (e.g., the Argentine Breccia's version of *Moby-Dick* or the inclusion of Hugo Pratt, the Argentinized Italian), particularly appropriate for a neighborhood in which street names are frequently cities and in which one can meet at the corner of Liverpool and Cádiz and where London is the continuation of Dublin. The two-part final episode of *Parque Chas*, "Final a toda orquesta" (Full Orchestral End), follows this transnational approach. Barreiro includes very specific national references, such as to a Ballester Molina, an Argentine make of semiautomatic pistol, alongside transnational references, such as the brief appearance of Casanova. Moreover, just as in *Ciudad*, the protagonist is shown a way out of Parque Chas by an imaginary creature, here the Latin American "cuco," a popular monster in Hispanic and Lusophone culture used to frighten children into going to sleep. When Barreiro expresses his surprise at being rescued from the final battle by this underground monster, "el cuco" reminds him that the monster's existence is dependent on the human imagination. That the head of "el cuco" is a television with its screen smashed is a reminder of the way in which *Parque Chas* places value on refashioning mass media. Once again, it is a shared prosthetic imaginary that saves the protagonist.

In *Parque Chas*, however, the characters do not escape the city but rather escape from it right back into its very heart: After climbing a spiral staircase and opening the door at the top, Barreiro and Aitana find themselves emerging from the Obelisco, the obelisk that is the city's most recognizable icon. Ever since it was built in 1936 to commemorate the fourth centenary of the founding of Buenos Aires, the Obelisco, now the material, geographic, and symbolic "center" of Buenos Aires, has often been a site that reveals tensions in the construction of Argentine national identity.[10] In recent years, Argentine cultural production has often either turned its back on such monumental iconography or turned it on its head, symbolized by the scene in *Pizza, birra, faso* (dir. Adrián Caetano & Bruno Stagnaro, 1997) in which the characters break into the monument to reveal its dark, phallocentric interior. In that sense, *Parque Chas* also turns the Obelisco inside out, seeing in it not the entry point to a restored national city but rather to the dark underground sewers that house ongoing urban conflicts. Such darkness is a reminder of the fact that the city in *Parque Chas* is often a threatening and violent space, an impression fueled both by the setting and Risso's drawing style. Not only are many of the stories set at night or indoors, often in underground spaces, but they are depicted via Risso's detailed and time-consuming use of gray scale (which he used because he was not permitted to use color), a style that creates rich contrasts between light and dark. Risso subtly captures the breaking of dawn in "Dueño alquila un ambiente: Parte 2" (Landlord renting apartment: Part 2); more than once he draws the character Barreiro writing at his desk illuminated only by a triangle of light coming down from the shade, and in "Un asesino anda suelto" he uses car headlights and a bonfire to great effect. These images sometimes exaggerate the oppressive and violent nature of the urban landscape, its uncertainty, and moral ambiguity.

At the same time, however, Risso's use of contrast also draws our attention to the spaces of light, not least in the final panel of "El subte" (The Subway), in which light streams out of the bar in which Barreiro has been listening to a story. Indeed, almost every episode begins in a bar since it is in these spaces that the character Barreiro listens to and collects stories about Parque Chas. The extensive use of bars in the comic symbolizes the way that many Argentines in the post-dictatorship period saw the local neighborhood rather than national sites as housing the spatial possibility for social equality and a restored democratic community (Menazzi, 2008). Bars and cafés in *Parque Chas* function as common spaces, locales in which stories can be exchanged. As in the rest of the comic, which provides a multisensory experience of the city via cityscapes, graffiti, advertisements, newspapers, and sounds (in "Un asesino anda suelto," for example, bars of music are reproduced in speech bubbles), Risso is careful to draw the reader into such encounters by including panels that depict close-ups of drinks being poured or sugar being added to coffee cups. In the first panel of "El libro," for example, figures being served drinks are reflected in a large beer glass sitting next to a bottle of Quilmes Cristal beer and Marlboro cigarettes. Risso details the beads on

Figure 3.4. Image from the episode "El libro" in *Parque Chas*, written by Ricardo Barreiro and drawn by Eduardo Risso.

the outside of the glass, the creases of the cigarette packet, and, in a further frame, the click of a lighter. That sensual experience of being in the
bar is exaggerated by the close-up in the second frame, in which we can
only see one hand taking a cigarette from the packet offered by another
hand amidst the things on the table, and, in a subsequent frame, by the
torso of the waiter and the tray he carries that partially block our view
of the characters. In contrast to the threats of the city, therefore, it is the
communal space of the bar that offers the opportunity for urban change
precisely because it is the setting for the palimpsestic layering of myths,
stories, and imaginaries that are told there. The point is intensified in the
final chapter by the inclusion of the writer Alejandro Dolina, famous for
the best-selling collection *Crónicas del Angel Gris* (1988), a collection of
neighborhood-based stories of the city.

The cities in Barreiro's two comics are worlds in which "the indis-
tinction of inside and outside leads to the discovery of another dimension" (Deleuze & Guattari, 1986, p. 8). Here too we find "blocks on a
continuous and unlimited line, with their doors far from each other,
[which] are revealed to have contiguous back doors that make the blocks
themselves contiguous" (p. 73). But whereas in *Ciudad* the characters are
confronted with an urban dystopia that they want to escape in an act of
anti-urbanism, in *Parque Chas* the homonymous neighborhood of the
title acts a kind of urban subconscious in which the city can be explored
through the imagination. The emphasis on the space of the bar, included
in this comic not as a national space but as a local, neighborhood space
of encounter that draws urban dwellers together to share stories, highlights how the commons of the urban imagination itself can lead to the
imagining of alternative urban futures. Thus the disconcerting nature of
the work's shifts in perspective, which include ground level images, bird's-
eye views, close-ups, long-distance images, images of characters from afar,
and images that put the reader in the position of the character, as well as
the blank spaces that sometimes appear in the comic grid, can gradually
be assimilated by the reader as part of the urban experience. The comic
book fragment is here put forward as a means of envisioning the way
that post-dictatorship fracture can be turned back into multiple acts of
storytelling that function in common to fashion new urban communities. Nevertheless, the decade that followed, characterized by an increasingly neoliberal urban landscape, would demonstrate that post-national
imaginaries could not always create the possibility for such exchanges
and encounters; on the contrary, they would often point toward a series
of urban commons based on exclusion.

Chapter 4

Neoliberal Urbanism

Anticommons in Common

The 1990s in Argentina was a decade marked by extreme neoliberal reform. The cornerstone of President Carlos Menem's strategy to reduce the impact of the state was the 1991 Plan de Convertibilidad (Convertibility Plan), which pegged the Argentine peso to the U.S. dollar at the rate of one to one. Allowing the market to determine social "equality" via the promise of opportunity, convertibility was initially successful in curbing the persisting threat of spiraling hyperinflation that had plagued the Alfonsín era. Before long, however, such parity became unsustainable, and the rising cost of the borrowing required to sustain the exchange rate was a major cause of the eventual economic collapse of 2001. The Convertibility Plan was symbolic of the way that the Menem administration restructured the state, reigning in public spending, deregulating the market, and carrying out a number of significant acts of privatization (most notably of public services, the railways, electricity, and communications infrastructure). For the wealthy these shifts meant that the 1990s were a boom period as the overvalued peso enabled them to purchase imported goods and expensive foreign holidays. For the rest, however, the 1990s were marked by dramatic increases in living costs and unemployment, intensified by the collapse of the support network of a welfare state that had been in steady decline since the apogee of the first Peronist administration (1946–1955). Buenos Aires, like the rest of Argentina, was now left, in Javier Trímboli's words, under "an open sky, without shelter, defense or protection" (2003, p. 189).

The rapid and far-reaching structural and ideological transformations of the 1990s were at their most stark in the city. The neoliberal logic of privatization meant that Argentine urban policy in the 1990s "accepted fragmentation as a given, as the necessary condition for a modernizing leap" (Gorelik, 2009, p. 75), highlighting that the city incorporated enclosure as the basis for progress, development, and internationalization. Whilst some forms of exclusive commons—such as gated communities—thrived under this urban logic, the inclusive potential of other commons—public spaces, nonstate entities, and transport—were undermined by their subjugation to the market. Buenos Aires turned away from what Maristella Svampa calls the " 'open city' model, essentially European, centered on the notion of public space and in values such as political citizenship and social integration [and] toward a 'closed city' regime following the North American model, marked by the affirmation of a 'private' citizenship" (Svampa, 2008, p. 14). Public policies over housing, for example, contributed to a crisis in territorial belonging. As Raúl Wagner (2008) has shown, the end of the "loteos populares" (working-class lots) during the dictatorship, a means by which low-income families without access to credit could own land via grants, had already reduced levels of home ownership. During the 1990s, with lower incomes and rising living costs (partly a consequence of the privatization of amenities such as gas, electricity, and water), an increase in middle- and upper-class land ownership on the urban periphery (traditionally areas inhabited by the working class), and privatizations such as that of the Banco Hipotecario, the country's leading mortgage lender, housing became increasingly inaccessible. Concurrently, alternative forms of accommodation boomed in Buenos Aires, evident in the growth of temporary lodgings such as cheap hotel rooms and sub-lets, the growth in squatter communities, and the expansion of the population of shantytowns.

At the same time, Buenos Aires, like many other cities around the world, underwent a process of bunkerization driven by concerns over the rise in crime under neoliberalism. The repressive geographies of the Cold War were now revamped into new modes of urban policing and division in a city increasingly characterized by inequality. During the 1990s security-conscious businesses and homeowners in Buenos Aires battened down the hatches, utilizing architectural design, fences and walls, private security firms, firearms, alarm systems, cars, and gated neighborhoods in a collated response to the perceived threat of this rapidly transforming, unfamiliar and threatening metropolis. Fueled by police corruption and a mass media that stoked the fear of crime far beyond actual figures, the city began to install a security system that ran parallel to that of the state (Smulovitz, 2003, p. 146). When not defending themselves against specific urban others, citizens sheltered themselves against the city itself, personified as hostile and indifferent. Urban life was inscribed by fear.

The growth in large-scale private land ownership, transformations in practices of consumption and public space, lack of access to housing, and discourses of fear all meant that the city was entering a phase of intense conflict between enclosure and common use, a conflict that went to the heart of the notion of the right to the city. That conflict would itself be played out via territory, whether in the spatial forms of protest that proliferated during the 1990s and beyond (Wagner, 2008, p. 74), or in the desire for territorial security evident in the ongoing spread of insular gated communities and security-conscious apartment blocks. The consequence, as Wagner argues, was an increasing link between (lack of) territory and identity construction. For the lower classes, for example, against a backdrop in which growing unemployment and the restructuring of work made it increasingly difficult to build identities around labor, the boom in informal housing created a concrete link to territory via localized informal construction networks and the use of new materials required to build and sustain housing without the support of the state. It is also within this logic that the neighborhood, or *barrio*, became a privileged locale for expressing political discontent and constructing alternative urban identities. The prominence of the neighborhood as a marker of identity was part of a broader geographical shift in which the urban center was replaced by a new set of urban nodes and peripheries. The growing prominence of the citizen as consumer, for example, went hand in hand with a boom in shopping centers, sites that offered an alternative set of confluences and trajectories to the centralized city of modernity but which also reduced the possibility for encounter with the urban stranger. Shopping centers epitomized the divisions of the neoliberal city, built for a mobile consumer class participating in a deregulated market via acts of consumption and simultaneously excluding those without the requisite spending power.

The structural transformations just described simultaneously intensified the importance of the urban imaginary, and the struggle over the right to the city was also played out in cultural representations of the city. Martín Rejtman's 1999 film *Silvia Prieto* depicted how urban decentralization and fluidity seeped into all facets of city living. A vision of Buenos Aires stripped of any semblance of filmic pamphleteering, the progressive aesthetic challenge of *Silva Prieto* demonstrates how the city of the 1990s transformed commons into commodity. Claudia Piñeiro's 2005 novel *Las viudas de los jueves* (Thursday Night Widows) further demonstrates how gated neighborhoods during the same period deployed spatial and social boundaries in an attempt to counteract a city stripped of community belonging. By building a community around immunization, however, the gated community of *Las viudas de los jueves* turns the violence it purports to exclude back on itself. Though very different in setting and aesthetics, both of these works demonstrate how the neoliberal city encourages the creation of commons that function as anticommons. Similar, albeit more subtle, kinds of exclusive communities that attempt to confront the threats of the urban present are evident in an array of cultural texts created toward the end of the 1990s and the beginning of the new millennium, not least the films that formed part of so-called New Argentine Cinema.

The City De-Centered

The transformation of the city over the course of the 20th century, from the locale of industry to the locale of postindustrial business to the very object of that business, has reshaped the city's relationship to its inhabitants. Marking the manner in which urban dwellers can frequently only engage with that city through acts of consumption, when the Argentine Constitution was rewritten in 1994 the consumer was entered as a figure of constitutional rank, highlighting the significance of consumerism to this newly defined social contract (Lewkowicz, 2004, p. 19). Though some theorists such as Nestor García Canclini (2001) have highlighted the democratic potential of a citizenship constructed around consumption, as Gareth Williams argues (2002), re-legitimizing the nation-state through a community model based on market forces reinforces the power of capital, excluding those without access to the means of consumption, let alone the means of production.

Alejandro Parisi's 2002 novel *Delivery* captures the rampant consumerism of the 1990s in Buenos Aires by highlighting how the protagonist Martín's entry into the world of drug trafficking enables greater purchasing power. In much the same way as when the dealers reward him for good work by telling him that he "went to the second level, like in a videogame" (p. 87), Martín's progression in the novel is marked by making his way up the urban pyramid of this newly configured citizenship via his growing involvement in dealing drugs. The style of the novel and its use of language highlight Martín's lack of civic consciousness. The shift between action and thought creates an interior monologue that does not reveal hidden meaning via free association so much as highlight the superficiality of the protagonist: "I invite him for a beer because I want to talk to him but Toni and Andrés hear me and ask if they can come with us. Fucking hell, I think" (p. 14). The novel's rather trite resolution with the drug dealers and Martin's departure from the city with one of his girlfriends is an unconvincing attempt to break the narrative cycle established by the protagonist's constant TV zapping and the references to the time display on his video machine. Quitting the city with expressly no destination in mind is symbolic of the way that Martín tries to escape his mapping of the city around consumption, money, and trafficking. Working as a fast-food delivery boy, he moves around the neighborhood delivering *empanadas* and cocaine. His urban geography is explicitly built around the street corners where he picks up the drugs, place names that become meaningless as one is replaced by the other in a neverending cycle of non-spaces in the here and now. In this city of the eternal present, mirrored by the stifling present tense in which the novel is written, urban geography and identity is not created via history but by wealth. When Martín accompanies a girlfriend to a party in Olivos, he is palpably unfamiliar with this affluent suburb in the north of the city. He states that "we go via an avenue that's called Maipú" (60), his jarring unfamiliarity with one of the principal thoroughfares of the northern suburbs a reminder of the sociospatial division of the city. Such division is also evident in a brief scene set in the Alto Palermo shopping center, where the security guard eyes Martín suspiciously. Martín resents the guard's suspicious gaze not because of some ideological critique, however, but precisely because he does, in fact, have plenty of ready cash that would allow him to participate in this space of consumption. Martín has interiorized the neoliberal logic of "good" citizenship.

Highlighting how the accumulation of money gives access to the new urban centers provided for the citizen as consumer, the novel's reference to a shopping center is a reminder that the urban dweller's right to transverse and negotiate the city is dependent on spending power. Built around a philosophy of consumption, shopping centers in Buenos Aires are not public spaces but private spaces revamped and marketed around the pretense of being public. Restricting access to "undesirable" citizens via security guards is hardly problematic for the shopping center if that restriction encourages a greater number of acts of consumption from others who have greater spending power; after all, as Lewkowicz argues, global capitalism does not try to multiply the number of consumers so much as the acts of consumption (2004, p. 79). Thus, when Sarlo states that shopping centers are "the monuments of a new civic-mindedness: agora, temple and market" (2004, p. 16), she not only highlights that the forum-turned-marketplace transforms public gatherings into an exclusive commonality based on consumption but also how the citizens who have access to such acts of consumption desire to share that commons with other citizens of the same "constitutional rank."

The locations for such shared experiences of consumption marked a significant shift in the urban geography of Buenos Aires. Whereas citizens used to visit the downtown area as a weekend outing, more and more people started visiting shopping centers (Sarlo, 2004, p. 11). Shopping centers in Buenos Aires can be found throughout the city, and taken as a whole they can be seen as creating an alternative set of urban centralities (Tella, 2005, p. 41), territorial nodes that offer alternatives to local businesses and the streets of the city center.[1] That the shopping center offers an alternative to the centripetal and centrifugal modern city, built around a unifying core, is not necessarily to be lamented. The problem lies with the alternative commonality it proposes, one based on unequal and exclusive acts of consumption. The commons that shopping centers promote is based on the stark contrasts between the space they offer (ordered, secure, homogenous, clean, etc.) to the space outside (disordered, unsafe, multiple, dirty, etc.), a separation intensified by subterranean parking lots that allow visitors to participate in a variety of acts of consumption without ever having to encounter the street. Once inside, the space's layout encourages acts of consumption by leading people past as many shop windows as possible, simultaneously disorientating the consumer, as if they were trapped in a neverending consumer world. Thus the shopping center purports to offer everything that the consumer could want, constructing "an idealized eternity, in the sense that an absolute present (presence) as absolute actuality within the interior of a space operates to obliterate the subjective sense of the exterior" (Draper, 2009, p. 38).

The absolute present of the shopping center, typified by constant temperature, lighting, and smells, does not do away with history entirely. As Hugo Achugar has demonstrated, for example, the Punta Carretas shopping center in Montevideo, formerly a penitentiary and detention center, remains a symbol of power, expressing the desire "to erase violence from the public stage in order to realize the ideal Uruguay" (2009, p. 199). At the same time, however, it simultaneously disappears all trace of the famous breakout from the prison undertaken by more than 100 left-wing Tupamaro guerrillas during the Uruguayan dictatorship. Thus, in Punta Carretas, "the memory that has been definitively erased is not the memory of power, but rather the memory of resistance to power" (Achugar, 2009, p. 196).[2] All shopping centers in the Southern Cone are

indirectly involved in the erasure of a contested past to foment a consensus which, in turn, turns consumption into both the raison d'être of
politics and also the means of expressing political viewpoints. Consumers
are encouraged to forget that it was the dictatorships of the 1970s and
1980s that instigated the economic framework that gave birth to the Latin
American shopping center (Draper, 2009, p. 38). Thus, though Sarlo is
right to highlight the functional similarity of shopping centers and the
way that they all offer the same concthey do not always create cities
absented of geography and history (2004, p. 15). Instead, particular geographies and histories are commodified and deployed as marketing tools
to encourage consumerism, and it is that deployment that de-historicizes
and de-politicizes urban life.

The logic of commodification, de-historicization, and de-central-
ization is evident, albeit in an entirely different way, in the production
that Sarlo chose to be her archetypal feature film of the 1990s: Martín
Rejtman's *Silvia Prieto* (1999). Similar to the trends described previously,
the film's city is stripped of any obvious landmarks that would provide a
clear urban identity. And yet the city is recognizably Buenos Aires, the
street scenes playing on the geography and emptiness of the city's residential *barrios*. The real is not just located in peripheral urban neighborhoods,
however. The real itself becomes peripheral, because references to it are
constantly situated as a means of highlighting the central irreality of the
film world. The innumerable shots of particular Chinese restaurants where
the characters eat, for example, eventually collapse into sameness. The
globalization of culture is not critiqued for producing a loss in national or
urban identities, but simply provides the stage for this anti-drama. Emilio
Bernini suggests that the city in the film "can never be rebuilt into an
imaginary whole" (2008, p. 54), and *Silvia Prieto* neither pretends that is
possible nor is it even concerned with such a problem.

The nondescript, marginal city neighborhoods utilized in the film,
filmed in a similar way to the setting of Rejtman's earlier film *Rapado*
(1992), which "radically eliminat[es] any references to historical or social
context through the extreme reduction of the frame, suppressing the out-
of-field" (Andermann, 2011, p. 19), are mirrored by a group of characters
who also lack identity and history, transformed, like the interchangeable
restaurants, into objects of exchange. Like the city, characters in the
film lack a clearly identifiable center, a loss of identity evident from the
moment that the protagonist Silvia Prieto discovers that she has a namesake in Buenos Aires. Initially Silvia appears indignant that there could
be any other Silvia Prieto, reacting angrily to her colleague Brite when

the latter asks whether Silvia uses her maiden name or her married name: Brandishing her identity badge, Silvia states vehemently, "What does it say here?! What does it say?!" And yet Silvia is quickly involved in a series of rearrangements and identity exchanges that reveal her identity to be precarious, even nonexistent: Brite starts dating Silvia's ex-husband Marcelo and then sets Silvia up with her own ex-husband Gabriel. Brite is later mistaken for Silvia because she is wearing Silvia's overcoat, which itself formerly belonged to Silvia's grandmother. This replacement or exchange of characters is emphasized by repeated side-on shots of them facing each other at tables in cafés, restaurants, Silvia's kitchen, or a prison—the characters are less important than their repeated replacements of each other.

Individual identity in the film, destabilized by these fluid interchanges, is intensified by the aforementioned collapse in work as a mode of belonging (Sarlo, 2003, p. 128). The jobs evident in *Silvia Prieto* are precarious, temporary, and require no training. Silvia's only means of trying to make sense of her work as a waitress is to keep a tab on the number of drinks she serves, eventually giving up her post because she can no longer keep count of the *cafés con leche* and espressos that she has served. When she next appears assisting Brite in handing out free sachets of washing powder on the street there is no indication of how she obtained the job—she simply appears in uniform from one frame to the next, fluctuating between jobs.

In this city of interchangeable places and inhabitants, objects are placed center stage. As Rejtman himself stated, a shot of an ashtray was as important to him as one of a lead character (cited in Fontana, 2002, p. 84). Indeed, the film is fascinated with the aesthetic of the everyday object, a means of emphasizing both the centrality of the object in urban life and the lack of any political resistance to that objectification. Oubiña argues that objects in the film "are commodities whose 'use value' tends to be eclipsed by their 'exchange value'" (2004). Silvia's "bottle lamp" is a case in point: Initially she tells Gabriel that "it's no longer a bottle, it's a lamp," but she then states that a "bottle lamp" refers to someone who serves no purpose; Garbuglia, an old school friend of Gabriel, adds that a bottle lamp is "not much of anything" since it is "a double device." The use value of the object is surpassed by the way it is interchanged between the characters, whether physically or even because it turns out that "bottle lamp" was Gabriel's nickname at school. Its identity, like that of the inhabitants of the city, is disrupted by a series of exchanges that depend purely on the present and not on past or intended use. Objects in the film thus circulate freely between the characters: An Armani jacket passes from Silvia, who stole it from an Italian tourist, to Gabriel, who sells it to Marcelo. In turn, Marcelo sells it back to the Italian for a profit of $25, calling the transaction "the best deal of my life." The circulation of goods creates profit with no effort from citizens, who act simply as market catalysts. Incessantly fluid, neither do these objects provide markers of identity. Silvia initially gives Gabriel the Armani jacket because it is collecting too much dust—as soon as the jacket accumulates a history it is passed on.

These history-less objects are further interchanged with people: Brite's name comes from the washing powder company for whom she works, and the Italian whose suit jacket is taken by Silvia simply calls himself "Armani." The figurine that Brite eventually gives Silvia because the statuette looks like her typifies the interchange between people and objects. Calling it Silvia Prieto, a further diffusion of her identity, Silvia eventually throws the statuette out of a bus window in a metaphorical attempt to destroy her namesake other, crying "Death to Silvia Prieto!" The statuette Silvia Prieto does not pass away, however; in a further level of flux and exchange it is picked up by a teenager who leaves home to go and see a band just as his mother is going to bed. After the recital, the lead singer of the band, tellingly named "El Otro Yo" (My Other Self), returns home to his mother, none other than Silvia's namesake, constructing a symbolic tie between the two Silvia Prietos.

The doll is the perfect commodity to symbolize the exchange of characters within a city constructed around the market: The figurine's static, expressionless face reflects the lack of emotional register and drama in the film. Brite and Marcelo's first kiss, for example, springs out of nothing, lacking any buildup or sexual tension. Similarly, just as there was nothing furtive in Silvia's initial "appropriation" of Armani's jacket, the original owner displays no anger when he has to buy it back from Marcelo. This lack of drama is intensified by the inability to create affective ties through communication. The answer machine gifted to Silvia, for example, is never taken out of its box, symbolizing how language, words, and (the lack of) human communication also become objects of exchange rather than expressions of drama and depth, a point intensified by the featureless style of speaking, characterized by an unsettling regularity and lack of register. As Emilio Bernini argues, "the proliferating dialogue [of the film] no longer guarantees the statute of identity, because here the characters, rather than being defined by what they say, are mere carriers of words" (2003, p. 94).

Certainly, as Andermann warns, when analyzing films like *Silvia Prieto* we should be wary of critiquing it for something that it never set out to do in the first place. As he has demonstrated, Rejtman's films steer away from any semblance of a social or political didactics but rather offer an alternative poetics: "[T]he everyday is made to release its absurd and hallucinatory qualities by closing off the wider frame of (socio-cultural) reference, the out-of-field, as soon as it is invoked—producing an intrafilm-ic real that is shot through with figments of contemporariness, but isolated, set free from their usual contexts" (Andermann, 2011, p. 25). And yet Rejtman's "abyss of meaning" (2011, p. 25), as Andermann calls it, is none-theless tied to a specific moment in Argentine history, and *Silvia Prieto* is a clear engagement with a society of hyper-commodification. As Constanza Ceresa suggests, the film's new cinematographic language confronts the logic of the market by fusing "the accelerated time of the market with anti-narrative," a move that draws attention to how reality is constructed (2014, p. 182). In that sense, it is worth pointing out that, though it is sometimes difficult to pinpoint the precise locations where *Silvia Prieto* was filmed precisely because of their generic qualities, one building, at least, is read-ily identifiable: the former Caseros Prison located in the neighborhood of Parque Patricios, which was eventually closed in 2001. The prison, while it was still functioning, was a symbol both of the dictatorship, when it first housed prisoners, and, subsequently, of the corrupt world and decaying urban fabric of the neoliberal era. Perhaps, then, the film does not so much close off the wider frame of sociocultural reference as singularly fail to do so—such references inescapably permeate the poetics. Thus the reduction of indexicality not only "allows for a different, more indirect and complex, mode of reference that exploits this 'irreality' to comic effect" (Andermann, 2011, p. 21), but also shows how what remains of the indexical constructs a complex mode of reference to the real.

Silvia Prieto's sparse dialogue, fixed camera angles, soundtrack with-out music, and lack of "drama" highlight the film's aesthetic intervention, a poetics that replaces a politics or, perhaps, a political poetics. For all of its aesthetic differences, the film does share with other films made at the same time what Gabriela Copertari called "narratives of disintegration (com-munitarian, political, social, economic, cultural, familial and personal) [that] articulate a social experience of loss" (2005, p. 279). Commenting on social relations in neoliberal Argentina, Lewkowicz suggested that citi-zens now exchange products rather than share a history (2004, p. 34), and the film portrays how both city and characters are characterized by a lack of depth, stripped of history and trapped in a forever-repeating world of perpetual exchange and interchange. The film concludes with an aesthetic shift, a handheld camera documenting a meeting of "real" Silvia Prietos. In the wake of the rest of the film, some of the "real" Silvias' statements, such as that "Silvias are calmer" or that she is "Silvia Prieto from Villa Luro," emphasize the pathos of these desperate attempts to construct individual identity. Just before this documentary sequence, Silvia puts on a video of Garbuglia and Marta's wedding for a friend, but when she discovers that the video is blank she secretly replaces it with the video of her own marriage. For a moment she wonders to herself whether he will realize before she resigns herself to her plurality: "By now, I really didn't care." Silvia's apathy symbolizes the film's dark vision of the de-centered city. What *Silvia Prieto* highlights, therefore, is the effect of this environment on characters who appear to form a commons around objects. It is precisely that this apparent commons is built around the exchange and not the use of goods that turns this city into an anticommons: Stripped of use, commoning becomes commodification. In turn, the characters are turned into automatons, directed by circumstance, television, and the market. Garbuglia's and Marta's passive acceptance of the power of the media dictates their future: First meeting on a lonely hearts show, they only go through with their wedding because the television channel has already paid for the party. The act of commoning has been turned into a commodity.

The Logic of Exclusion

The commodification of the commons and the sharing of products rather than history are especially evident in gated communities, which, along with shopping centers, are perhaps the archetypal urban development of post-dictatorship Argentina. In Claudia Piñeiro's 2005 novel *Las viudas de los jueves*, one of the shrewdest takes on the enclosed neighborhoods of Buenos Aires, the characters see the city as the place where history happens: Political events, corruption, or the deaths of famous people are always perceived to occur on the other side of the fence. The gated neighborhood of Altos de la Cascada in which the novel is set, on the other hand, is where history is forgotten: "Entering La Cascada produces a certain magical forgetting of the past" (p. 30).[3] The neighborhood purports to offer a space where past indiscretions, including domestic abuse, can be left behind simply by buying a new house. The community is thus based on an eternal present. Ultimately, however, though the erasure of history and memory initially offers a sense of liberation, the characters suffer the return of the repressed, discovering that they are simply unable to cut themselves off from life outside the gates.

The novel begins precisely with references to irruptions from the out-side world, namely the attacks on the World Trade Center and the anthrax poisonings of 2001 (p. 11). Not just an indication of how the outside to the gated community is included in its very exclusion, since the way gated communities are marketed are forever dependent on reminders of reasons to fear the outside, these references are also symptomatic of the wider paradigm of immunization that permeates the novel. Roberto Esposito takes 11 September 2001 as indicative of his argument about immuniza-tion, suggesting that the immunity drive set in motion in the wake of the attacks resulted in a destruction of life brought about by "an excess of defense" (2008, p. 9). Esposito argues both that the immunity paradigm, intensified by a globalization that increases the points of human interac-tion and thus the desire for immunity, structures contemporary society, and that unbridled immunization ultimately ends up not protecting but destroying life. It is the destruction brought about by excessive immunity that characterizes the gated commons of *Las viudas de los jueves*.

Gated communities are now a common sight in Latin American cities, located in the urban peripheries that historically housed poorer sec-tors of the population, creating a new urban landscape in which extreme wealth sits alongside highly impoverished communities.[4] The founda-tions for the development of country clubs and private neighborhoods in Buenos Aires were laid in the 1970s and 1980s, the expansion of the motorway network making weekend getaways accessible for those who desired safe havens from the country's uncertain political situation. After the explosion in gated communities that took place in the 1990s, by 2004 there were almost 300 *countries* (country clubs), *barrios cerrados* (enclosed neighborhoods), and *emprendimientos* (large-scale enterprises) covering a total area approximately twice the size of Capital Federal (Janoschka, 2005, p. 97). Over the course of this period, gated communities became, for many, permanent residencies: If in 1979 almost none of the com-plexes had a permanent population, by 1999 some 20,000 people were living in country clubs, and by 2004 there were approximately 110,000 living permanently in the various types of residencies (Atlas Ambiental de Buenos Aires, n.d.). The services offered by these neighborhoods encour-age residents to stay within the confines of the walls. Located near the motorways that carry residents directly to their jobs in the city, the small-est neighborhoods offer various services and leisure activities, including tennis courts, swimming pools, and small golf courses, in addition to neighborhood organizations and social events; the largest include super-markets and schools. In addition, peripheral urban expansion—particularly in the northern sectors of the city—has generated a new network of private schools, universities, and commercial and shopping centers. The growth in secondary and tertiary regional banks in the urban periphery between 1994 and 2004 is indicative of a trend by which urban outskirts are transformed into autonomous suburbs, since these financial institutions tend to have a close territorial relationship to their clientele (Atlas Ambiental de Buenos Aires, n.d.). Furthermore, sports provide a means by which gated communities run inter-*country* competitions, constructing an inward-looking network. Gated communities in Buenos Aires have thus created an "archipelago city," formed by a series of nodes or "small *publics*, each of which may be thought of as a collective consumption club" (Low, 2004, p. 186), that work together to territorialize socioeconomic divides.

The autonomous network built up by gated communities emphasizes a material and imagined separation from the rest of the city. The *barrio cerrado* is normalized around "a clear separation between the 'inside' and the 'outside,' an unmistakable register between 'us' and 'them'" (Svampa, 2008, p. 254). Indeed, in *Las viudas de los jueves,* residents of the gated community constantly remind themselves that they are explicitly not part of Buenos Aires. The characters go "to the city," a phrase that positions the city as an other space; once there, one resident feels like "a tourist, visiting a place that didn't belong to her, as if she were spying from behind a curtain" (p. 199). The emphasis on the otherness of the city plays into the reasons behind the initial flight to the gated communities of the urban periphery. As Guy Thuillier suggests, residents of gated communities turn their back on what the city has to offer: "The new suburban residents now value more domestic space, nature and family life, rather than the urban landscapes, the opportunities for recreation and contacts provided by the city" (2005, p. 262). María Cecilia Arizaga has further pointed out that children who live within the *megaemprendimiento* of Estancias del Pilar refer to the built "town center" of the gated community as "the city," whereas they refer to Buenos Aires by name, a difference that reinforces geographical and social difference (2004, p. 67).[5] In particular, the appeal of the gated community in terms of separation from the city, and the alternative commons that it offers, can be divided into four overarching lures, all of which are evident in *Las viudas de los jueves*: the desire for nature; the provision of leisure activities; the fear of the city and its accompanying security measures; and the desire to be part of a community.

The name of the private neighborhood in the novel, Altos de la Cascada, emphasizes the importance of nature to the community, evident also in the streets named after birds or the way the hedges are cut irregularly to increase their "natural" aspect (p. 26). The enclosed neighborhood also offers protection from the perceived dangers of the metropolis. Not only are Latin American urban dwellers dominated by the fear of violence, but that fear has also been transformed into fear of the city itself. For the citizens of fear that live in gated communities, security becomes a point of commonality. In the aftermath of the strikes, mass protests, and supermarket sackings of 2001 and 2002, the ultimate aspiration of gated communities in Buenos Aires is even more loaded in favor of sophisticated security measures (Svampa, 2008, p. 278). Thus the narrator praises the fact that in Altos de la Cascada you can leave the front door unlocked (p. 20) or that you can walk around whatever time of day with complete confidence, whereas in the city you spend your time worrying about being assaulted (p. 27).

Security also allows the inhabitants to exaggerate difference with the city by enabling them to function as a partially independent state. The residents speak of "infractions" ("crimes" would imply the need for state intervention) that are dealt with internally by the Discipline Committee; state police are replaced by the neighborhood's private security guards and "the country's justice system, the external one, the one that's out-side, in the courts, in the Palace of Justice, almost never manages to get involved" (p. 241). The gated community also uses security to frame its more immediate "other," the poor neighborhood called Santa María de los Tigrecitos located next door. The inhabitants of Altos utilize the difference of poverty to justify their existence: "The unpaved streets, the lack of suf-ficient parking space, but above all the distance that separates them from the security hut at the entrance to Altos de la Cascada makes us keep our distance. They say there are thefts every day in Los Tigrecitos" (p. 110).

In reality, however, the residents of Altos are involved in a precari-ous relationship of difference and dependence with Los Tigrecitos, not least since residents of the latter form the service community of the *bar-rio cerrado*: "Those living there depend on the work we provide them in Altos de la Cascada" (p. 108). This phrase is suggestive of the way that residents of Altos see themselves as providing a service rather than the other way around, symptomatic of the way the wealthy expiate their guilt by organizing charity events to help the residents of Los Tigrecitos who work in the *barrio cerrado*. That charity even stretches to a semblance of possession of the urban poor, one of the inhabitants of Altos referring to "other poor people, not ours" (p. 128). Residents of gated communities in Buenos Aires, Svampa suggests, believe "not only in the meritocratic vision but also in the pedagogical, even civilizing, task that the upper classes should undertake in relation to the poor" (2008, p. 224). Her comments highlight once again that the gated community needs poverty to justify its own enclosure.

The pretense of enclosure dismantled by the relationship with Los Tigrecitos is just one of the façades that permeate the novel. The shaping of the hedges and the planting of imported trees highlights how nature is manufactured. The literary classics that line one resident's shelves turn out to be just covers with blank pages. The concern with one's own image is further evident in imported branded goods such as Twinings tea or Calloway golf clubs, the narrator's concern that she cannot afford to keep her maid full-time, or Juani's quizzing of his parents after he is caught smoking marijuana and is put on the neighborhood committee's list of truant children: "But what is really bothering you, that I smoked pot or that I'm on the list?" (p. 205).

The sense of a façade that hides nothingness is intensified by the style of the novel itself, located between plot and description. If the novel begins with the evening that will later be revealed as the key moment in the plot, an evening further inscribed with the historical encroachment of global fear, then description soon overwhelms the plot. It is no accident that the principal narrator of the novel, Virginia, works as an estate agent within and for the gated community, a role symbolic of the self-perpetuation and subsistence of the neighborhood as real estate. The presence of Virginia's voice means that the novel reads as if the community were being marketed to the reader. In a statement that reveals how the narrative is stripped of fiction, Virginia says that in September "everything smells like star jasmine [which] isn't a poetic phrase but a purely descriptive one" (p. 28). The filmic level of detail saturates the novel almost to the point of meaninglessness. The opening of Chapter 24 is a case in point:

> In autumn the Bermuda grass turns yellow. It doesn't dry out, doesn't die, it just hibernates until the summer, when the grass turns green again, and the cycle starts once more. Meanwhile there are two options. . . . The first is to look for color elsewhere: golden or red sweetgums, golden oaks, yellow ginkgos, fire-colored *rhus typhina*. . . . And the other is ryegrass, a grass that lasts a season, with a color that's false it's so intense, like cold-store apples, or chickens fattened under electric lights. But flawless; not so much grass as a carpet. (p. 177)

The level of detail in this passage is soporific, taken to such an extreme that it is almost stripped of meaning and narrative. It is as if the novel's intention is not to narrate a set of events but the *barrio cerrado* itself, which, in its own world of no history and no past, has no narrative. And yet, at the same time, the detail sets up codes and symbols that are in fact overdetermined within the context of the gated community. The line following the extract above—"That year wasn't a year for ryegrass in the Urovich household"—reinserts narrative back into the description, demonstrating how detail is meaningless and how the meaning of the novel is precisely meaninglessness. And yet even in their meaninglessness, the façade of objects and words cannot suppress the violence that the gated community attempts to push beyond itself. The point is made in Chapter 46, in which the group of husbands discusses the possibility of killing themselves and faking their deaths as an accident so that their families can take advantage of their life insurance. The discussion takes place over a game of *truco*, the Argentine card game based on deceit and sleight of hand. The narrative mixes the conversation with the calls in the card game, creating a tension between the light-hearted nature of the friendly encounter and the gravity of what is being suggested (p. 303). As the passage continues, however, the card game gradually peters out until it is left unfinished with an unanswered "truco" (trick) (p. 305) hanging mid-paragraph before the heated discussion ends with the disgusted Ronie leaving his friends to their plan. The passage highlights how the game cannot suppress the pressing reality of the possibility of life insurance, a decision that only has meaning given the context of the Argentine economic crisis.

But it is crime, security, and fear that really demonstrate how the gated community is a false commons built on inequalities and subject to collapse. The way the community attempts to handle crimes that take place within its walls in the novel demonstrates that the ideal of security is not what it purports to be. Fear and security highlight not just the breakdown of the community idyll but also how that breakdown is dependent on the act of immunization. Reflecting Esposito's observation that "the harder ['the self'] tries to include what is located outside itself; the more it tries to introject every form of negativity, the more negativity it reproduces" (2008, p. 6), characters in the novel not only attempt to construct a clear inside-outside dichotomy but also perceive layers of otherness within the gated community. Thus the wall the residents want to build around the entire zone keeps the residents in as much as it keeps others out.

The tangible network of security barriers, walls, and fences is mapped onto a set of conceptual boundaries within. The inhabitants are involved in a constant process of demarcating their land: "With each step he marked his territory; it was evident. If he'd been an animal he would have pissed" (p. 39). The underlying racism of the neighborhood spills over when a member of the only Jewish family in the community marries the daughter of a devout Catholic family. Justifying their discrimination by laying claim to Argentina being "a free country" (p. 146), the inhabitants, as the narrator states, "end up saying things like 'this is a lay club, obviously, but the families who come here are, in the main, Catholic'" (p. 147). As Setha Low writes, "gating also involves the 'racialization' of space, in which the representation and definition of 'other' is based on human biological characteristics" (2004, p. 143). Here, race is deployed to define internal relations, and the Jewish family in question, the narrator acknowledges, fulfilled "a fundamental role in the neighborhood: that Jewish friend that guarantees that we don't discriminate" (p. 143).

As the novel progresses, the dangers of this introspective immunity become increasingly apparent. Juani's girlfriend Romina is aware that the perimeter of the enclosed neighborhood is problematic: "Which is the inside and which the outside?" (p. 184). The electronic collars that give a shock to dogs if they get too close to the outer fence, a territorial limitation they learn to respect even when the collars are eventually taken off, is a reflection of the way the inhabitants learn to stay within the confines of the community. If the first chapter concludes with the narrator's husband Ronie saying that he is afraid, expressing the fear that the gated community purports to suppress, the novel gradually reveals that his fear is not of the outside but rather of what lies within: We eventually discover that he has just witnessed the beginnings of the suicide pact. Unable to escape the impact of the 2001 economic collapse in Argentina and on the verge of having the façade of their idyll existence stripped away, the men, in an act of male bravado and protectionism, sacrifice themselves to enable their partners to live off the life insurance and exist precisely as widows, that is, as women whose identity depends on their marital status. The men's actions are based on the gender inequalities and exclusions around which the gated community functions, and it is not by chance that one of the men who kills himself physically abuses his wife. There have been a number of high-profile instances of violence directed toward women in gated communities in Buenos Aires, perhaps most famously the murder of María M. García Belsunce, who was found dead in her bath in the gated neighborhood "Carmel." Initially said to have died from drowning after slipping and knocking herself out, a later autopsy revealed that she had been shot five times in the head. In her later novel *Betibú* (2010), which is also set in a gated community, Piñeiro refers to the García Belsunce case (and other crimes against women that are either unsolved or involved miscarriages of justice) as being illustrative of a lack of justice toward women in Argentina. Thus, in both *Las viudas de los jueves* and *Betibú*, Piñeiro demonstrates how the gender politics of the gated community reveals this particular commons to be based on inequality, abuse, and lack of opportunity for women. Indeed, that violence is what the men ultimately turn on themselves to perpetuate the unequal commons they have created. Thus the novel concludes with the narrator asking Ronie if he is afraid to go out when they are about to denounce the crime to the state police. As the narrator states: "I felt like I was in one of those films where those who've broken the law have to cross the frontier" (p. 317).

The acts of self-harm with which the novel concludes, therefore, highlight how "the violence of interiorization—the abrogation of the outside, of the negative could be reversed into an absolute exteriorization, in a complete negativity" (Esposito, 2008, p. 11). In the depiction of this absolute negativity, *Las viudas de los jueves* demonstrates not just the dangers of immunity but also of constructing a community of the immunized. The novel explores immunity not just as a withdrawal from the community but also as an act of withdrawal that provides the foundations for another community, which, in turn, re-instigates the immunity paradigm. Gated neighborhoods are often marketed in terms of the sense of community they will provide: "[T]he desire for social homogeneity is probably one of the strongest attractions of the gated communities" (Thuillier, 2005, p. 262). And yet community as homogeneity is precisely the expulsion of difference on which immunity is based. The act of being in common, a commons that does not exclude difference, cannot be built on immunity since immunity is not only an act of self-destruction and an act of protection against *the* community but also an act that disassembles communities working in common.

The immunity imaginary of the gated community stretches far beyond the *barrios cerrados* of the urban periphery of Buenos Aires. With Latin American cities increasingly inscribed by ever-larger gated communities, some settlements stretching beyond 30,000 inhabitants, the notion of a *barrio cerrado* may need replacing with a term such as *ciudad vallada* (fenced-in town) (Borsdorf & Hidalgo, 2008, p. 154).[6] These gated communities are not only reminders of how the city threatens to become a series of separate city-states but also of how the logic of the gated community is encroaching on urban life more broadly: "[P]rivate neighborhoods [have] emerged as . . . a *total social act*, within which one can see the functioning of society in general" (Svampa, 2008, p. 291). In a physical sense, gated communities are mirrored in the city center by *las torres jardín* (garden towers), high-rise blocks built within the dense urban fabric and which some have labeled "vertical gated communities" (Borsdorf & Hidalgo, 2008). Like the gated neighborhoods, these constructions promote themselves as secure and enclosed private residences, ones that retain the attractions of the traditional *barrio* as well as being able to offer 24-hour security, vehicle access directly into parking lots, swimming pools, gardens, recreation rooms, tennis or squash courts, gymnasiums, and sometimes even rooftop heliports. But, as Esposito suggests in terms of the all-pervasive nature of immunity, the real threat is that the paradigm of the gated community, the fear of the other and the withdrawal to communities that refuse to act in common, becomes established as the urban norm.

The Alternative Families of New Argentine Cinema

A number of films released between 1997 and 2003 also use Buenos Aires to depict and sometimes advocate, albeit in more subtle ways than *Las viudas de los jueves*, communities based on exclusionary commons. Andermann is right to be wary of simply assessing recent Argentine films for contemporary events since that risks "fail[ing] genre cinema for something it never claimed to deliver in the first place," emphasizing instead that "we need to assess genre narratives by their success in crafting figurative expressions for particular forms of historical experience" (2011, p. xvii). Nevertheless, it is still pertinent to ponder why, at a time when political communities were constantly being refashioned in expansive as well as exclusive ways, so-called New Argentine Cinema constantly resorted to the latter. Furthermore, though audiences "are perfectly capable now of understanding and appreciating generic devices for what they are: a play, a rhetorical game the purpose of which is not to 'represent reality' but through which contemporary reality can be alluded to in an indirect, ironic or critical fashion" (Andermann, 2011, p. 148), that does not mean we should shy away from evaluating figurative expressions and allusions as a means of assessing the kind of political communities that are depicted.

Key studies of Argentine cinematic production from the mid- to late 1990s until the present, films that make up the so-called New Argentine

Cinema, have discussed what this broad and varied corpus of films might have in common (Aguilar, 2006; Andermann, 2011; Aprea, 2008; Page, 2009). If anything, the films can be said to share two overarching elements: (1) that they emerged from a renewed cinematic landscape brought about by highly promoted and popular film festivals (Mar del Plata, BAFICI), by the establishment of film schools, by a reinvigorated body of cinema critics and critical output (especially via print and online magazines), by a growing body of cinema goers, and by improved access to imported cinematic equipment and films as a consequence of the policy of convertibility; and (2) a preoccupation with the present, which is to say that the films were engaging explicitly with the social, political, and cultural moment of the time they were made, whether in terms of cinematic realism, albeit a fictionalized and mediated one, or more explicit displacement via, for example, aesthetic shifts or what Gonzalo Aguilar called a "new creative regime" (2006, p. 14).

One further trait of New Argentine Cinema highlighted by these studies has been the different kinds of communities established both within and beyond the film world. As Aguilar and others after have noted, New Argentine Cinema is characterized by a rejection of "the demand for identity and politics" (2006, p. 28). In particular, that rejection has taken the form of a cinematic rejection of the political demands of films produced in the 1960s and 1970s, especially the project set out under the banner of Third Cinema. Notions of identity are, as highlighted above, increasingly problematic in an environment that has transformed so many of the traditional markers of identity construction and belonging, leading Aguilar to add that the films reject "the people as the privileged political subject and cinema as one of its possible weapons" (2006, p. 144). But whilst New Argentine Cinema tends to critique the national-popular model and presents urban environments endemic with brutal division and hostility as one of the few things citizens have in common, the films do offer a wide range of alternative communities. Thus, if it is true that characters in the films suffer "a certain orphanhood" (Aguilar, 2006, p. 41), then the protective structure of the family is replaced not by the political communities of the 1970s but by other smaller communities that tackle their local, threatening (urban) environment (Aprea, 2008, p. 73). What I want to highlight here, however, is that those small groups more often than not appear to exist in isolation rather than acting in common with other communities. They react against the transformations of urban life during the 1990s at the same time as being heavily influenced by a desire to escape the grand communities of filmmaking in the 1970s, concluding that the only possible means of survival is a kind of community bunkerization, forming groups that are hermetic entities of self-defense and exclusion.

One such community is epitomized by *Los rubios* (The Blondes; 2003, dir. Albertina Carri), a seminal film within contemporary Argentine memory politics and one that has already produced much analysis and debate about its treatment of the documentary genre and foregrounding of the vagaries of memory and the impossibility of re-presentation (see, among others, Kohan [2004]; Nouzeilles [2005]; Page [2005]; Sarlo [2005]; Aguilar [2006]). Sarlo, for example, has critiqued the film for its failure to try to understand what led Carri's parents to join the left-wing guerrilla group Montoneros, a decision that ultimately led to their disappearance. Sarlo's frame of reference, however, remains rooted in the cultural politics of the 1970s and the documentary militant cinema groups of the 1960s and 1970s, such as Grupo Cine Liberación and Grupo Cine de la Base. Not just questioning the manner in which the documentary form purports to truth, however, Carri also problematizes the notion of political filmmaking in terms of a shared cinematic project, a point made by her vision of the film family. Carri's film family is offered as an alternative to other kinds of belonging and community building, namely the blood family, the community of collective memory, the political community espoused by Carri's parents, and the community of political filmmaking.

Unlike the expansive philosophy of filmmakers in the 1960s and 1970s, who believed that their films would draw together support for the revolutionary cause, Carri's alternative family is not open but exclusionary. The viewer is left outside the process of remembering, which remains impossible in any collective sense, a point made evident in the impasse between Carri and the Instituto Nacional de Cine y Artes Audiovisuales (INCAA), who decide not to fund the film because it lacks the "documentary rigor" of truth-seeking they believe would contribute, one assumes, to their vision of collective memory. The failed project of collective memory is further evident in the urban landscape itself, which provides tenuous and problematic markers of identity and location, a point emphasized by the contrast between the entry in *Nunca más* that describes the detailed location of the Sheraton, the detention center where Carri's parents were held, and the confused reality of actually trying to arrive at the place described.[7] Even the house where the film crew first stop to talk to someone who remembers the Carri family has two numbers on it—"Husares 473" and "Husares 375 ex. 473." As Javier Trímboli has argued, the Carris's decision to move to Villa Tesei, the working-class neighborhood where they were arrested, was fueled by their belief that doing so would help them shed their middle-class background. In practice, however, as the mistaken memories of the former neighbors—particularly their erroneous belief that the Carris were blonde—make clear, the militants were palpably out of place. The ongoing dislocation is continued in the present when the film crew don blonde wigs, emphasizing the impossibility of constructing a community around memory.

Not only emphasizing the collapse of "the people" as a site of belonging (Aguilar, 2006; Trímboli, 2006), the film also suggests that the city itself contributes to that collapse, a point highlighted by the contrast between city and country in the film. Inverting Sarmiento's dichotomy, Carri portrays the city as the setting for the barbaric outcome of "civilization," whereas withdrawing to the country offers a refuge from that brutality: After their parents' disappearance, the Carri daughters lived with relatives in the country, a place that provides Albertina with happy childhood memories. In the film's final sequence Albertina and the film crew walk away from the camera down a country track wearing wigs, a defiant display of Carri's film family. By turning their backs on the viewer, the ending symbolizes how this film family turns its back both on the spectator and on the barbaric city *tout court*. Carri's film family, based on a friendship of aesthetics, performance, and generational togetherness, offers an important political alternative to other forms of memory-based belonging and political filmmaking. The price of that alternative, however, is the ongoing rejection of any semblance of an inclusive urban commons.

Whereas *Los rubios* has a clear political objective behind its exclusive community, other films of New Argentine Cinema appear to be motivated simply by providing aesthetically innovative readings of contemporary urban life, symptomatic of the trend Malena Verardi described as replacing "a political demand (what to do)" with "a demand over identity (who we are)" (2009, p. 183). More often than not, that demand is explored predominantly in and through Buenos Aires, since the city houses the films' varied political, social, cinematic, and aesthetic actualities. The vast number of films that engage with turn-of-the-millennium Buenos Aires mirror the growing importance of urban territory to political struggles and the redefinition of cultural identities since the early 1990s. Andermann has argued that the displaced or indirect realism, as he sees it, evident in many of the films being produced during this period is a direct consequence of "the estrangement that all inhabitants of Buenos Aires experience as a result of urban crisis" (2011, p. xvi). Much of New Argentine

Cinema has reconfigured the urban imaginary of Buenos Aires to generate a broader cinematic portrait of the city than had been evident before in national production. Turning their back on the symbolic heart of the national-popular city, the films frequently use both outlying *barrios* of Capital Federal and the lesser-known districts of the vast urban cordon that makes up Gran Buenos Aires.

The early films of Pablo Trapero are a case in point, the director emphasizing how he turns the Province of Buenos Aires and particularly La Matanza in Gran Buenos Aires into a character in and of itself: "Everything I am and do was born in San Justo, district of La Matanza, Province of Buenos Aires. Or why else do you think my producer is called Matanza Cine?" (Serra, 2002, p. 85). In *Mundo grúa* (Crane World; 1999) the outlying neighborhoods provide the contrast between construction and unemployment in a city that has lost its core and in *El bonaerense*[8] (2002) a dialogue is constructed between a provincial town of the interior and the metropolitan area of La Matanza. The film depicts Zapa's journey from provincial locksmith to metropolitan policeman. Duped into being the fall guy for a robbery, his only means of escaping a jail sentence is to head to the city to become a cadet in the infamous police force of the Province of Buenos Aires. Zapa's journey to the metropolis is also a shift from the friendly world of the rural town, to the highly localized and exaggeratedly anonymizing nature of Buenos Aires. Thus, whilst the recruits must shout together that they are from La Matanza, a large district that forms part of Gran Buenos Aires, that geographical entity only offers Zapa protection when it is filtered through the localized Mafioso police network. Zapa is characterized precisely by lack of will: He allows himself to be taken from one situation to the next, getting deeper and deeper into the corrupt world of the police before he is fully institutionalized. The only time that he appears to act with anything resembling self-fulfillment is during the violent sex he has with his partner, an act of near rape that is indicative of the way the violence of the institution he works for begins to seep into his everyday life. Politically disenfranchised, economically marginal, the city allows him no other form of expression other than a violence that emphasizes the inability of the state to regulate its own watchmen. Thus it is not exactly that *El bonaerense* is stripped of all community—the police workers, after all, celebrate Christmas, get drunk together, and (in the main) look after their own—but that the community it presents, one which is supposed to serve *the* community according to its own motto, operates as an introspective, defensive body, a group that defends itself *from* the community, whether law abiding or law breaking.

Adrián Caetano's urban western, *Un oso rojo* (Red Bear; 2002), also picks up on the filmic possibilities of the urban margins—La Boca, marginal to the center of Capital Federal, and San Justo, marginal to the entire city of Buenos Aires—to emphasize the lawless, frontier town atmosphere of the film and the city. In his 2000 film release *Nueve reinas* (Nine Queens), Fabián Bielinsky chose a different geography to stress the transnational nature of the city (and the film), filming several sequences in the Hilton Hotel, built in 1998 and inaugurated in 2000. Located in Puerto Madero, the epitome of neoliberal urban development construction in the city, which packages history into a consumable commodity for the nomadic elite, the Hilton offers transitory accommodation for the transitory subjects of the global economy, just a short walk from the shantytowns of Barrio Rodrigo Bueno or Villa 31. In all these films, therefore, there is a conscious shift in the urban imaginary of Buenos Aires—a shift away from the traditional urban iconography of the city.

The departure from that Buenos Aires is best symbolized in the film often seen as ushering in New Argentine Cinema, *Pizza, birra, faso*, (Pizza, Beer, & Smokes) the film poster for which stated "There's a new Argentine cinema." Similar to the image of Buenos Aires captured in the short "La Querencia" (1998, dir. Nicolás Saad) featured in the collection *Mala época* (Bad Times; 1998, dir. various), in which two brothers from the rural interior are confronted with the murderous potential of the metropolis, the city in *Pizza, birra, faso* is a dog-eat-dog, survival-of-the-fittest world in which national narratives fail to generate a sense of community or to overcome urban unemployment. *Pizza, birra, faso* undoes the national and architectural iconicity of the city by filming the dirty inside of the Obelisco. In the film, the structure's phallic erectness is satirized in a parody of male fantasies of the national: Pablo tells Cordobés that he once knew "a chick who was turned on by the Obelisco" because she thought it "a kind of dick that captured all the cock vibes that circulate through the city." Cordobés's response, his nickname emphasizing his regional background, critiques the symbol's centrality: "I don't get putting a gigantic cock in the middle of the city—you've got to be *porteño* to think like that." Soon after the characters break into the structure, ogling the pornographic photos pinned up inside before climbing to the viewing platform at the top of the internal ladder, where they get high smoking marijuana and reflect on unemployment in the neoliberal city as they look out over the lights of Buenos Aires. As if to remind us of the tragic failure of previous forms of political engagement, we catch a glimpse of a graffitied "P/V" on the wall, the symbol for "Perón vuelve" (Perón will return) which was used by the left to rally support during Perón's exile in the 1960s and 1970s. Here it appears only hidden away in the dark interior of the monument. With the further irony that the white limestone of the Obelisco was mined in Cordobés's home province of Córdoba (Dirección General de Patrimonio, 2003, p. 193), the Obelisco is here turned inside out, its pure white façade debased by highlighting how the structure's implied narrative of a collective national identity is shown to be an exclusionary commons because it is based on a highly centralized national imaginary, one that is blind to its own overt masculinity (the pregnant Sandra, after all, is left on the pavement outside).[9]

Claudio España in *La Nación* praised *Pizza, birra, faso* for its "anthropological" inclusion of the language of the street and the way it "talks about what's happening to us" (1998, p. 13). Horacio Bernades in *Clarín* stressed that the characters, the situations, the dialogues, and the city were all "believable," the city itself a welcome departure from the middle-class city so typical of Argentine cinema and transformed into "a city-hunting ground" (1998a, p. 8). The scene that symbolizes such conflict most starkly is when Cordobés and Frula steal from the amputee street beggar, a moment when the urban world of betrayal and survival (introduced in the very opening sequences, which depicts a robbery followed by treachery) surpasses any false semblance of a community of the poor. As Bernades highlighted in a review published in *Los Inrockuptibles*, the world of the margins is itself structured around a corrupt hierarchy, and whilst he is right to point out that "the principal group of *Pizza, birra, faso* functions as an alternative, and not entirely dysfunctional, family" (1998b, p. 63), that family is nonetheless introspective and exclusive.

A similar understanding of family is evident in *Un oso rojo*, where the protagonist Oso is involved in a series of robberies and gunfights in the peripheral "wild west" communities of Buenos Aires in an attempt to recover the money owed him so that he can give it to his daughter (Scorer, 2010). It is also in *Un oso rojo* that we find a satire of the nation, depicted as a failed (urban) community. Oso's violent fight for his family is further justified by the failure of the nation to provide security or togetherness in this marginal city: As the robbery of the factory takes place, Oso's daughter is acting as the bearer of the national flag in a school ceremony, the sounds of the gunshots from one scene interspersed with the children singing of the nation's glory in the other.

Whereas most films either critique the national community or avoid it altogether, Gabriela Copertari has persuasively argued that another film, *Nueve reinas*, enacts the desire for national justice via the ultimate simulation that ekes revenge on the swindler Marcos. In this "parentless family" (2005, p. 283) the community is restored via a charade ostensibly formed around bonds of friendship; however, as Copertari highlights, the newly reformed (national) community is unstable: "the symbol of articulation of community is in itself a simulation whose truth or falseness is undecidable" (2005, p. 290). Thus, while Joanna Page highlights how the film's emphasis on artifice and fiction is entirely coherent with the realities of an economic system that is itself "[dependent] on fiction and belief for its stability" (2009, p. 91), the fact that *Nueve reinas* was read as a national drama, despite Bielinsky stating that this was not his intention, does indicate that the nation was an ongoing concern in the context of the kind of communities prevailing (and waning) in neoliberal Argentina. Once again, however, even if the film's community is symbolic of a national desire, the community is only ever manifest behind closed doors, coming together in a sort of backstage prop room hidden away from the economic realities taking place outside. This family, like all national families, is based on exclusion, the creation of an inside that separates order from disorder, and those who belong from strangers.

The dark side of the national family is starkly portrayed in Adrián Caetano's *Bolivia*, a film that Pablo Scholz in *Clarín* called "a complete picture of a society in crisis, a country in a state of emergency" and which demonstrates that "solidarity is an asset in disuse midst a society sick with selfishness" (2002, p. 9). The film depicts the struggles of a Bolivian immigrant who has found a job working as a cook in Buenos Aires. Poorly paid because the owner overlooks his illegal status, Freddy has his affability tested by the racial and xenophobic abuse he suffers from nearly everyone except the Paraguayan waitress, Rosa. Set in a restaurant-bar in the *barrio* of San Cristóbal (though actually largely filmed in Villa Crespo), located southeast of the *microcentro*, the film utilizes the *parrilla* as a microcosm of a working-class Argentina put under immense strain by the country's economic situation and who survive by engaging in shady deals and failing to pay loans. Those workers perceive the illegal immigrants who come to Argentina to send home their earnings in the form of remittances to be a direct cause of their financial woes. Caetano here taps into the way that race became an integral part of the discourse of crisis during the 1990s and at the start of the new millennium. As Ignacio Aguiló has pointed out, anxiety over the inherent exclusions and inequalities of neoliberalism were vocalized via a critique of an internal outsider identified on racial grounds (2014, p. 180). That *Bolivia* was filmed in black and white only adds a further layer of symbolism to a work that addresses the fluctuating visibilities of race in Buenos Aires at the time it was made. Here the national commons is shown to be not just an exclusionary form of belonging, one that pushes the racial other beyond its metaphorical limits, but also one that suppresses forms of solidarity that might otherwise develop between two disenfranchised, working-class groups that, in fact, have a great deal in common.

The setting of the film, the *parrilla* bar (bar and grill), heightens these racial tensions by working on two levels. On the one hand, it functions as a national-urban symbol, a locale based around the archetypal Argentine product of meat in a cyclical process of preparation, cooking, eating, cleaning, and urinating. On the other, it functions as a local-*barrio* symbol, a hyper-localized space frequented by regular customers and from which the camera rarely strays. As Andermann points out, the neighborhood bar becomes a space "of uneven encounters between multiple trajectories between place and the out-of-place," a displacement as true for the *porteño* (native of Buenos Aires) as for the migrant in the wake of a city that has experienced a rapid transformation of the familiar into the strange (2011, p. 60). The bar is thus a space that captures the tensions between global, national, and local: Eating and drinking in a quintessential *porteño* space, vehemently partisan customers watch a heavyweight boxing title fight between Evander Holyfield and Mike Tyson (a fight that locates the events in 1996 and which introduces another layer of race to the film) while they are served by a Paraguayan and a Bolivian, the latter having lost his job at home due to the U.S.-promoted policy of spraying coca farms as part of the "war on drugs."

The tensions between nations are clear from the outset, the credits interspersed with an international football match between Bolivia and Argentina. The choice of the Andean nation as the film's racial other is especially potent in an Argentine context because Bolivian immigrants "call up an indigenous otherness that could not be further from Buenos Aires's self-image" (Grimson & Kessler, 2005, p. 127). Moreover, it is no accident that Caetano chooses a clip of the teams entering the pitch in which the commentator introduces the Argentine captain as "El 'Cholo' Simeone," a nickname that is itself racially loaded. Indeed, as Alejandro Grimson and Gabriel Kessler point out, the fans of the Argentine football team Boca Juniors are sometimes disparagingly called "Bolivians," a name that blends racial stereotyping with the working-class background of the club's supporters (2005, p. 127). But national and racial stereotypes are mirrored by other stereotypes based on sexuality and gender: The restaurant owner warns the young gay man who frequents the bar to stop checking out Freddy, and when he refers to the area of Palermo where the names of the streets are "all Central American countries, Peru and all those," his ignorance about the geography of the Americas is linked to him trying to describe where the transvestites work. That discussion is also marked by his own unfamiliarity with Buenos Aires geography since, as one of the other customers points out, he cannot be right when he says that the transvestites are to be found at the intersection of Charcas and Nicaragua since the two streets run parallel to each other.

City and nation are not the only failed commons here, however, since the clientele at the bar also reflect the manner in which other forms of belonging are collapsing. Friendship—if it can be called that—is constantly tested by financial obligations and debt, and there is no wider structure of work on which to rely. In an interview published in *Veintitrés*, Caetano suggested the film was not so much about xenophobia as about a populace that "is alone, lost and needs to grab onto somebody" (Lictira, 2001, p. 38). In the same interview he went on to discuss the collapse of Peronism (which he calls "being a fan of a club that doesn't exist anymore"): "Until I was 23 I was even active in the JP (Peronist Youth). But because of that I started having problems in the factory, and when they got rid of me I went to the union to ask for help and no one moved a finger, and that's when the disillusion kicked in" (Lictira, 2001, p. 40). The film also, therefore, demonstrates the failures of political belonging. Once again, the state is absent until the simmering tensions of the film spill over and result in Freddy's violent death. High on cocaine and drunk on beer, one of the regular customers, who constantly blames his lack of work on Uruguayans, shoots Freddy in an act of revenge for the latter breaking his nose after the two were involved in a scuffle in the bar. After the shot of Freddy's body lying prostrate on the bar floor, seeping blood as if he too was now just another slab of meat to be served up to the Argentine customers, the film then includes a scene in which the owner of the short-term hotel in which Freddy spent the previous night tidies up his belongings. The scene is a reminder of another family tragedy, as Freddy leaves behind his wife and children in Bolivia, introduced in the film via an international call he makes and in the glimpse of a family photo. Indeed, the strains placed on that family are intensified not just by the nature of transnational work but also because Freddy's night in the hotel is a direct result of his getting drunk and sleeping with Rosa.

In most of these films of New Argentine Cinema, the biological family has become an unstable, disrupted entity: In *Un oso rojo*, Oso must deal with the gambling problem of his ex-wife's new partner; in

Pizza, birra, faso, Cordobés relies on the family of his friends before his death leaves his yet-to-be-born child an orphan; in *Nueve reinas,* the parentless brother-sister duo are supported by a network of friends and acquaintances; and in *Bolivia,* Freddy betrays his wife. Similarly, in Diego Lerman's *Tan de repente* (Suddenly), the characters reach Rosario after a road trip from Buenos Aires and form what Alan Pauls calls "another one of the 'alternative families' . . . through which Argentine cinema reflects on the present" (2003). And in Trapero's *El bonaerense* Zapa's only means of existence in a brutal Buenos Aires is the parallel Mafioso state of the police force that forms a substitute family to replace the mother he leaves behind in his provincial home. In this urban landscape, which Trapero describes as "devouring" Zapa, the police are, in his words, "mafioso, but show solidarity" (Serra, 2002, p. 84), emphasizing how links are constructed via corruption.

Perhaps unsurprisingly, therefore, given the legacy of the disrupted, disappeared families of the dictatorship, these film families replace the nuclear family with ones based on friendship, business, convenience, sexuality, or corruption. Of course it might be argued that such defensive families are a necessary strategy of resistance to the threat of the metropolis. But whereas nonnuclear families might offer the potential for expansion rather than reproducing the inward-looking nature of conjugal family ties, the end result in New Argentine Cinema seems to nearly always be the creation of communities that fail to think about how they might work in common with other communities. Similar to the film family found in *Los rubios,* such alternative, introspective families are not only found within the film world but also permeate into the world of cinema production itself. In one of the earliest studies of recent Argentine cinema, Sergio Wolf cited a common response to a question posed in a 1994 questionnaire in which young directors were asked about their Argentine cinematic roots: "[W]e're a generation of orphans" (2002, p. 29). Wolf goes on to suggest that in the productions of New Argentine Cinema "that 'generation of orphans' has stopped drifting and found itself in a state of brotherhood" (2002, p. 39). But this sense of brotherhood never stretches beyond the world of cinema production, not even within the cities depicted in the films themselves. On the whole, therefore, New Argentine Cinema imagines communities but not communities working in common.

The point is made by comparing these films to Pablo Trapero's 1999 film *Mundo grúa,* in which the affective, larger-than-life Rulo makes his way through the hostility of the neoliberal city via a more expansive notion of friendship and family, however complex and problematic his relationships are. Confronted with the mechanical cranes that dominate the opening sequences and that symbolize the ties between neoliberal industrial construction and unemployment (the cranes standing in for the seemingly absent worker), it is Rulo's physicality that provides a touching reminder of the transformation of work in Argentina in recent decades. Trapero's deliberate decision to use a nonprofessional actor, Luis Margani, to play the part of Rulo only exaggerates how the film family of the production/acting team functions within this hostile city. In his review of the film for the newspaper *Clarín*, Diego Lerer wrote, "[I]t's not only a very good film; I'm sure that it's made by some very good people" (1999, p. 9). Lerer's conviction about the "good people" of the film highlights how the film generated a sense of friendship not just within the film world but also between Rulo and the cinema goer. Rulo seemed to be the friend that everyone wished they had. As Diego Batlle wrote in *La Nación*, *Mundo grúa* is "a film that pays homage to chatting among friends and the small day-to-day acts of solidarity" (1999, p. 4). His palpable affability turns what might otherwise be nostalgia—he is, after all, the former bassist of a rock band—into possibility for other friendships. Despite the film's potential romanticization of what Batlle called "small day-to-day acts of solidarity," therefore, the commons of friendship to be found in *Mundo grúa* is not one based on exclusivity.

Nonetheless, the overriding urban imaginary that emerges from the films discussed here presents the urban landscape of Buenos Aires as one to confront not by looking toward wider social or political communities but by building enclaves, exclusive communities, and reduced film families, a point symbolized by the oft-cited scene in *El bonaerense* in which Zapa, recently arrived in the city, cuts through a protest march on his way to signing up with the police. The fact that the film was released in 2002 and filmed during the economic crisis and social protests of the new millennium in Argentina only serves to exaggerate the manner in which Zapa turns his back on politics as a means of change. Zapa's choice is rather symptomatic of the films discussed here, since, unlike documentary film, which did explore the relationship between urban cultural imaginaries and social protest in films such as *Espejo para cuando me pruebe el smoking* (A Mirror for Trying on My Tuxedo, 2005, dir. Alejandro Fernández Mouján), fiction film hardly ever put those protesting the economic crisis on screen. Sharing a landscape of disenfranchisement and alienation, Argentine fiction film at the turn of the millennium preferred to look to other strategies of survival (such as urban nostalgia, crime, urban flight, etc.) in the neoliberal city. Whereas other cultural products being created at a similar time were able to construct, even at a highly localized level, possible imaginaries for a city in common, films made around the time of the crisis only rarely turned their strategies of survival into the possibility for more open, outward, and forward-looking urban communities. Perhaps such cinematic urban imaginaries were necessary and logical responses to a city whose potential common nature was being increasingly corrupted and dismantled in favor of enclosure and privatization. Even if, then, these urban imaginaries did not put forward inclusive communities in the face of urban fragmentation, they did express deep-seated discontent with the trajectory of the exclusionary urban landscapes that dominated Buenos Aires both before and after December 2001.

Chapter 5

Neighbors and Strangers
in Gran Buenos Aires

Given the hostile nature of the neoliberal city, it is unsurprising that city dwellers, community organizations, and urban imaginaries would turn to territory itself in an attempt to provide markers of identity in the context of urban uncertainty. As the city went global, those living in Buenos Aires often turned to increasingly localized urban environments. As David Harvey suggests, when confronted with large-scale urban transformations that attempt to appropriate territory to create a surplus in capital, urban dwellers over the past half century have often turned to "a localized neighbourhood aesthetic" (2008, p. 28). Out of the transformation of the labor commons experienced in Argentina during the 1990s, therefore, came a transformation in the commons of land: Stripped of labor, urban dwellers deployed various practices to re-appropriate territory.

Published in 2000, just before tensions between state, the financial sector, and citizens reached melting point, Sergio Chejfec's novel *Boca de lobo* (Lion's Den) highlighted how the writing of territory engaged precisely with the pivotal transformation in labor relations that had been taking place over the previous decade. Describing the novel as a homage to the working class in a city that is precisely no longer working class (Siskind, 2005, p. 43), Chejfec tapped into the precarious nature of labor and unemployment in Argentina, not least at a time when so many forms of protest were not only spatial in nature but were also based around labor, notably worker-led factories or the *piqueteros*. Set on the de-industrialized edges of the city, the novel is narrated by a middle-aged, middle-class man recalling his brief relationship with a 16-year-old factory worker called Delia. As a result, the novel probes not so much the nature of the working class in Buenos Aires as the manner in which a middle-class man narrates that working class, a point emphasized by the fact that Delia barely has a voice in the narrator's memories. The narrator loves Delia above all because she is a worker (2009, p. 12), and other markers of identity have no importance to him. Such objectification is intensified by the narrator's acknowledgment that he is aroused by hands that "hours earlier had been occupied with operating machines, manipulating tools or carrying future merchandise" (p. 12), making Delia part of the narrator's machine fetish.

The narrator's fascination with the working-class Delia means he worries about a postindustrial future in which she will be destroyed because the comforting numeratory structure of the factory will collapse into "something certain and intangible at the same time, like a feeling" (p. 13). The narrator's ultimate concern, however, appears to revolve around his belief that "Delia would lend me life" (p. 127), an expression that inserts a permanent bond of debt between their bodies. By describing the figurative shadow that Delia throws over him as "charitable" (p. 128), it is as if the narrator is disturbed by the manner in which charity is shown toward the middle class rather than emerging from it, no doubt also why he describes his impression that "Delia exerted a similar power over me, one simultaneously absolute and faint" (p. 127). There are frequent references in the novel to the increase in "value" created by coming together or shared use: The group of workers are described as being "more than the sum of its parts" (p. 35), and uniforms "increase in collective value" (p. 29) as they are lent among workers. And the narrator goes so far as to admit that workers' bodies have constructed an infinite and unpayable (because uncountable) debt to humanity (p. 38). That the narrator is unable to bear the unpayable debt or the life that Delia lends him is made manifest in the way that he callously discards her after she becomes pregnant with their child (which the narrator always calls "the child" rather than "my child"). Not only does his gendered perspective on women and labor mean that he sees motherhood to be in tension with being a worker (p. 71), but the way he treats his child also symbolizes his rejection of the way that their bodies came together and produced unquantifiable life in common. And yet it is the fact that their son is conceived in a disused factory, making him a product precisely of the postindustrial landscape (the factory where Delia works is described as being "old and in ruins" [p. 90]), that strikes at the heart of the novel. Just as people and objects create a network of exchange, a trait already seen in *Silvia Prieto* in the previous chapter, the city in *Boca de lobo* is also a layered space of exchange. The desolate working-class industrial cordon of the novel, inhabited by shantytowns, is full of liminal spaces where the boundaries between city and country are so blurred that it is unclear whether buildings are half-constructed or in ruins. The importance of this desolate periphery to the novel is emphasized by the fact that the only name mentioned in the novel other than Delia's is that of Borges, the writer who sought a premodern city untouched by modernization via that "imaginary corner of the suburb invented by Borges in the images of *las orillas*, an indeterminate place between the city and the countryside" (Sarlo, 1993, p. 13).

The reference to Borges, one of whose most famous poems, "Fundación mítica de Buenos Aires" (The Mythical Founding of Buenos Aires; 1929), presented the city as mythic and eternal, taps into a view of geography—the writing of space—that initially appears to have much in common with the views of Chejfec's narrator:

> It's always disturbed me that geography does not change in spite of time, in spite of our changes and the changes that are produced in it. We preserve something immaterial, equivalent to what geography conserves, also immaterial. And nevertheless, although it does not change, geography is the measure of change. (p. 7)

And yet the rest of the novel undoes that rather disingenuous claim, since the urban periphery, the beginning of the urban beyond where streetlamps run out and the darkness begins, is what gives the imagination possibility: "[A] place made of remnants, promises of houses and imaginary crossings' (pp. 60–61). It is not just the plural voice of the landscape (p. 44) that dismantles the narrator's view of geography, however, but also Delia herself. Recognizing that her silences are "something alive, eloquent, as if they had been worked" (p. 15) and that she herself is beyond enumeration (p. 111), the narrator admits that Delia alters the landscape: "[W]alking with Delia was to participate in a change of geography" (p. 168). As they walk, the characters engage in the creation of meeting places, adding value to the landscape, just as the landscape gives value to them.

Such a negotiation echoes the blurred boundaries that permeate the novel: buildings and emptiness, order and disorder, memory and forgetting, darkness and light, night and day, all of which become fluid concepts rather than dialectical opposites. The liminality and uncertainty of the urban night, suspended between streetlamps and the threatening darkness of the *boca de lobo*, are symbolic of the novel itself, described by Alfonso Mallo as being on "the frontier of writing" (Mallo, n.d.).[1] Thus the narrator speaks of the way his phrases "appeared and disappeared . . . just like the landscape did as we moved on" (p. 86), emphasizing how the writing of space is tied to the creation of space enacted by the narrator and Delia.

That creation is cut short by their separation, the narrator admitting that parting from Delia has resulted in an exhaustion of the landscape (p. 171), epitomized by the final line of the novel in which Delia and her son enter "la boca de lobo" (p. 180).

Chejfec's novel is important not just because it portrays a disjunction between middle and working classes or because it highlights transformations in the nature of labor, but also because it demonstrates, via the character of Delia, how factory labor has been transformed into the production of space itself. If, on the one hand, Delia disappearing into the darkness of the urban unknown typifies the narrator's cold-heartedness, on the other, her constant transformations of geography offer a semblance of possibility for the mutual production of a city in common. In that sense, Chejfec's novel captures the mood of turn-of-the-millennium Buenos Aires, which, as the previous chapter demonstrated, mirrored Harvey's claim that "individualized capital accumulation perpetually threatens to destroy the two basic common property resources that undergird all forms of production: the laborer and the land" (2011, p. 106). Even though the geography of *Boca de lobo* emphasizes the indeterminate nature of its spatial setting and certainly does not make geography a form of resistance, Chejfec's novel is suggestive of a localized aesthetic in as much as it is clearly located within the trope of the urban periphery in Argentine culture, one that includes the writings of Borges, the photographs of Horacio Coppola in the 1920s and 1930s, and, more recently, work by Juan Andrés Videla, whose blurred oil paintings and graphite drawings of suburban neighborhoods are suggestive of a ghostlike, oneiric city, and by Cristina Fraire, whose photographic series *Donde la ciudad se interrumpe* (Where the City Is Interrupted), portrays a decaying periphery of rubble where cars rust alongside passing horses and carts (Malosetti Costa, 2007). These recent works—and other representations of Gran Buenos Aires, such as the films *El bonaerense* and *Un oso rojo*—are hardly sympathetic portrayals of the urban neighborhood, however, and are in stark contrast to the way that, with the growing territorialization of urban politics in Argentina in recent decades, localized zones within the city have taken on political significance from both above and below.

As the economic crisis moved toward collapse at the turn of the millennium, neighborhood meetings—"asambleas barriales"—were suggestive, at least for a while, of a more grassroots political organization that demanded a localized response to the crisis. Though the *asamblea* movement has stagnated in recent years, its impact is nonetheless evident in the attempt by the Gobierno de la Ciudad de Buenos Aires to tap into this desire for more localized, decentralized urban governance by creating 15 *comunas*, agglomerations of different *barrios* that would have a certain degree of regulatory autonomy (Gobierno de la Ciudad de Buenos Aires, 2015). Despite attempting to emphasize local autonomy, however, the *comuna* remains a purely administrative entity, since it is to the *barrio* that citizens continue to have the greatest sense of social, cultural, and political belonging.

Barrios have long been privileged sites of urban identity in Buenos Aires, and histories of the city are often organized around the history of its neighborhoods. Cultural texts also regularly turn to the *barrio* as a site for exploring the city's imaginaries. In *Rep hizo los barrios: Buenos Aires dibujada*, for example, the artist Rep creates a series of comic illustrations of maps of the city's neighborhoods. The map of San Telmo, for example, includes captions reading "occupied house," a reference to squatters; "National History Museum: Future antiques shopping center for tourists"; and "someone who has a loft apartment and thinks he lives in Soho"; the latter jibes at the gentrification of the neighborhood that began in the 1990s (2005, p. 49). The importance of *barrio* identity is established by an anecdote included in the introduction: "A friend was convinced that he was born in Floresta. When I told him that actually it was Parque Avellaneda, it changed his view on life, which had been built on a lie" (Rep, 2005, p. 17). Other recent examples of the city being imagined via its neighborhoods include the collection of short stories *Buenos Aires/Escala 1:1: Los barrios por sus escritores* (Buenos Aires/1:1 Scale: The Neighborhoods by Their Writers; Terranova, 2011) or the three-volume best-seller series *Buenos Aires es leyenda* (Buenos Aires is Legend; Barrantes & Coviello, 2009, 2010a, 2010b). The latter is a compilation of highly localized myths and stories relating to Buenos Aires, the entire work being organized around the *barrios* from which the stories come, as if the neighborhoods were repositories for urban myths that exaggerate the fable-like dimensions of a Borgesian city. Indeed, the work itself perpetuates certain myths about these neighborhoods, such as presenting the stadium Monumental as if it were in Nuñez when officially it is in fact in Belgrano. All these works thus highlight the ongoing importance of the *barrio* to the Buenos Aires imaginary (and, indeed, of the imaginary to the lived experience of the city). When considered alongside the prominence of territory to identity formation, protest, and self-defense in Buenos Aires during the 1990s and the new millennium, symbolized by the entrenchment of both gated communities and shantytowns, then the geographical significance of the neighborhood is intensified.

Recent Argentine cinema also contributes to the interest in the *barrio* as a site of belonging. As seen in the previous chapter, many films, including *Mundo grúa* and *Bolivia*, emphasize the significance of the neighborhood in their urban dramas. Indeed, Batlle praised *Mundo grúa* for celebrating the *barrio* "without falling into exacerbated local color or the conservative view of the neighborhood set out by both the producers of Pol-Ka and the television programs of the Telefé group" (1999, p. 4). If Daniel Burman's *El abrazo partido* (Lost Embrace; 2004), in which the neighborhood of Once provides a multiethnic but emphatically middle-class microcosm for an inward-looking community, is a good example set in Capital Federal of this trend to use the hyper-local as a means of defense against the alienating effects of contemporary urban life, then Juan José Campanella's film *Luna de Avellaneda* (2004) is the pre-eminent example of this urban vision in Gran Buenos Aires. In Campanella's film, inscribed by the atmosphere of economic crisis, the middle-class Román attempts to save a social club in Avellaneda that is threatened with closure, a romanticization of love, friendship, and the *barrio* of Gran Buenos Aires as the potential site of lost community values. As Andermann indicates, Campanella turns the Argentine crisis into the necessary trigger for Román to restore those traits of compassion and friendship that had taken a battering during the 1990s (2011, p. 41). The neighborhood is, however, as Andermann goes on to argue, carefully constructed and managed: "The self-proclaimed capacity of Campanella's films to allegorically represent the nation's plight sustains itself precisely on the occlusion of the margins and the poor: the only image in Luna of the shantytown where Dalma lives is shot from afar, literally 'from across the river' from where Darín's Ramón calls her after deciding to allow her free access to the club" (2011, p. 42).

Another set of rather different films that are explicitly located in Gran Buenos Aires make up Raúl Perrone's trilogy set in Ituzaingó, comprised of *Labios de churrasco* (Churrasco lips; 1994), *Graciadió* (Thank God; 1997), and *5 pal' peso* (5 Cents Short; 1998). Andermann has persuasively argued that the trilogy plays on the marginality of the slacker movie to "[open] up in Argentine cinema itself a 'marginal space' set free from the testimonial politics of the cinema of transition" (2011, p. 16), a negation not just of consumerism "but also, and just as importantly, of the prefabricated answers and conventional wisdoms of the 'political cinema' which had predominated in Argentine film for over a decade" (2011, p. 17). Indeed, the fisheye lens used in *Labios de churrasco*, the image incorporating the black edges, not only distorts the landscape but also exaggerates the distance between viewer and character. This distancing, reminiscent of the way that the actors turn their back on the audience in *Los rubios*, is symptomatic of what Andermann calls a "politics of refusal" (2011, p. 16). Part of that refusal is encapsulated by the decision to set the films in such a hyper-localized, domestic, and marginal neighborhood.

Despite the importance of these filmscapes of Gran Buenos Aires, however, the imaginaries of Capital Federal continue to dominate the way Buenos Aires is depicted. In the prologue to *Buenos Aires/Escala 1:1*, Terranova acknowledges the lack of literary depictions of Gran Buenos Aires, sometimes referred to as the *conurbano*, when he writes that "Argentine literature is still, despite some honorable exceptions, in debt to the constantly expanding universe of the Conurbano" (2011, p. 7). That debt, almost an echo of the debt to the working class Chejfec writes about in *Boca de lobo*, has only intensified in recent decades with the growing divide between the two parts of the city. Ever since Capital was granted autonomous status as part of the 1994 constitutional reform, the frontier between Capital and Gran Buenos Aires has become increasingly politically and symbolically loaded. This transformation in the delimitation of national political territories was accompanied by Menem's intense neo-liberal reforms, and it was Gran Buenos Aires that suffered most from privatization, unemployment, and the withdrawal of state protection. Gran Buenos Aires thus continues to be particularly representative of urban tensions that configure the city, because it is there that the vast panoply of Argentine society is evident. From the supermarket sackings that accompanied the economic collapse of 2001 to the attempt by residents of the wealthy neighborhood of San Isidro to build a wall between them and the neighboring poorer *barrio* of San Fernando in 2009, the *conurbano* encapsulates the way Buenos Aires is played out, mapped, and imagined. As a result, to ignore Gran Buenos Aires when speaking of the imaginary of contemporary Buenos Aires is to risk not speaking of the city at all.

The texts analyzed here engage with the tensions between these two areas of the city, with Capital Federal traditionally regarding Gran Buenos Aires as the locale of violence and disruption, often in the form of the Latin American immigrant, and the former regarding the latter as elitist and, more often than not, anti-Peronist. Pablo Trapero, who stated explicitly that *El bonaerense* was a film about the difference between living in the Province of Buenos Aires and Capital (Peña, 2003, p. 201), an interesting statement given that the film never sets foot in the latter, has said that if you come from Gran Buenos Aires, "you feel like a foreigner in Capital" (quoted in Lerer 2002, p. 68). The boundary between the two, the raised motorway flyover named General Paz, creates an imposing physical frontier that is policed as if it were the crossing point between civilization and barbarism, and Sarmiento's classic dichotomy percolates throughout these urban visions.

Rocking the Suburbs

The "politics of refusal" is certainly a significant and symbolic form of living on the margins in the contemporary city. It is present in several cultural forms affiliated with the imaginary of Gran Buenos Aires, most famously the music of *rock barrial*, which incorporates the *barrio* as an alternative to the politics of grand revolutionary communities. In Perrone's trilogy referred to previously, for example, music by the band Caballeros de la Quema plays a key part in the creation of the neighborhood aesthetic of the films. The song "Mientras haya luces de bar" (While the bars still have their lights on), for example, is used diegetically and nondiegetically, its lyrics speaking of homeless wandering through the city drinking from one bar to the next. Such themes are typical of *rock barrial*, sometimes known as *rock chabón*, one of the most significant post-dictatorship cultural forms in Argentina. As sociologist Pablo Semán stated in a seminar in 2005, when one takes into account that in Gran Buenos Aires "there are fewer schools than radios, fewer teachers than musical leaders and singers, and more Pentecostal pastors than university lecturers, you start to realize that you learn a lot of things from religion, corner bars and music that you don't learn anywhere else" (Pedroso, 2007, p. 29).

Building on Argentina's strong tradition in rock music, *rock barrial* has its origins in *rock nacional*, the music that emerged during the late 1960s and 1970s in Argentina. *Rock nacional* developed as a form of cultural resistance to and rejection of the political right, marked particularly by the military dictatorships of 1966–1970 and 1976–1983. Receiving greater exposure during the Malvinas/Falklands conflict, *rock nacional* came to be one of Argentina's pre-eminent cultural forms of the 1980s, gathering a fan base that stretched throughout Latin America. The lyrics of *rock nacional* frequently turned to the urban, expressing the notion of "naufragar" (foundering) through the city (Franco, 2006, p. 26), illustrative of the period's sense of loss of meaning. The city also provided the meeting points that allowed rockers to share that sense of loss, turning it into a countercultural urban movement and, later, into a celebration of the re-appropriation of the city streets post-dictatorship. Though *rock barrial* continued *rock nacional's* interest in the city, however, it had a number of significant differences with its predecessor. Darío Calderón reads Argentine rock as a series of expressions of how the young are being excluded from the city, suggesting that prior to 1973 exclusion in rock is dealt with symbolically, becoming explicitly physical between 1974 and 1980, no doubt influenced by the practice of disappearance, before that exclusion is countered by a sense of re-appropriation after 1980 (2006, p. 84). He goes on to suggest that the sense of exclusion that returns after 1985, and which intensifies after 1990, is more markedly social. Rock in the 1990s "stops being a countercultural experience and starts being a 'refuge,' a means to take shelter in the face of the collapse of social welfare" (Enghel, Flachsland, & Rosemberg, 2008, p. 5). Thus the sense of lack with which *rock barrial* pulsates vocalizes the enforced absence from the city being experienced during the neoliberal 1990s and turns it into a marker of identity. As a result, *rock barrial* moves away from the production of an imaginary of the city as a whole and instead makes explicit the importance of localized sites and areas within that city to a disenfranchised urban youth.

The most significant influences on *rock barrial* are singer-songwriters such as Bob Dylan, suburban electric blues bands, figure-headed by the guitarist Pappo, and The Rolling Stones, who gave concerts in Buenos Aires in 1995 as part of their Voodoo Lounge tour and in 1998 as part of their Bridges to Babylon tour, using the local band Viejas Locas as a support band. Thus, *rock barrial* produced a fusion of heavy rock, blues, and poetic lyrics. The themes of those lyrics are often centered on drugs and alcohol, women, music, and conflicts with the police and other gangs and groups. Unlike the earlier *rock nacional, rock barrial* was no longer a critique of the alienation of the working day or of capitalist accumulation so much as of a world in which the worker is no longer a figurehead of the urban poor (Semán, Vila, & Benedetti, 2004, p. 263). Leaving aside the irony that the very economic shifts they were critiquing were in fact a major contributor to the boom in rock, the economic policy of one-to-one convertibility between the Argentine peso and the U.S. dollar making musical instruments, amplifiers, and recording equipment accessible to a much wider percentage of the population (Semán, Vila, & Benedetti, 2004, p. 264), *rock barrial* made the marginality of the neighborhood the pre-eminent alternative space for those dominated by consumption.

The neighborhood here functions on several specific levels. First, it is portrayed as a space within which Peronism survives: that is, if neoliberalism in the 1990s is also the period that marks the nail in the coffin of the Peronist welfare state, then rock turns to the neighborhood as the space within which the popular imaginary can continue. The ongoing support for Peronism in Gran Buenos Aires (as opposed to, say, Capital Federal, whose mayors are traditionally conservative) is a reminder of the lasting power of a Peronist political imaginary.[2] Second, the neighborhood is also a space of nonconsumption: that is, communities are built around not doing anything (Semán, Vila, & Benedetti, 2004, p. 274). Inactivity, a result of not working, allows the possibility for an alternative politics (or anti-politics) based around friendship and family, and *rock barrial* also venerates the possibilities for neighborhood pleasure, particularly focused on the body (Semán & Vila, 2002, p. 79). Third, the neighborhood is not just a local space but also a national one. Semán stresses that *rock barrial* expresses strong allegiance to the national, whether in lyrics influenced by the tradition of populist politics, in the banners unfurled at concerts, or the inclusion of folkloric rhythms and songs within the rock songs (Pedroso, 2007, p. 31). Finally, the neighborhood is in constant struggle with other parts of the city, antagonistic relationships that can sometimes explode into pitched battles.

Rock barrial is, therefore, often a combative cultural form, one that places certain territories against others, whether that be one *barrio* against another, or the *barrio* against the city. The resulting urban landscape created by this music is an antagonistic one, the neighborhood becoming a site of resistance both from and to the city. Such a politics of expansive withdrawal is formulated around reinforcing territorial entities that delimit certain communities from others. The 2004 Cromañón (or Cromagnon) disaster, which marked a watershed in Argentine music, encapsulates this territorial antagonism. The most visible way in which the tragedy, which resulted in nearly 200 people being killed on 30 December as a result of a fire in the Cromañón nightclub in Plaza Once, has been played out in territorial terms has been the various conflicts over memory sites and practices that emerged in the wake of the fire. Soon after the deaths, themselves "out of place" (Enghel, Flachsland, & Rosemberg, 2008, p. 7), an urban sanctuary was erected outside the club, cutting off Calle Bartolomé Mitre. The sanctuary, an example of popular religion by no means endorsed by all survivors or relatives, soon became a site of tension between mourning families, who demanded their right to remember in the face of impunity and official shortcomings; local residents, who complained about the rerouting of bus services and reduced access; and the city government, which created its own memory space. The depth of feeling generated by the disaster was manifest outside the trial of those implicated in the fire, where families and friends of the victims entered into a pitched battle with supporters of Callejeros, the band playing the club that night, and with the riot police.

But Cromañón also typified the nature of territorial tensions in Buenos Aires in other ways, not least since the owner, Omar Chabán, had been well known for providing concert spaces for non-mainstream bands (Flachsland, 2006, p. 63). Clubs such as Cromañón were thus important because they offered an alternative to the growing number of privatized music venues in Buenos Aires and the way that the state, especially the Gobierno de la Ciudad de Buenos Aires, was becoming more and more involved in the creation of mega-recitals such as Buenos Aires Vivo, Buenos Aires no duerme, Creamfields BA, Quilmes Rock, and Pepsi Music. An increasingly disenfranchised urban youth gathered in places like Cromañón to listen to bands that lent them a voice. Indeed, the name Callejeros itself played on territorial deprivation, meaning both "street," the newly privileged gathering place for the young, and "stray," a reference to the way that young people had become waifs. Moreover, however, given that that disenfranchised urban youth was often to be found in Gran Buenos Aires, it was significant that not only were Callejeros from Gran Buenos Aires but also that 60% of the victims in the Cromañón disaster lived in Gran Buenos Aires (Enghel, Flachsland, & Rosemberg, 2008). To some degree, therefore, Cromañón was a disaster of the *conurbano* acted out in Capital, one that demonstrated how multiple layers of territorial struggle could be encapsulated in cultural production and its environs.

Villa Celina

Callejeros hail from Villa Celina, a neighborhood that is located just outside of Capital Federal, in the metropolitan district of La Matanza in Gran Buenos Aires. The neighborhood is delimited on two sides by the major traffic arteries of the Avenida General Paz and Avenida Ricchieri, and on the other two by the Mercado Central de Buenos Aires, which is the country's major fruit and vegetable trading center, and the river Riachuelo. These major physical structures mean that Villa Celina's territorial limits are quite clearly demarcated, though its historical growth is a result of its proximity to wider transport and commercial networks. It is this neighborhood that is situated at the heart of the narrative output of the writer Juan Diego Incardona, whose semi-autobiographical novels and sketches collectively form a portrait of Gran Buenos Aires in the run up to the new millennium. Incardona's writings construct an imagined geography in which the treatment of the unknown within his own neighborhood allows for a highly localized and yet simultaneously expansive and welcoming urban commons. Even though Callejeros themselves do not form part of his work, *rock barrial* plays a key role in his imaginary of the neighborhood. His references to Viejas Locas, a band from the neighboring *barrio* of Villa Lugano in Capital Federal, and their frontman Cristian "Pity" Álvarez, later of Intoxicados, not only express his own personal friendships but also demonstrate how Incardona uses rock music to express an urban vision of openness and togetherness.

Certainly, there are tribal, divisive, and combative elements in Incardona's work. The narrator, Juan Diego, refers to street fights between Peronist factions (2010a, pp. 56–57) and to a rumor that the residents of Villa Lugano are planning to attack Villa Celina, demonstrative of the tension between Gran Buenos Aires and Capital (2010a, p. 63). It is music in particular that offers a means for Villa Celina to express its identity in the wider city, as in the way that fans graffiti band names on walls or place stickers on public transport. These activities take Gran Buenos Aires to Capital ("before long, the music of our pavements had been exported to Capital" (2010a, p. 58)), indicating how rock is a potent symbol for the *conurbano* in its struggle against other territories and cultural forms. Incardona goes so far as to call those who participate in such actions "militants" (2010a, p. 58), as if being a music fan was a new form of political activism, a point emphasized by the way that rock becomes a verb: "Rockeaban pasos que volaban las tejas flojas" (They rocked steps that sent loose tiles flying; 2010b, p. 73).

Stronger than these territorial struggles, however, is the collective spirit that is built up around music. Sometimes that spirit emerges from a celebration of playing on the street corner, but more often it emanates from a carnival atmosphere, what Sandra Contreras calls "festivo" (festive) (2009, p. 6), such as when the Peronist banners move musically to the beat of *murga*, the traditional Argentine carnival (Incardona, 2010a, p. 81). At times such elements of the carnivalesque appear to be little more than the defiant romance of those who are "immersed in post-work culture and abandoned without any protection" (Enghel, Flachsland, & Rosemberg, 2008, p. 2), existing beyond the consciousness of the city at large: "Tetrapak, beer, pot, raviolis, intoxicated, we just wanted to sing and dance in our little forgotten south-west town, everyone in the midst of a piss-up on a perfect, starlit night" (2010a, p. 88). At others, however, the atmosphere is less inward looking and more inclusive. In one scene in *Rock barrial*, for example, Juan Diego relates the events of a concert that emphasizes how rock forms new communities in the postindustrial landscape: "[B]etween the cemeteries of factory buildings and workshops, we flapped our way through indigenous dances and blues and rocknroll songs like old chickens, every one of us with their fringe cut short and neckerchief flying, circling our hips and frenetically shaking our heads, asking for who knows what, maybe rain, or sun, or nothing in particular" (2010b, p. 64). The festive expression of community is emphasized by the shared physical movement, the open space of the street, and the music of the description. Writing itself has to adapt to the forms in which togetherness is expressed, such as when the chant sung by fans of Viejas Locas is transcribed in a manner that emphasizes the physical act of singing in a group: "Vieeejas Looocas es un sentimieeeento, no se expliiica, se lleva bieen adeeentro" (Vieeejas Looocas is a feeeeeling, you can't explaaain it, it's deeep insiiide; 2010a, p. 106). That Incardona uses the band from Villa Lugano to express togetherness in Villa Celina, moreover, highlights how music can span territorial divisions between Capital Federal and Gran Buenos Aires. Both neighborhoods, despite their differences in administrative affiliations, share a common working-class history and cultural-territorial imaginary.

Incardona thus presents *rock barrial* as a form of cultural commons, a point made evident in the chapter from *Rock barrial* entitled "La mejor banda de los barrios" (The best neighborhood band). Playing on the word "banda," a reference to both a rock band and to a group of young people, a term that Silvia Duschatzky and Cristina Corea used to emphasize how children in Argentina were forming groups to confront the lack of institutional support in the country (2002), Incardona relates how a group gathers on top of the disused water tower that lies at the heart of Villa Celina and ends up creating a large improvised rock orchestra: "Not long ago . . . came an unknown band asking to play on the roof of the Tanque de Celina, one, two, three, a thousand songs, whatever the rest of the night allowed. It was made up of fifty people: fifty drummers, fifty bassists, fifty guitarists and fifty singers . . ." (2010b, p. 74). Via rock, the *barrio* here opens its arms to an expansive orchestra, drawing the reader in to share the magic of the spontaneous, improvised nature of the gathering, in which being a musician is stripped of its stardom and 50 people share instruments.

Critics of Argentine rock have suggested that the innovative quality of *rock barrial* is precisely that it expresses belonging both to the neighborhood and to the nation (Semán, Vila, & Benedetti, 2004, p. 279). Whether

national symbolism expresses concrete national desires is, I think, questionable, though it lends credence to those who saw the use of national
flags during the 2001 economic crisis as symptomatic of a reaffirmation
of national identity. Either way, Incardona's treatment of *rock barrial* in
his work places little emphasis on the national and, in that sense, the view
that *rock barrial* "es nacionalista, pero su patria es el barrio" (is nationalist,
but its fatherland is the neighborhood) (Enghel, Flachsland, & Rosemberg,
2008, p. 5), is more helpful. In Incardona, rock functions not as a means
of reaffirming national identity beyond the city but rather to determine
neighborhood belonging within the context of the wider metropolis at a
specific moment in the city's history. As Horacio Bilbao writes, *rock barrial* can be seen as a form of resistance to the fact that "in 2001, walking
through the *conurbano* was walking through a cemetery, with all those
factory buildings" (2011), a connection that Incardona makes explicit:
"When they closed the factories and the skilled lathe operators committed suicide en masse, we children, lounging under the sun smoking one,
two, three joints, we confined ourselves to the street corners and played
our first songs" (2010b, p. 55).

The indifference of both the state and the city at large to Villa Celina
is particularly tied to transformations occurring in the 1990s, the period
in which the works are set, a point made clear in the episode entitled "El
ataque a Villa Celina" (The Attack on Villa Celina), which describes how
a series of gas explosions and subsequent fires ravage the neighborhood.
The opening sets the scene with a series of telling references:

> On 5 November 1992, three years and almost four months after
> Carlos Saúl Menem assumed the Presidency of the Nation,
> exactly three years before the attack on the Fábrica Militar de
> Río Tercero, nineteen months after the Ley de Convertibilidad
> del Austral was passed, fifty-three days before the privatization
> of Gas del Estado, a sinister plan was carried out that still
> today remains unpunished and kept from public opinion: a
> sabotage, an attack on the most colorful neighborhood of the
> south-west sector of the *conurbano*. (2010a, p. 53)

Incardona here ties together the explosions in Villa Celina to a narrative of economic neoliberalism, privatization of state entities, corruption,
and state impunity.[3] Indeed, the explosions are only stopped when the
volunteer firemen cut through the doors of the gas substation with axes
(2010a, p. 54). The explosions, just as the floods that occasionally plague

Villa Celina, are symptomatic of a state that is uninterested in helping its citizens, almost allowing the neighborhood to "disappear." Indeed, that only one local newspaper covers the event indicates how Villa Celina remains beyond the imaginary of the city.

Incardona further emphasizes state and city indifference to Villa Celina by stressing the ways that other forms of protection have been enacted during the neighborhood's past, "before the era of compulsive construction" (2010b, p. 15). Thus he refers on several occasions to the local "sociedad de fomento," a nonprofit organization that works for the benefit of the local community, and on the first page of *Villa Celina* he mentions the early Peronist social housing projects, the *monoblocks* of Barrio General Paz, Barrio Ricchieri, and Edificios Estrellas that continue to dominate the landscape (2010a, p. 11). Thus at the same time as expressing urban togetherness, Incardona simultaneously emphasizes the particularities of the areas of the city he is focusing on, using a wealth of proper place names to re-insert within the imaginary of Buenos Aires the urban geography of Villa Celina and Gran Buenos Aires, from its waste grounds and shantytowns to its street corners and riverbanks.

Incardona's hyper-localized geography is created in the idiosyncrasies of both Villa Celina and Gran Buenos Aires, which he uses to express the potent sense of belonging that he himself feels and also to reinforce the particularities of these territories in comparison to Capital Federal. One way Incardona establishes difference is via his references to popular religion and myth. In the first episode of *Villa Celina*, in which the narrator is taken to see a medicine woman, he notes that Juan Diego is the name of the Indian who discovered the Virgin of Guadalupe, and that his birthday (27 July) is the Saint's Day of San Pantaleón, not only the patron saint of physicians but also one of the Fourteen Holy Helpers whose faith was more important than science when combating disease. The incident introduces a neighborhood that is populated with ghosts and monsters, from the "hombre gato" (cat man) or rampaging Dantean dogs (2010a, p. 99) to the beast who lives in "El túnel de los nazis" (the tunnel of the Nazis).

Such a strong localized sense of place is further created through a careful rendition of the language of the *conurbano*, introducing slang, sound ("jajajá se había atado un pañuelito, jajajá se había cortado el flequillo" (hahaha he'd put on a neckerchief, hahaha he'd cut his fringe) (2010b, p. 71), and mixing direct speech into the narrative: "[H]e says hey man help us out with ten centavos, I'm not here to rob you, I'm asking, and take that you fat cock, trying to pull one over me in my own neighborhood, and what neighborhood's that, asks the guy, and I reply proudly Villa Celina, and he says you're messed up and then disappears" (2010a, p. 45). Here the lack of punctuation makes it difficult to unpack the dialogue, blurring the boundaries between the two speakers. Likewise, Incardona infuses his narrative with the lyrics, rhythm, and form of *rock barrial*. In *Objetos maravillosos* (Wonderful objects; 2007), for example, the first chapter is called "La pentatónica" (the pentatonic), the scale used in blues, and lyrics are often worked into the narrative proper, such as the line "Mucha tropa riendo en las calles con sus muecas rotas cromadas" (A great horde laughing in the streets with their broken chrome faces; 2010a, p. 88), which is taken from the song "Nuestro amo juega al esclavo" (Our master plays at being a slave) by Los Redondos. The following extract also draws on song lyrics, on this occasion from the song "Preso en mi ciudad" (Prisoners in my city), also by Los Redondos:

> Bajé la escalera cantando tum tum tum *una vez le hice el amor a un drácula con tacones* y los escalones hacían uno dos uno dos hasta que me metí de lleno en el sótano de la Matanza, cerca de la General Paz y la Richieri, atrás de la zanja grande que va a la Villa Lucero, tana tana tana tatá *era un pop violento que guió el gran estilo siniestro*, entre Celina y Madero, Celina y Lugano, Celina y la Mesopotamia (2010a: 44; emphasis added).

> (I went down the ladder singing dum dum dum *once I made love to a dracula with heels* and the rungs did one two one two until I was fully inside the basement of la Matanza, near General Paz and Richieri, behind the big ditch that goes to Villa Lucero, dada dada dada deda *it was a violent kinda pop that steered that great creepy style*, between Celina and Madero, Celina and Lugano, Celina and Mesopotamia)

Incardona here captures the music within his narrative style, using onomatopoeia to render the singing of the lyrics.

The particularities of Gran Buenos Aires are also expressed via a forceful Peronist imaginary. Villa Celina, like most of Gran Buenos Aires, is markedly Peronist in its politics and has been inscribed both by its supporters and its opponents. Following Perón's exile in 1955, for example, the housing complex known as "17 de Octubre," a reference to the most important day in the Peronist calendar, had its name changed to "General

Paz." Indeed, in that very complex lived Gustavo Rearte, founder member of the radical left-wing group Juventud Peronista (Peronist Youth), which was formed in the late 1950s (Biaggini, 2014).[4] That Peronist history permeates Incardona's works, from the very first episode in Villa Celina when Juan Diego asks his mother to explain the difference between "Yanquis," Marxists, and Peronists (2010a, p. 15). As Hernán Vanoli and Diego Vecino argue, Incardona sees Gran Buenos Aires as the locale of persistent, authentic Peronism, "possessor of symbolic potency and its own mythic system" (2010, p. 270). The point is emphasized by the inclusion in *Villa Celina* of images by Daniel Santoro, an artist famous for his diverse portraits of Peronism, including, as Alberto Petrina has demonstrated, the Peronist architectural projects carried out between 1946 and 1955, particularly large-scale state building projects and social housing (Petrina, 2006). Whereas Sarlo describes Santoro as a "nostalgic painter of images of Peronist happiness" (2012), Vanoli and Vecino argue against seeing Incardona's work in that nostalgic vein, suggesting that the social relations presented by Incardona are less a portrayal of "aguante," roughly translatable as "resistance," than the construction of a more positive form of resistance through the symbolic world of national populism, itself reinvigorated and updated via new cultural forms and practices (2010, pp. 270–272). But Sarlo is right to hint that Incardona does not simply reproduce a Peronist community (2012). Indeed, in similar fashion to the way that he treats *rock barrial*, the popular in Incardona appears to have little to do with popular nationalism and more to do with what Peronism—its myths, tropes, and symbols—allow him to express about the neighborhood's identity within the wider context of Buenos Aires. In that sense, Sandra Contreras evaluation is more accurate when she emphasizes that Peronism in Incardona is "affective, social and familiar [both 'familiar' and 'of the family'], not party based" and which is ultimately based around a solidarity where collaboration and help takes sway over defending "the flag linked to the identity of a territory" (2009, p. 5). Thus Incardona builds on the idea of the famous Ciudad Evita, the Peronist housing project supposedly designed to look like Evita's head from the air, by referring tongue-in-cheek to how the characters were aware of abandoned neighborhoods dating from the era of Perón shaped like San Martín, Rosas, and Perón himself (2010a, pp. 19–20). His treatment of such neighborhoods is neither defensive nor nostalgic, however, but rather a humorous celebration of the mythic potential of Peronism. Especially noteworthy is the fact that these lost neighborhoods are unknown precisely to those who live in Gran Buenos Aires. Indeed, the political force of Incardona's narrative emerges precisely from the way in which the hyper-familiar local is set alongside the strange and the stranger *within the neighborhood.*

Writing the Internal Stranger

Cosmopolitanism, a sense of belonging balanced precariously between borderless universality and the need for boundaries for the cosmopolitan act to come into being, is useful for thinking through the relationship between stranger, neighborhood, and the city in common. The city is the cosmopolitanism space par excellence, not just as the privileged site of transnational and transregional encounters between strangers, but also because of its history as a site of hospitality, which, as Jacques Derrida argued, is a key tenet of the cosmopolitan ideal (Derrida, 2001). Narratives of the local—in Incardona's case, the neighborhood—might be seen to venerate the local in the face of the global, reinforcing internal frontiers and thus undoing the act of hospitality. And yet the city (or neighborhood) must be demarcated by a frontier for the act of hospitality toward the stranger to come into force. The arrival of the stranger, as Puspa Damai has highlighted, is the moment in which the city is opened up, when insides and outsides are both highlighted and transcended (2005, p. 75). Esposito takes a similar line, arguing that shutting down borders is a response to the perception that the foreign body, usually the alien or the immigrant, harbors the threat of contamination (2008, p. 11). Such acts of immunization, Esposito adds, ultimately negate the life that they aim to protect, turning the cosmopolitan place of immunity—to which, as Derrida wrote, "one could retreat in order to escape from the threat of injustice" (2001, p. 9)—to a space not just of protection but also of self-destructive exclusion.

So how is it possible to inscribe a bounded neighborhood and yet avoid exacerbating the antagonistic relationship with the stranger, not least since, as Kurt Iveson argues, the stranger 'is the cause *and also the effect* of boundary-drawing efforts conducted by those who have assumed the status of 'host' or 'native' " (2006, p. 75)? How can writing the neighborhood avoid returning to a time when places were demarcated by, in Doreen Massey's words, "internally generated authenticities" and "their difference from other places . . . beyond their borders" (2005, p. 64)? And how can the urban dweller offer hospitality to the stranger without reinforcing a power imbalance brought about by the act of charity, either "imposing conditions on the arrival of the other in its own name," as

Damai warns (2005, p. 92), or, ultimately, intensifying indifference to the difference of the stranger? Incardona is able to generate a strong sense of place and of community without excluding the stranger because he writes a community marked by fluctuating narratives that always recognize strangers and the strange within both neighborhood and narrator. Writing place as, in Massey's term, "a simultaneity of stories-so-far" (2005, p. 24), meeting points that sometimes take on material form, Incardona turns the frontier into a more protean entity, accommodating the fact that the urban dweller is affiliated to a network of different places and entities, sharing points of narrative convergence with both neighbor and stranger.

Three particular kinds of strangers and "the strange" emerge in Incardona's work. First, he writes from the neighborhood that is itself outside the city's imaginary, not just because of its expressly immigrant history, but also because it is inscribed as a space beyond the idea that Buenos Aires is merely Capital Federal. Second, he himself writes from a present in which he stands outside the neighborhood and has, in turn, become a stranger. Returning to Villa Celina after a nomadic decade traveling the country, the narrator expresses his surprise at coming across a group of kids in front of his parents' house whom he does not recognize (p. 52). He goes on to note that "now I'm a stranger in my own country. . . . I spent my time writing story and poems about this, and now I'm disorientated' (2007, p. 62). This distance is especially evident in the incidents related to the mysterious figure that scales trees and rooftops and who sends the neighborhood into a frenzy of fear and lynching. Later acknowledging that the "hombre gato" is a creation of the neighborhood's imagination (2007, p. 12), symbolic of the collective desire to expel the stranger, in *Villa Celina* Incardona expresses his admiration for this outsider, hoping he does not get caught. Watching the pursuit on television after having left the neighborhood—"And me on this side, so far away" (2010a, p. 30)—Incardona emphasizes his affiliation with the stranger that he himself has partly become.

Third, whether inside or outside the neighborhood, he constantly engages with the familiar and the strange, aware not just of the stranger beyond the familiar, but also the stranger within. Both *Villa Celina* and *Rock barrial* begin with narratives of strangers that inhabit the geographic imaginary of the frontier zone: In the former, Juan Diego and his family embark on a journey to an unknown part of their neighborhood in search of a cure for shingles; in the latter, Incardona describes a football match between his friends and a group of albinos who live nearby—their physical difference turns out to be the result of pollution in the Riachuelo, highlighting their shared state of marginality. Thus, despite the hyper-local nature of Incardona's work, his stories are frequented by strangers and the unknown *within the neighborhood*. Likewise, the whole of *El campito* (2009) is based around the journeys made by the rubbish-picker Carlitos around the southwest of Gran Buenos Aires, during which excursions he comes across a whole number of lost Peronist neighborhoods built along similar lines to the actual Ciudad Evita. Similarly, there are several stories in which the characters engage with zones that appear to be no man's lands, such as the space under the crossing of Avenida General Paz and Avenida Ricchieri, inhabited by drug dealers and prostitutes and where it is unclear which police department has jurisdiction, or the tunnels under the motorways that are described as "una boca de lobo" (a lion's den; 2010a, p. 26). Indeed, at one point during a conflict between the youths of Villa Celina and neighboring Villa Lugano the locals describe the *barrio* itself as temporarily a "no man's land" (2010a, p. 96).

Thus, if one initially takes the narrative voice to be an expression of Villa Celina, it quickly becomes apparent that even the narrator is unfamiliar with all aspects of his *barrio*; the neighborhood continually surprises him and the reader. And it is precisely in the encounter with the internal stranger that a potential community can be formed—in one chapter, Juan Diego encounters a thief who threatens to take his shoes and guitar. Refusing to give up his precious instrument, the narrator instead offers to play the potential mugger a song. Juan Diego ends up spending the whole night playing music with the young people there, delighted when he wakes up to find he still has his guitar and his shoes, admiring the fact that "those kids had codes" (2010a, p. 110). The narratives of Incardona imagine spaces and moments in which the contemporary urban choice between the cosmopolis and the gated community is bypassed. Engaging with the internal stranger both accepts the strangeness within and avoids inscribing a fixed frontier. The neighborhood thus becomes not the last line of defense in the struggle against an encroaching global culture, but works together with other neighborhoods in the construction of the city in common, a city in which being strange is itself a site of togetherness. Moreover, Incardona's way of writing the neighborhood is itself simultaneously highly localized and generic to the city, contemporary sketches that are built around sharing stories of urban life. Incardona here echoes Kwame Appiah's suggestion that shared narratives are the foundation of cosmopolitanism (2001, p. 224). The point is reinforced when Incardona, describing himself as a pariah among the students of Puan for wearing dungarees and having long hair (2007, p. 12), overcomes difference by convincing his classmates to share his innovative reading of the text they are studying.

But it is also the way that Incardona writes his neighborhood that offers a means of moving beyond exclusion: "During its nighttimes you're aware of a light fog, partially lit up by the old lamp-post lights, you hear dogs (which abound) barking, gunshots far away and up close, and a kind of murmur that's difficult to identify and that frequently interrupts the conversation on the pavements, perhaps a kind of past, a sound of the past, a goal by Tino on the wasteground mixed up the laughter of the boys of the band Perseverancia and the swearing of Carlitos the drunk" (2010a, p. 12). On the one hand, the narrator emphasizes with some romanticism what is his own, a localized geography that constructs a neighborhood, and a particular gaze toward the past and its characters; but, on the other hand, the invitation is to share the story of that neighborhood, inviting the reader, themselves strangers, to draw on Villa Celina as one *barrio* among many. A similar sensation is created in the following sentence: "a bloke as big as a giraffe, measuring some three meters or more, I swear on my mother, and I'd never seen anything like it and even Carlitos *superpancho de Giribone* wasn't a patch on him" (2010a, p. 47). Even without knowing Carlitos, his identifier (hot dog on Giribone Street) is enough for the reader to be brought into and share the particularities of Incardona's world.

Incardona's work is thus balanced between an emphasis on difference and the means to transcend that difference via writing and the imagination, an approach that allows him to inscribe a specific geography back onto the cultural map of the city not simply as an act of defense, which perpetuates exclusion, but also as an act of inclusion. Incardona himself has pointed out that his writing should be seen as an intervention into Argentine literary history, which has tended to write about the *conurbano* from the perspective of someone taking a day trip from the city center, whereas he tries to write the periphery with "the voice of the native, the neighbor, the inhabitant" (Incardona, 2012).[5] This element of his work emphasizes the power of the local, the way that he takes his literature to be read in the schools where his mother teaches as a means of highlighting that those children too have an urban imaginary that relates specifically to them. For that reason, the section in *Objetos maravillosos* in which his parents sell the house that his grandparents built is followed by a chapter entitled "La hemorragia" (The Hemorrhage) in which he describes the unstoppable flow of blood created by pulling a tooth out, a metaphor for the depth of his roots. And yet at the same time, Incardona is at odds to write the neighborhood into a wider urban imaginary and cultural history. *Villa Celina*, for example, includes references to Mark Twain's *The Adventures of Huckleberry Finn*, Pachelbel's *Canon,* and Jonas. Incardona has also explained that the references he makes to Roberto Arlt, Jorge Luis Borges, Leopoldo Marechal, and Héctor G. Oesterheld in his work are there not just to tap into the wider historical imaginary of Gran Buenos Aires but also because "I like the fact that this story goes beyond the boundaries of General Paz and Ricchieri" (Bilbao, 2011).[6] The way in which Incardona's works are structured around stories and vignettes of urban life makes his ties to Arlt particularly strong. As well as writing novels, a considerable portion of Arlt's written output was formed by sketches known as "Aguafuertes," written for the newspaper *El Mundo*. Published between the late 1920s and early 1930s, the majority of these sketches depicted the broad spectrum of life in Buenos Aires at the time. The inclusion of Santoro's illustrations in *Villa Celina* further emphasizes Incardona's link to Arlt since, as David Viñas points out, the latter's depiction of the city was influenced by the artist Facio Hebequer, whose work encapsulated "the aggressive and multitudinous technique of the engraver" (1998, p. 7).

Thus, Incardona writes both from and beyond the neighborhood, writing a *barrio* that goes beyond itself to become and transform Buenos Aires at large. Villa Celina enables Incardona to explore the writing of Gran Buenos Aires, both because of its position on the imaginatively rich edges of the city, full of "bocas de lobo" that allow for fictional possibility, and because it incorporates the delirious imaginaries of Peronism, turning storymaking into the foundation of a new urban geography. That urban geography is vital to any understanding of Buenos Aires and, indeed, Argentina, as he pointed out in a radio interview: "I always think that the neighborhood can tell the history of the country, and the country can't tell the history of the neighborhood" (Lavaca, 2009). Moreover, it is also vital for the city in common, since the ever-present, internal stranger breaks down the frontier of exclusivity that the celebration of the neighborhood threatens. Confronted with the possibility of the unknown, Incardona invites the urban dweller to form part of a commons in which narrative intensities and itineraries are exchanged with neighbors and strangers alike.

Chapter 6

Transforming the Commons, Recycling the City

The presence of cultural discourses stemming from the areas beyond Capital Federal is a great test for Buenos Aires as a city in common since its imaginary has always been dominated by the smaller, now independent entity formed within the borders created by the Riachuelo and Avenida General Paz. The difficulty Capital has in incorporating an imaginary that draws on the whole of Gran Buenos Aires is intensified since the latter is often seen as harboring, as the previous chapter illustrated, cultural, racial, political, and class traits that do not sit well with the more affluent residents of Capital. Thinking the city through the urban poor and the disenfranchised dwellers living on the boundaries of the urban imaginary is a task fraught with deep-seated, perhaps irreconcilable dangers, not least that of romanticizing urban poverty. Nevertheless, to fail to address and, indeed, imagine the urban poor would be to ignore the very real extremes of poverty and inequality that continue to dominate the Latin American city. One very visible face of that poverty in Buenos Aires in the lead-up to and the aftermath of the 2001 crisis, were informal rubbish collectors, known as *cartoneros*. With their daily commute into Capital Federal, *cartoneros* created tensions over the right to move in the city and, in the process, engaged with and transformed three kinds of urban commons—street, movement, and rubbish—that all tapped into notions of urban recycling.

Informal garbage collection and scavenging has a long history in Buenos Aires: *Cirujas*, a word derived from *cirujano*, meaning surgeon, a pejorative term believed to stem either from the prong used to pick up discarded rubbish or the ability to cut up bones collected from the streets, were a well-established urban phenomenon by the end of the 19th century and in 1899, when the city had a population of about 750,000, an estimated 3,000 people in the city were already living off rubbish (Fundación

Metropolitana, 2004, p. 7). At the turn of the new millennium there was a dramatic increase in the numbers of *cartoneros* as a result of growing unemployment and urban poverty in Buenos Aires. *Cartoneros* moved through the heavily populated areas of the city, sifting rubbish left out for the waste collection companies. The 2001 devaluation of the Argentine peso hiked the cost of importing raw materials such as paper and plastic, making local recycling economically advantageous and encouraging the informal collection of recyclables such as metals, glass, and cardboard, which are transported via trolleys and carts to central collection points where they are bought up by weight. Estimates of the number of *cartoneros* operating in recent decades peaked at over 40,000 in 2002, before declining to a number less than 10,000 (Whitson, 2011, p. 1409).

Rubbish pickers have been confronted with laws specific to Capital Federal, such as that forbidding animal-powered transport, which prevents them from using a horse and cart to collect rubbish. Police at the entry points from Gran Buenos Aires stop such carts from entering the city, a symbolic reminder of the strained relationship between "civilized," modern Capital and "barbaric" rural Gran Buenos Aires. When the number of *cartoneros* increased, train companies were faced with surging demand, and other passengers complained at having to share space with supermarket trolleys and carts. As a result, the companies began to run special services for these *cartoneros*, who were, in turn, prohibited from using regular trains. Running a limited service of one train in and one train out per day, the companies put back into service old passenger trains stripped of seating and in varying conditions of decay. Functioning with deplorable safety standards, some train windows were locked shut after the death of one *cartonero*, killed leaning out of the train as it entered a station (Anguita, 2003, p. 97). This parallel transport service highlighted the conditional nature of traveling through the city, a key element of the right to the city.

The train that symbolized these special services, running until its suspension in 2007, was the Tren Blanco, the subject of both a film, *El tren blanco* (The White Train; 2003, dir. Nahuel García, Sheila Pérez Giménez, & Ramiro García) and the photographic essay *Tren blanco: el tren de los cartoneros* (White Train: Train of the Rubbish Pickers) by José Enrique Sternberg (2004). Sternberg's photographs in particular highlight both the political impact of the *cartoneros* and their ongoing entrapment within the cycles of waste and recycling, as well as serving as a reminder of the problems raised by cultural interactions with the urban poor. On the one hand, *Tren blanco* captures the latent trajectories of the *cartone-*

ros, the transformative movements that will be released onto the city as the passengers get off the train. On the other, it is a reminder of the way that *cartoneros* are trapped, both in photographic time and in terms of social mobility. The train makes movement possible, but it is also a space of confinement. From the very first image, *Tren blanco* creates a contrast between stasis and the promise of movement. Here the bodies move toward the stationary train, creating, together with the train, the electricity cables, and the clouds, lines of actual and potential movement, in similar fashion to the way other photographs capture other forms of transport, such as innumerable supermarket trolleys stored in the carriage (image 4) or an upturned bicycle wheel (image 9). But the static nature of these makeshift, human-powered forms of transport creates a stark contrast with the powerful machine of the train. As the *cartoneros* board the train and move to their destination, they appear precisely to lose their mobility. The rigidity of the train and its tracks, running from periphery to center along predetermined routes regulate and restrict the freedom of movement. The potential for dissent is captured by the tensions between the train company's official paintwork and the graffiti on the side of the carriages (image 6).

As the series progresses, not only is the photographer located inside the carriages, but the subjects begin to look back at the camera, establishing a dialogue with the camera. If in the second image the figures talk to each other, ignoring the camera such that the eye is drawn away down the empty aisles, in the fourth image they look at the viewer, demanding a photographic conversation. Highlighting the ability of the subject to decide whether to return the gaze, Sternberg reminds us of the active role that *cartoneros* can play in the cultural imaginary of the city. The active gaze establishes a photographic subjectivity that, in Barthes's terms, animates the viewer (1993, p. 20). At the same time, however, the returned gaze establishes difference and distance as much as reinforcing any semblance of a commons on based on poverty and inequality. Thus, in the final image of the series, the viewer is confronted by a child looking directly at the camera through the bars of the supermarket trolley in which he sits. Ending with this image, a symbol of the way that the *cartoneros* are themselves sometimes turned into products produced and consumed by the global market, unsettles any temporary intimacy that the photographs might have established.

Many images in the series portray the train not only as an enclosed space but also as detached and estranged from the city. Images 3, 5, 7, and 10 all portray figures standing by windows, barriers between the inside of the carriage and the outside of the city, reminiscent of the enforced movement of humans in cattle cars. The city beyond remains invisible, beyond the frame or "appearing" as a white, ethereal light pouring in through the windows, an otherworldly light in direct contrast to the train's murky interior. The portrayal of the interior of the carriage, not least with the inclusion of impoverished children, reverses the famous scene in Fernando Birri's 1960 film *Tire dié*, in which destitute children risk injury by running alongside a passing train begging from the wealthy travelers who lean out of the train window. Far from the freedom of train travel, *Tren blanco* symbolizes the way that the *cartoneros* are at once part of and removed from the city, pushed beyond its imaginary in much the same way as the rubbish they collect.

Many citizens responded to the influx of *cartoneros* into the city at the turn of the millennium with disapproval, as if the urban poor were disrupting the image of the city in much the same way as they had done during the first period of Peronism. In Capital Federal, in particular, many middle- and working-class neighborhoods were fearful that the boom in *cartoneros* would lead to an explosion of shantytowns, where many *cartoneros* live, in the city (Chronopoulos, 2006, p. 175). The fear of the shantytown "encroaching" on the city is a reminder of how informal housing, and, indeed, *cartoneros* are constantly located as entities that are not of the city, rather than being recognized as integral to the urban system. The fear of "strange bodies" encroaching on the city, with citizens using terms such as "invading" or "taking over" (Whitson, 2011, p. 1420), is inscribed within the wider discourse of the "threat" of Gran Buenos Aires to Capital Federal, a discourse linked to the dichotomy of civilization/barbarism and, as Adrián Gorelik has suggested, with the manner in which Buenos Aires fears "Latin Americanization" (2002, p. 7). For Capital, *cartoneros* had no place disrupting the order and image of the modern city they imagined Buenos Aires to be.

Despite initial hostility, *cartoneros* came to receive much wider social acceptance in the city, and a change in legislation legalized informal rubbish collection in 2002. As Alejandro Grimson notes, the drastic and tragic nature of having to live off rubbish "should not hide from view [that] poverty and the relationship among social sectors are now visualized differently," a shift that has resulted in the transgression of two boundaries, "a spatial one by the cartoneros and a symbolic one by middle class sectors in order to rearticulate the social link" (2008, p. 507). The established presence of the *cartoneros* is illustrated by the Atlas Ambiental de Buenos Aires, which lists informal (such as that of the *cartoneros*), formal, and illegal garbage collection and disposal as part of the city's mechanisms of dealing with rubbish, clearly opposing informal to illegal rubbish collection. Moreover, the interaction between *cartoneros* and refuse, particularly through recycling, is further indication of the way they have influenced the understanding of the city. Garbage, much like *cartoneros* themselves, threatens the very premise of the modern city, becoming, in González Stephan's words, "one of the metaphors that complemented the great axiom of 'barbarism' " (cited in Moore, 2009, p. 430). As a result, garbage offers political opportunity, troubling the boundaries between, as Sarah Moore suggests, "clean and dirty, order and chaos," creating possibilities "for political acts that expose the unstable and fragile nature of the imposed categories of modernity and the institutions responsible for upholding them" (2009, p. 429).

In an article reflecting on the right to the city, Sharon Meagher offers a more cautious reading of rubbish, taking up Moore's premise that garbage can be a means to demand the Right to the City, but suggesting that whose right and which city the term refers to is not so straightforward (2010, p. 428). She goes on to argue that the rubbish protests Moore studies in Oaxaca are not examples of "systemic" or "revolutionary" change, since most of the participants are not demanding a world in which their lives no longer revolve around rubbish (2010, p. 430). *Cartoneros* in Argentina might be considered in similar fashion as they too can hardly be seen as dissenters or protesters in the manner of other turn-of-the-millennium social protests in Argentina. Instead, they offer a caveat to the city in common, reminding us that the commoning of the public street can also be turned into a practice of social exclusion and desperation, one that might be described, as Sergio Chejfec suggests, as a Sisyphean act (Chejfec, 2002). In that sense, *cartoneros* highlight the limitations of the cross-class alliance that erupted into the streets of Buenos Aires in December 2001. *Cartoneros* are not just the return of the repressed for the urban middle and upper classes, the social rubbish that cannot be thrown away, but they also function on the edges of the change demanded by the protest movements. After all, the legalization of *cartoneros* and the incorporation of informal rubbish picking into state politics of rubbish collection, though obviously welcome, is hardly a radical change in outlook for the urban poor.

And yet to recognize the transformations brought about by *cartoneros* is not always to "get down with the cartoneros and cheer for the unemployed," in the words used by Francine Masiello in her acerbic critique of postcrisis cultural production (2007, p. 202). The disruption caused by *cartoneros* in the longstanding urban imaginary of Buenos Aires has been significant and perhaps even productive. Moreover, *cartoneros* are not just further examples of the growing importance of space to the sociopolitical realities of Buenos Aires at the turn of the millennium; they have also reshaped three different kinds of commons that form the focus of this chapter: the street, walking, and rubbish. *Cartoneros* do not make of the street a productive civic space simply because they force urban dwellers to engage with them as strangers, though that is a significant element of their transformative potential, but rather because the habits, rhythms, and multiplicities that they release transform the street. In particular, *cartoneros* mobilize bodies in space by walking, a tactic that is itself transformative. They instigate political change in their interactions with nonhuman elements of the street, namely rubbish. Cartoneros restore to rubbish, itself a marker of the strange and the unwanted, a marker of value, highlighting how the city can itself be recycled from the ruins of politics. That politics of recycling was taken up by culture and cultural practices in the wake of 2001, seeing in the *cartoneros* a means of revising cultural politics. Certainly it is vital, as Masiello writes, to avoid exploiting the "cultural capital" of the poor and the "short-lived fascination with the lives of others," but cultural representations of the *cartoneros* are not simply part of, in her words, the "trafficking of faith" brought about by 2001, nor "part of a larger agenda to renew a sense of feeling" and "reinvigorat[e] our passions" (2007, pp. 202–207). They also stimulate recognition that different political subjectivities enact urban change, not least at a time when other urban recycling projects threaten to turn the city into a historyless experience for the nomadic elite.

Walking the Streets

The presence of *cartoneros* on the streets of Buenos Aires has highlighted differences in the way that certain urban dwellers understand these public spaces. Some citizens of Buenos Aires recognized the right of *cartoneros* to carry out rubbish collection, establishing bonds of solidarity that encouraged and assisted the work of the pickers. Many *cartoneros*, for example, working in the more affluent areas of the city where inhabitants were more likely to discard valuable rubbish, built up relationships with apartment block porters. Themselves lower-income workers, porters act as an interface between residents and the outside, particularly the service community. As a result, they were in a privileged position to help *car-*

toneros collect valuable recyclables and sort the rubbish. In other areas, however, such as the wealthy residential areas of the northern suburbs, where there is less traffic and less interaction between the single-plot home and its outside, the street is less "shared." Not only do security railings protect residents, but the streets are policed by private security guards keeping watch in street-corner cabins. Perceived to threaten the security and the aesthetic and socioeconomic "feel" of these streets, *cartoneros* were unwelcome because they offered a reminder of the urban inequality that wealthy residents constantly try to omit from their conceptual and material cityscapes.

Linebaugh notes the historical tradition of the street as a commons, observing that "the street was the public realm of the unpropertied, or the urban commonage—the location of laundry, the place of commerce and street peddlers, the scene of courtship, children's playground, beauty salon, outdoor parlor for housewives" (2008, p. 262). *Cartoneros*, at least, as well as stimulating debate over uses of public space (Chronopoulos, 2006, p. 171), showed the city streets to be a problematic commons, with residents appearing to take "ownership" of the streets outside their homes, hoping to protect them from the incursions of other, undesirable publics. Linebaugh's comments highlight why considerable expectation continues to be placed in physical public space, and how the impact of those urban commons has been transformed by privatization, surveillance, and the growth of other kinds of public spaces, including cyberspace.

Certainly the ongoing use of city streets and squares as privileged spaces for expressing political dissent demonstrates that physical spaces still allow for the gathering of bodies en masse, a bringing together that disrupts the smooth running of the urban machine. Nevertheless, as urban theorist Ash Amin suggests, "in an age of urban sprawl, multiple usage of public space and proliferation of the sites of political and cultural expression, it seems odd to expect public spaces to fulfill their traditional role as spaces of civic inculcation and political participation" (2008, p. 5). Amin probes precisely the conceptual distance between those cultural and political theorists (as he sees it) who suggest that urban public space "has become one component, arguably of secondary importance, in a variegated field of civic and political formation," and the urban theorists who continue to argue that there is "a strong link between urban public space and urban civic virtue and citizenship" (2008, p. 6). Taking a middle line between these two positions, Amin suggests that the unpredictable nature of meeting strangers, the traditional aim of civic urban planning, means that solidarity may or may not emerge from such encounters (2008, p. 7), a point supported by the varying response to *cartoneros* in Buenos Aires. He goes on to argue that if there is political promise in public space then it is as likely to be found "in the entanglement between people and the material and visual culture of public space, rather than solely in the quality of social interaction between strangers" and that "the collective impulses of public space are the result of pre-cognitive and tacit human response to a condition of 'situated multiplicity,' the thrown togetherness of bodies, mass and matter, and of many uses and needs in a shared physical space" (2008, p. 8). The encounter with strangers in public spaces is full of potential for political solidarity, and it is the way that *cartoneros* use public space, particularly through walking and interactions with rubbish, that transforms the city.

Growing unemployment and economic inequality in Argentina prior to and after the crisis were often linked to the growing significance of territory in urban life from housing to public space. Neoliberal Buenos Aires, like many other cities, began to accommodate extremes of immense velocity, epitomized by Carlos Menem, a president who liked to drive his Ferrari at illegal speeds (Guillermoprieto, 1994, p. 119), at the same time as growing restrictions on movement were imposed on the urban poor, such as the privatization of the motorways, instigated in 1989. The flows tied to an increasingly mobile middle and upper class, evident in commuter travel, flights, mobile communications, and money transfers, were offset by other constrictions and limitations: "[N]eoliberalism in practice is *not* simply about mobility: [I]t too requires some spatial fixes" (Massey, 2005, p. 86). Moving around Buenos Aires required negotiating a network of frontiers, turnstiles, and security fences.

Given their ties to the territorialization of poverty and urban movement, therefore, *cartoneros* have much in common with another set of actors that came to symbolize the 2001 economic crash: the *piqueteros*.[1] It would be the *piqueteros*, groups of organized unemployed persons forming blockades on major thoroughfares, that epitomized the importance of space and movement to social protest, using the roadblock to demand the right to social and physical mobility, at the same time as making dissent tangible by restricting movement. Their stationary bodies, located at strategically placed roadblocks, antagonize the rest of the city, restricting traffic, people, and capital. As one *piquetero* stated, "capitalism can't last long against the roadblock" (cited in Massetti, 2004, p. 52). But the self-consciously dissenting nature of the *piqueteros* emphasize that they are palpably different from the *cartoneros*. Whereas *piqueteros* were directly involved in social protest and fueling debates over the future of political representation, *cartoneros* were trying to eke out a living off rubbish, demonstrating not the desire for social transformation but rather the pressing realities of destitution. In that sense, *cartoneros* and *piqueteros* represent two very different sides of the crisis. The direct political interventions of the latter make it difficult to recognize the political impact of the former because political change is more obvious when seen in terms of insurrection, protest, and armed revolution.

I want to suggest, however, that the *cartoneros* nonetheless enact political change insofar as we recognize how, on the level of their everyday habits and rhythms, they constantly transform the city, albeit in less perceptible ways. In his three-volume *Critique of Everyday Life*, Henri Lefebvre sought, in a renewed celebration of the everyday, an alternative to the urban alienation brought on by a rampant consumer culture. Lefebvre saw creative possibility in the quotidian, adding that a true revolution cannot occur purely in economic or political terms but must place everyday life at its core, both as its ultimate aim and its medium of change (2008, vol. 3, p. 29). His comments help refine Hardt and Negri's uneasy tension between what they call the "ontological" multitude and the "historical multitude or, really, the not-yet multitude" (2004, p. 221). The habits and everyday practices of the *cartoneros* show that the multitude itself can be everyday, a "mode of being" (Virno, 2004, p. 26) that transforms the commons more in line with Hardt and Negri's belief that "habits form a nature that is both produced and productive, created and creative—an ontology of social practice in common" (2004, p. 198).

Looking more closely at *cartoneros* and *piqueteros*, therefore, highlights that, in spatial terms, the habits of everyday motion used by both transform the city streets. The nature of the *piquete* roadblock, during which the road is used as a place for, among other activities, voting, saying mass, and eating and sleeping, highlights how *piqueteros* "actively re-create imaginaries, practices and projects that challenge the structures of neoliberal globalization" (Motta, 2009, p. 84). Thus, whilst the roadblock limits physical movement, it expresses at the same time the desire for social mobility. As Amin suggests, particular rhythms and multiple temporalities foment the "civic culture of tolerated multiplicity and shared commons" of each individual public space (2008, p. 9). It is precisely those repeated actions that make such spaces recognizable as such. Moreover, rather than settling into a status quo that threatens their transformative potential, repetitions, and habits, Amin suggests, are constantly creating new permutations in a simultaneous "process of ordering and disruption" (2008, p. 12). Recognizing the different ways in which stasis can produce movement and movement stasis highlights how the repeated urban rhythms of practices and habits such as those enacted by the *cartoneros* can have political potential.

In particular, *cartoneros* transform the city through the habit of walking, another commons. Linebaugh, noting that travel is one of the five foundations of the Magna Carta (2008, p. 245), indicates the foundational role of walking in the formation of the commons, both as a perambulation—the marking of the forest boundary as a delineation of common land—and as a form of protest against enclosure (2008, p. 75). Of course, we should not assume that walking is always affiliated with "openness" or "public ownership" (Solnit, 2002, p. xi); a wide range of different people and groups, from policemen to street vendors to prostitutes to those wanting to keep fit, deploy walking with varying political, social, and economic ends. Nevertheless, walking enables *cartoneros* to inhabit the street, not just highlighting how the city is divided by access to and deployment of movement, but also how they leave their mark on that space.

Michel de Certeau famously analyzed a number of different urban practices, including walking, to think about how such practices might combat the authority of those up high who are in a position to read the city. Down below in the city, he argued, "beneath the discourses that ideologize the city, the ruses and combinations of powers that have no readable identity proliferate [and] are impossible to administer" (1988, p. 95). As a nonlinear set of Brownian movements (1988, p. 40), the random and unpredictable motion of particles in a fluid, walking eludes legibility. Whatever the specific, necessary, and essential destination, the simple joining together of multiple and contiguous trajectories enacted by walking has an impact on the city. Walking has the potential to contribute to the city in common precisely because it enables bodies to mobilize against structures of power without the need for any other form of mediation. Placing bodies into space is a key site of commonality for social struggles surrounding the 2001 crisis (Zibechi, 2003, p. 34). From worker-occupied factories to roadblocks organized by the unemployed, from local neighborhood street assemblies to pots-and-pans marches, contemporary protest is often characterized by deploying bodies to enact or prevent movement in and through the city. Like the *piqueteros*, therefore, the paths created by the circulating bodies of the *cartoneros* both produce and restrict flow. Whether producing stasis or flow, when *cartoneros* walk they reveal above all how the street "becomes the setting for . . . the building up of political solidarity" (Dinerstein, 2001, p. 6). They reconstruct the street as a site of commonality by employing innumerable, habitual steps in the manner of Francesco Careri's description of Richard Long's 1967 *A Line Made by Walking*—"a straight line 'sculpted' on the ground simply by treading on grass . . . disappearing from the ground when the grass returns to its original position" (2002, p. 142). Amin makes a similar point: "The lines of power and separation somehow disappear in a heavily patterned ground, as the ground springs back as a space of multiple uses, multiple trajectories and multiple publics, simultaneously freeing and circumscribing social experience of the urban commons" (2008, p. 12).

Thus, even if it does not always leave material traces, walking perpetually transforms the city streets and their meaning. The bodies of the *cartoneros* create an uncountable mesh of layered trajectories and an amalgamation of footsteps, which "*cannot be counted* because *each unit has a qualitative* character: a style of tactile apprehension and kinesthetic appropriation. *Their swarming mass is an innumerable* collection *of singularities*" (De Certeau, 1988, p. 97; emphasis added). Walking emphasizes the here and now of physicality, the "innumerable collection" of bodies moving in common, and the transformation of discarded bodies into recycling bodies and bodies recycled. *Cartoneros* thus not only created a debate over the nature of public space but also transformed it, both in strict legislative terms and insofar as they introduced a new set of rhythms and paths into the urban environment. As such, they emphasize how the practice of commoning continues to transform the street.

Garbage and Recycling

The way in which *cartoneros* transform the city is also related to a third form of commons: garbage. Referring to the common potential of rubbish as a form of exchange and barter, Linebaugh goes on to argue that "the allure of commoning arises from the mutualism of shared resources" (2008, p. 103). Informal garbage collection thus becomes a means, albeit a desperate one, of establishing one's presence within the urban network. It also lends credence to Amin's suggestion that the civic qualities of public space are also built via interactions between the human and the nonhuman. *Cartoneros* enacted changes in the value and understanding of rubbish and, in turn, in the legal and conceptual understanding of the street.

Just as the informal collection of rubbish is not a new phenomenon in the city, neither is recycling. At the beginning of the 20th century, for example, an ordinance in Buenos Aires demanded citizens sort their organic rubbish and the aforementioned *cirujas* collected bones, glass, metals, and paper, either reusing them or selling them on to factories (Fundación Metropolitana, 2004, pp. 6–7). The nature and quantity of rubbish has, however, changed over time. The growth in mass production, mass distribution, and consumer culture over the course of the 20th century has generated more objects, more trash, and an ideological transition from re-use to disposal, such that rubbish becomes directly associated with poverty (Strasser, 1999, p. 17). Rubbish and rubbish collection is an evermore dominant element of urban politics and management, with citizens often measuring the efficiency of local government on the basis of their ability to process rubbish.

It is unsurprising that, within this culture of consumption and disposal, the garbage dump is the end of the road for the consumer's product, the place where those that consume can discard unwanted memories and hopes: "In the dump's squalid phantasmagoria, the same commodities that had been fetishized by advertising . . . are now stripped of their aura of charismatic power" (Stam, 1997). Likewise, recycling highlights the fact that garbage can also be reinserted back into the cycle of materials and goods. The public nature of rubbish explains some of the unease generated by *cartoneros*: The discarded object often reveals a great deal about the person discarding, who neither wants a stranger to be in possession of *their* rubbish nor wants to be confronted with the potential return of *what is no longer theirs*. Rubbish should stay out of sight, out of mind. Thus the processes of recycling create, like walking, another set of urban flows. Like the emergence of *trueque* (barter), an exchange system that had a temporary revival during the cash-poor period of the 2001 crisis, by engaging in this activity of recycling *cartoneros* have reconfigured the monopoly on rubbish, participating in the body of knowledge on, for example, the comparative value of recyclable materials, the amount of rubbish produced in different parts of the city, and the most effective and economical ways of constructing durable carts and trolleys. Constantly adapting to changes in the market and the spaces they transverse, *cartoneros* became key figures in urban waste collection, generating self-run organizations to gather and distribute recyclables and working with groups such as Tren Blanco and Etilplast to establish fair, sustainable prices for recyclables.

The value of such rubbish has been a particularly contentious issue in Buenos Aires. The question posed by the sociologist Horacio González— "Who owns society's rubbish?"[2]—is especially important when, not long after the crisis, some 12.3 million tons of rubbish were being produced annually in Argentina, with the cost of collection in Capital Federal alone reaching 13 million pesos every month (Magnani, 2006, p. 2). Rubbish is big business. No wonder the major refuse collection companies were so concerned about informal garbage collection, especially when it is estimated that already in 1995 *cartoneros* gathered between 10 and 15% of the city's rubbish—worth approximately 10 million pesos (then equivalent to U.S. dollars). The 1976–1983 military dictatorship is a case in point. On the back of the 1974 closure of the city's incinerators, unable to cope with the quantity of rubbish being produced and struggling to work properly in the humid climate (Fundación Metropolitana, 2004, p. 9), the military regime created CEASME (Cinturón Ecológico del Área Metropolitana Sociedad del Estado) on the riverbanks of the city. Using huge quantities of urban waste as landfill for new recreational spaces on the edge of the city epitomized Osvaldo Cacciatore's project for a clean—and cleansed—city. Cacciatore realized that collecting rubbish would not only further the image of the ordered city but also that it would generate huge income for the government. Consequently, he implemented a law against the informal collection of rubbish in the streets and oversaw the creation of Manliba (Mantener Limpio Buenos Aires [Keep Buenos Aires Clean]). Manliba is owned by Grupo Macri, and during his unsuccessful first run for mayor of the City of Buenos Aires in 2003, Mauricio Macri, son of the company's founder, objected vehemently to *cartoneros*, stating that they would be imprisoned for "steal[ing] from the trash" (Chronopoulos, 2006, p. 180), comments that demonstrated how precious informal rubbish collection was even after formal ratification.[3]

Macri's comments not only echoed the 1988 ruling by the U.S. Supreme Court that trash is not private and that the police need no authorization to search citizens' rubbish (Strasser, 1999, p. 7), but they also indicated how garbage is a highly charged area of urban politics. Just as walking has the potential to revise public space, garbage offers the potential for urban dwellers to reposition themselves within the city. Garbage is especially potent in that regard since, as Cacciatore's "ciudad blanca" (white city) shows so clearly, it functions as a threat to urban "order" and as a reminder of the waste that modernity produces but which it refuses to acknowledge. Such a dynamic is especially loaded in Latin America precisely because the region's cities were founded with the inherent objective of ordering the subjects of colonial society (Moore, 2009). As such, garbage can become a political tool, because urban dwellers can exploit the gap between the expected order of the city and its disordered, out-of-place realities. Garbage threatens order in much the same way that recycling can threaten the logic of consumer culture.

Culture and the City Recycled

After 2001 the transformation of garbage carried out by the *cartoneros* had a significant impact on cultural production. The website liquidacion.org, for example, played on the notion of value by offering objects found by *cartoneros* for sale over the Internet, illustrating how *cartoneros* could turn garbage into symbols of urban culture (Liquidación.org, 2013).[4] Accompanied by a recording of where and by whom the object was found, rubbish was reinserted back into market circulation, gaining value not from its use value (many objects are broken) but from the stories that accompanied them. The editorial collective Eloísa cartonera, set up in 2003, was also set up around the practice of *cartoneros*, publishing Latin American literature in editions made from cardboard bought from the rubbish pickers.

Latin America has a long tradition of incorporating garbage into cultural production, as can be seen in the work of Hélio Oiticica, Antonio Berni, and Francisca Nuñéz, to name but three artists. The Argentine artist Ricardo Longhini also used recycling as part of his sculptures that reflected on December 2001, gathering physical remnants—stones, bullet shells, glass—of the protests. Robert Stam argued that cultural discourses in Latin American and the Caribbean have been characterized by an aesthetic of inversion, redeeming "the low, the despised, the imperfect, and the 'trashy' as part of a social overturning" (1997). Beginning with what the Brazilian underground filmmakers of the 1960s called the "aesthetics of garbage" (estetica do lixo), Stam suggested that garbage was an apt metaphor for urban exclusion, poverty, and the everyday need to recycle what wealthier urban dwellers discard. Latin American culture thus often uses rubbish (and its collection) as "a metaphorical figure for social indictment—poor people treated like garbage" (Stam, 1997), a notion encapsulated by the story of Daniela Cott, a discarded "garbage body" taken up by the fashion industry and "recycled" into a model (BBC, 2008).[5]

Cultural productions—like the fashion industry—are always open to accusation of aestheticizing poverty when engaging with *cartoneros*. The point, however, is not to celebrate informal rubbish collection but rather to recognize how the practice of the *cartoneros* forces us to rethink the city and its established social, political, and economic relations. To conclude this chapter, therefore, I want to look at one cultural production—the poem *El carrito de Eneas* (Aeneas's trolley) by Daniel Samoilovich—that uses informal rubbish collectors to think through postcrisis Buenos Aires and its relationship to culture. As editor of the publication *Diario de poesía*, Samoilovich has long advocated "neo-objetivista" poetry, one that is opposed to the lyricism of the neo-baroque poets, a form of poetry "without linguistic heroics" (Prieto, 2006, p. 452) and which tries, in the words of Francine Masiello, to recover "a fluid voice, without excesses and against the brimming over of the neo-baroque" (2012, p. 145). Indeed, even though *El carrito de Eneas* appears on the face of it to draw on a certain poetic romanticism and classical imagery, it is in fact typical of neo-objectivist poetry in its fascination with objects and the inclusion of marginal urban dwellers. Indeed, it is that engagement with the pressing realities of urban materiality and poverty that dismantles the mythic framework within which this Buenos Aires is housed.

El carrito de Eneas is set in the aftermath of the fall of a city. The myth of Troy, the paradigmatic demise of a city, is used as a symbolic foundation for a poetic exploration of the fall of Buenos Aires after 2001. Samoilovich creates a number of specific comparisons and transformations from Troy to Buenos Aires: Constitución, for example, formerly a square of colossal statues, a market and temple where sacrifices were made to the gods, has now lost its civic, political, and spiritual significance (2003, p. 25). The old city wall, a symbol of the city's political entirety and security, has been destroyed, leaving "the stumps / of the old wall" (p. 11), suggestive of an incomplete, amputated body of the city. Walls that used to be built like the old fortresses of the Incas—"an electrical *pucará* at the frontiers"—are now "stone walls of cardboard, / but weak, negotiable" (pp. 15–16). These cardboard walls of the city, vulnerable and unstable, have become the latest commodity. The fall of Buenos Aires, however, opens the door to a new city, in which the Greek Agamemnon and the Trojan Hector work side by side as *cartoneros* (p. 16). The emphasis on a new city is encapsulated by the poem's principal object: Aeneas's trolley. A variation on the myth in the *Aeneid* in which Vulcan makes weapons for Aeneas, the most significant of which was a shield, here Vulcan makes the trolley for Aeneas (p. 22). Jorge Monteleone (2003) reminds us that, in this sense, the book follows the tradition of relating figures depicted on a hero's shield, as in Hesiod's description of Hercules or Homer's of Achilles. In Virgil's *Aeneid*, furthermore, the particular significance of Aeneas's shield is that it foretold the founding of Rome by Romulus and Remus, a mythic cross-reference that heightens the idea of a new city being born from the ruins.

The role of the *cartoneros* in this new city is evident from the index page, which includes a drawing of a handheld, two-wheeled trolley broken down into its various parts, each part representing a section of the poem: As the major transport hubs in the city and those that see the greatest numbers of *cartoneros*, the two sidebars and the base represent Plaza Constitución, Retiro, and Plaza Miserere; the three crossbars represent glass, paper, and tin, the three main products collected by *cartoneros*. The trolley both foreshadows the city to come (like Aeneas's shield), and constructs a city that revolves around *cartoneros* and their practices. Furthermore, by associating each section of the poem with a piece of the trolley, the illustration also creates a link between the trolley, the city streets, and the book itself. Indeed, that tie is intensified by the way in which the walking of the *cartoneros* is connected to poetry in terms of rhythm. To use walking as art reveals "the rich potential relations between thinking and the body; . . . the way walking reshapes the world by mapping it, reading paths into it, encountering it; the way each act reflects and reinvents the culture in which it takes place" (Solnit, 2002, p. 276).

Cartoneros also reveal the importance of recycling the city's ruins: "what New Troy . . . / needs is a good recycling" (p. 53). Aeneas's trolley is illustrated with stories related to recycling—from the story of the invention of paper, to the process of making tin. Paper is the material on which the poet creates and which the *cartonero* collects, a point made by the aforementioned Eloísa Cartonera. Thus it is through paper that poets and *cartoneros* recreate the city, and it is paper that gives them the means to work.[6] Paper becomes a point of commonality, transformed from rhyming dictionary to yogurt carton (p. 43). It becomes a body of words, fluid and nomadic: "their own bodies / are transient, recyclable" (p. 42). Thus the poet sees in the *cartoneros* a practice of recycling that transforms the city. The poem does not offer a solution to poverty nor sees in the *cartoneros* a solution to the problems in the city. Instead it engages with the practice of the *cartoneros* to reinvigorate cultural practice as a means of reconsidering and transforming the way that we think about the city. Thus Samoilovich is careful to avoid romanticizing poverty and the activities of the *cartoneros*, a point he made in an interview: "The backdrop against which the book works for quite a while is my own fear of producing an aestheticization of poverty" (Aguirre, p. 2003). The way he avoids that aestheticization is precisely through his parodic use of myth. The poem places itself in dialogue with the epic tradition from the very first line: "Look, Marforio, look down there, / in the gloomy, acidic air" (p. 11), an opening reminiscent of Homer's *Iliad*, which relates to the fall of Troy.[7] But the comparison between the mythic city of Troy and contemporary Buenos Aires is bathetic and estranging: "The one you see lying there on the tall pile / of corrugated iron is Achilles himself" (p. 11). Myth in the poem, then, makes the *cartoneros* of Buenos Aires precisely un-mythic: "The mythologizing does not make them models but rather removes pathos through sarcasm and, in this way, de-naturalizes them" (Monteleone, 2003). These figures, lacking any semblance of the epic in their struggle to survive, highlight how the mythic idea of the city itself has collapsed. In much the same way as the *cartoneros* played a part in dismantling the idea of Buenos Aires as a "European" metropolis, the poem satirizes Troy precisely to highlight the end of the myth of Buenos Aires.

Samoilovich's poem was published in 2003, in the midst of economic crisis. In many ways, therefore, the promise of a new city that emerges through the poem is very much of its time, a moment when the promise of 2001, the sensation that an entirely new city was on the horizon, lingered in the air. The sensation that a new city, recycled out of the ruined politics and urbanisms of the past, was intensified by numerous urban recycling projects, such as La Fábrica, a working factory "recycled" into a cultural center at weekends, the factory storeroom used as a theatrical stage. Certainly, as Adrián Gorelik has argued, we should be wary of projects that market poverty as part of this recycling of the city (2006, p. 33), but such projects did, at least, engage with the pressing realities of urban crisis and try to connect culture and the urban imaginary to that reality. Moreover, they offered a more productive vision of urban cultural recycling than that evident in other recent projects such as the creation of the Faena Art District in the redeveloped area of Puerto Madero. Vision of developer Alan Faena, the Art District, that includes a hotel, apartment blocks (one designed by Norman Foster), and a cultural center, is designed for the wealthy nomadic elite of Buenos Aires, selling itself as a revised way of experiencing the city at the same time as it turns its back on Buenos Aires and the impoverished shantytowns on its doorstep. Such projects remind us of the importance of incorporating the practice of the *cartoneros* into the urban imaginary because they force all urban dwellers to think through different ways of recycling the city. As Horacio González has suggested: "*Cartoneros* are today the city, and Argentina is *cartonero*, Buenos Aires is *cartonero*," an experience that invites us "to think in common about how to remake the country."[8]

Chapter 7

Shantytowns

Beyond the Pale?

In April 2009, the municipality of San Isidro, a wealthy neighborhood in the northern suburbs of Buenos Aires, constructed a 3-meter-high concrete wall on its boundary with San Fernando, the adjacent working-class neighborhood. Erected after complaints by residents of San Isidro over rising levels of crime, inhabitants of San Fernando soon knocked the wall down with sledgehammers. The incident not only exemplified urban fragmentation in the form of a material barricade designed to impose and reinforce social divisions within the city, but also symbolized the ongoing struggles within urban communities to inscribe and erase territorial fixity in terms of rich and poor, safe and unsafe, self and other.

The urban settlement that encapsulates urban exclusion, class division, and territorial struggle most starkly is the shantytown. A recurring presence in Argentine urban historiography and cultural imaginaries, shantytowns—known locally as *villas miseria*—lie at the heart of the tension between urban commons and enclosure in Buenos Aires. Ever since they were first built in the 1930s, city dwellers, *villeros* (inhabitants of shantytowns), sociologists, anthropologists, journalists, urban designers, and artists have traced—sometimes unwittingly—the expansions and contractions of *villas* as both a threat and a solution to the city. Shantytowns are both in common, mutually constructed by the urban poor and forever seeping back into the urban imaginary of Argentine culture, and also placed outside the city, enclosed spaces pushed beyond its real or imagined boundaries. But in this very act of negation, in which the city is constructed as a space of order and harmony and the shantytown as chaos, the *villa* is included through its very exclusion.

The constant struggle over the relationship between shantytown and the rest of the city has serious political and social implications, and challenges the premise of a city in common. Political security, the political scientist Carl Schmitt claimed when writing in the early 1940s, is dependent on paradigms of friend and enemy and on borders that divide "a pacified order from a quarrelsome disorder, a cosmos from a chaos, a house from a non-house, an enclosure from the wilderness" (2003, p. 52). Following such a philosophy and positioning the *villa* as one side of a series of dichotomies in opposition to the city at large—disorder/order, illegality/law, nature/city, barbarism/civilization, enemy/friend, and so on—constructs a city based around an exclusionary set of commons: The city becomes in common but forgets the act of exclusion on which it is based, and that act of exclusion eventually destroys the city in common.

Ultimately, of course, the flows of people, goods, and labor emanating into and out of the shantytown highlight that the city can never sustain a material reality in which the shantytown is a separate entity. But the city can, and frequently does, sustain an urban imaginary that constantly portrays the *villa* as an exception and, crucially, "what the city is *not*" (Diken, 2005, p. 311). In some texts already analyzed in this book, notably in the work of Juan Diego Incardona, the shantytown is what lies beyond the neighborhood, a space that lies beyond narrative (Vanoli and Vecino, 2010, p. 266). In *Rock barrial*, Incardona uses the very word "deshacer" (undo) to describe how the edges of the neighborhood merge into shantytowns (2010b, p. 70). That is one response to the informal settlement, an expression of a belief that narrating what lies beyond is not only impossible but also politically problematic. Others, however, have tackled the precarious task of narrating the shantytown, and this chapter focuses on three: Cristian Alarcón's book of reportage, *Cuando me muera quiero que me toquen cumbia* (When I die I want them to play *cumbia* for me; 2003); the musical genre originating from the shantytowns known as *cumbia villera*; and César Aira's novel *La villa* (2001). If the first two, which engage with concepts of realism and purport to speak the truth, are narratives of exclusion, albeit in different ways, Aira's fantasy space reminds us that narrating the shantytown need not necessarily push it beyond the urban imaginary and thus undermine the city in common.

From Villa Esperanza to No-Go-Out

The first *villa* in Buenos Aires dates from 1932, a result both of the widespread unemployment brought about by the effects of the Wall Street Crash in 1929 and continuing high levels of immigration from abroad and the interior (Crovara, 2004, p. 35).[1] The lack of housing for the large influx of immigrants resulted in the military government of Agustín Pedro Justo constructing the temporary accommodation known as Villa Esperanza, located near Retiro and the port complex. To combat rising levels of crime perceived to originate from the *villa*, the temporary shacks were destroyed by judicial decree in 1935. A few years later, however, with housing for immigrants still unresolved, further *villas* were built by those unable to afford rental costs, some on the former site of Villa Esperanza (De la Torre, 2000, pp. 273–274). Shantytowns grew steadily throughout the 1940s and 1950s, bolstered by immigrants attracted by the growth of industry under Perón and refugees escaping political upheaval in neighboring countries such as Paraguay (Puex, 2003, p. 39). The 1946–1955 Peronist administration financed both single- and multifamily housing but was unable to provide for the huge numbers of immigrants. Consequently, as during the 1976–1983 dictatorship, walls were built to hide *villas*, notably along the new motorway to Aeropuerto Ezeiza. By 1958 the population of *villas* had reached approximately 200,000 (Salvatori, Savarí, & Raggio, n.d., p. 3).

The huge expansion of the *villa* population in the 1950s and the growing power of the working classes meant that many *porteños* feared the disruption of the modernizing project of the Argentine capital by a perceived "Latin Americanization," the sense that Buenos Aires was being threatened by barbaric, dark hordes, reinforcing the idea that the city should be racially "white." This fear, Adrián Gorelik suggests, was so great that since the mid-20th century the *villa* has often been perceived to be the origin of all the city's problems (2004, p. 121). But shantytowns had become permanent features of the urban landscape, not just materially but also socially, via clubs and organizations, and politically, via links to trade unions, left-wing guerrilla groups, and certain branches of the Catholic Church, not least the Movimiento de Sacerdotes del Tercer Mundo and the so-called "curas villeros" (shantytown priests), figures affiliated with the Equipo Arquidiocesano Pastoral de Villas de Emergencia (Salvatori, Savarí, & Raggio, n.d., p. 4). Confronted with greater organization in the *villas*, governments tried to confront the growing settlements and populations.

In 1955, in tacit acknowledgment that "villas de emergencia" were becoming more permanent than their official title suggested, the government began compiling statistics on *villas*. The Comisión Nacional de la Vivienda, formed in 1956 under the Aramburu government, was the first state organization to set itself the task of eradicating—sometimes literally—what was increasingly perceived as the "problem" of the shantytown (Blaustein, 2001, p. 21). Although the Frondizi administration (1958–1962) recognized the Federación de Villas de Emergencia, it too continued a policy of eradication and, in 1968, the Onganía dictatorship (1966–1970) instigated the most comprehensive demolition policy to date, the "Plan de erradicación de las villas de emergencia de la Capital Federal y del Gran Buenos Aires." These policies, however, were all destined to fail in the face of inadequate provision of alternative housing and the stubborn resistance of *villeros* to give up their homes. The attempted eradication of shantytowns continued during the 1976–1983 dictatorship, another aspect of its institutionalization of disappearance, forming part of Osvaldo Cacciatore's desired *ciudad blanca*. The 1978 World Cup also loomed large in the minds of the city planners, and Bajo Belgrano, located close to Monumental, the showcase stadium for the event, was the first *villa miseria* to be razed to the ground (Blaustein, 2001, pp. 67–68). Where eradication could not be implemented in time, walls were constructed to hide the *villas* from tourists.

The desired *ciudad blanca* was a *white* city not only in an aesthetic sense, but also in religious (whiteness = Christian purity), racial, and moral terms. Slums and shantytowns have always been perceived as spaces lacking morality as well as harboring physical and social disease (Davis, 2006, p. 22). The shantytown's threat to moral health was made explicit in a 1976 government report, which stated that *villas* threatened the general population's health since they were in tension with "elemental material and spiritual necessities of human life" (cited in Blaustein, 2001, p. 57). The 1974 assassination by the Alianza Anticomunista Argentina (AAA) of Padre Mugica, the most famous of the *curas villeros*, and the later destruction of the shantytowns, was part of a perceived moral and physical "bleeding" of the city, not least because, during the 1976–1983 military dictatorship, *villas* were regarded as seedbeds of subversion (Calveiro, 1998, pp. 90–91).

Since the end of the dictatorship, shantytowns in Buenos Aires have grown once again, a response to the growing difficulties in purchasing land and accessing affordable loans (Wagner, 2008, p. 66). During this post-dictatorship period, the *villa* has been articulated "around an internal/external dialectic, with the creation of a more and more rigid frontier" (Puex, 2003, p. 41). Nathalie Puex argues that post-dictatorship the *villa* has undergone two periods of widespread stigmatization: First, during the hyperinflation of the late 1980s, which heightened poverty and increased unemployment, in turn resulting in supermarket sackings, increased violence, and a break-down of social relations; and second, during the 1990s, which brought further unemployment, drug trafficking, drug use, and crime. In the mid-1990s the *villa* became synonymous with urban violence, a perception fueled by an ever-more sensationalist mass media, trapping the shantytown within an ever-increasing spiral of violence (Puex, 2003, pp. 42–46). No longer a springboard for upward mobility as it had been in the 1950s, the shantytown has become a permanent place of residence, transformed into an inescapable "no-go-out area" (Diken, 2005, p. 308). Symbolized in material terms by the growing number of brick-built dwellings in shantytowns, *villas* are no longer "de emergencia," a temporary solution to the failures of the wider urban system, but are a permanent exception.

Inside/Outside

Villas have come a long way since the days when they were "beyond the pale," located on the urban periphery or behind high walls built to keep them from view. Or perhaps they have turned full circle. Like the *porteños* of the 1930s, who took excursions to satisfy their curiosity about the first *villas* and their inhabitants (De la Torre, 2000, p. 273), the *villa* has once again become a site for fascination, as indicated by the emergence of shantytown tourism (Peralta, 2005). Such fascination with the Latin American other, however, not only affects the foreign tourist but also the urban dweller, who experiences difference as an integral part of the urban landscape. For many *porteños* the perceived "Latin American" nature of *villas*, whether in terms of race or socioeconomics, constructs them as "other" to Buenos Aires. For nonresidents, therefore, Villa 31, located in the neighborhood of Retiro between the railway tracks and the motorway, is forever looked at through glass. From behind car, train, and long-distance coach windows, travelers stare at the constructions and passageways running away from them and imagine the poverty within. Even if rubbish pickers, in-house maids, or the news of an armed robbery remind those living in other areas of the city of the *villa*'s presence, the shantytown is nearly always perceived as lying beyond the city's limits. This boundary between shantytown and city is reinforced by the nicknames given to certain *villas*, such as Ciudad Oculta (Hidden City), implying invisibility. Despite its physical proximity to the rest of the city, then, the *villa* is surprisingly distant, always lying *beyond*—beyond the railway tracks, beyond the avenue, beyond the river, even beyond the bus route.

The perception that the *villa* lies beyond is emphasized by its alternative spatial configuration: Unlike the grid of city blocks, the regular pattern of squares that create an apparent order and regularity to Buenos Aires, the passageways of the *villa* crisscross and weave irregularly. As a perceived threat to the desired city of social and spatial order, the *villa* bears many similarities to its forebear, the *conventillo*, housing for the poor that emerged toward the end of the 19th century and which "disrupted" both the traditional houses of the wealthy and the downtown area. Similarly, the shantytown's lack of "order" threatens the perceived inclusiveness of the traditional city grid (Silvestri & Gorelik, 2000, p. 466). The point is made in the policy document, "Plan de urbanización en villas y barrios carenciados" (Development Plan in Shantytowns and Deprived Neighborhoods), published by the Gobierno de la Ciudad de Buenos Aires in 2003, which argued that the physical characteristics of the *villa* are inherently socially anomic:

> These precarious settlements are characterized by a spontaneous, unplanned occupation of space, resulting in an irregular and intricate outline. This outline is linked in a different way to the urban weave that surrounds it, producing, in the majority of cases, a discontinuity between the urban weave and the internal outline of the *villas*. This provokes a fracture that makes integration difficult. (Ciudad de Buenos Aires, 2003)

Similarly, an internal document of the Comisión Municipal de la Vivienda del Gobierno Autónomo de la Ciudad de Buenos Aires defined *villas* as "illegal family settlements on fiscal lands and in some cases of third parties, with construction standards that do not comply with basic municipal norms of habitability and hygiene that are compatible with urban life" (cited in Crovara, 2004, p. 37). Both documents imply that the *villa* is not an urban space but rather an outside space that has somehow found its unwarranted way into the city.[2]

But far from being "outside," *villas* emerge precisely in the fissures in the geological strata of the city, "clustered in the liminal zones or 'in-between' spaces" (Podalsky, 2004, p. 104). The methods and materials of construction for these in-between (and not outside) spaces also originate from the cyclical flows of the city as a whole. Inhabitants of the *villa*, many of whom are *cartoneros*, often recycle what is left over from the rest of the city, creating a material connection. And the shantytown is connected with other flows: Every day a huge number of people commute to work from the *villa* and return home carrying objects and materials that are assimilated into their living spaces; domestic servants, bus drivers, and other low-income earners commute from the *villas*, bolstering the service sector; money circulates into and out of the *villa*; music, police, information, and television images of the *villa* and *villeros* all pass in and out of the *villa*. The fluidity of workers and the commodity form is suggestive of "a world in which . . . the dialectic between inside and outside has come to an end" (Diken, 2005, p. 315).

The Shantytown's Secret Heart

Cuando me muera quiero que me toquen cumbia recounts the attempts of investigative journalist Cristian Alarcón to penetrate the mysteries of the shantytown, a move that unwittingly only reinforces the very dichotomy of inside and outside that it sets out to dismantle. The book takes its festive title from a line belonging to the favorite song of the work's protagonist, Víctor "El Frente" Vital. Aged 17, El Frente was shot by the police in a *villa* in the neighborhood of San Fernando after he and two friends had been pursued there following a robbery. Alarcón initially visits the *villa* in an attempt to trace the story of El Frente, whom he calls "a particular type of saint" and "a new pagan idol" (p. 15). The death of Víctor Vital was the canonization of El Frente as a popular saint, a Robin Hood figure who shared his spoils with fellow *villeros*, made an exhibition at parties out of squandering stolen money, and whose tomb has become a shrine to the figure it is believed can protect local residents from bullets. The central miracle in the pagan hagiography of El Frente is the hijacking of the truck belonging to the dairy firm La Serenísima and the subsequent sharing out of the goods. Alarcón is complicit in the mythification of El Frente when he employs the same pathetic fallacy as the *villeros* when referring to the day El Frente died: "Like an all-powerful sign . . . the sky suddenly turned black, black clouds closing until it seemed as if night were suddenly falling over the shantytown. And it began to rain" (p. 33).

El Frente, then, was (and is) a figure of resistance in as much as he retained the old codes and criminal ethics, mediating between the strong and the weak of the *villa* to preserve order and gaining respect for constantly opposing the police. The inhabitants of the *villa* mark a clear before-and-after to the death of El Frente, Alarcón himself adding that 2 years after his visit to the *villa* the children who had grown up without the order promoted by El Frente were robbing old women and children; without El Frente, the *villa* is described as being overrun by lack of respect, betrayal, robbery of neighbors, and even madness. The threat

El Frente posed the police, then, was not so much a threat to order per se as the threat of an alternative order, adhered to with the utmost respect by the self-same figures who disregard the police and state law.

It is only by citing the name of El Frente that Alarcón gains access to the farthest reaches of the *villa*: "Invoking his name was almost the only passport to access the narrow roads, the small internal territories, the veiled secrets and truths" (p. 16). Alarcón frequently refers to the "secrets" of the *villa*, its unknowability and, simultaneously, his ability to integrate himself with the *villa* and thus unravel its "truth" (p. 176). Mirroring his territorial foray into the *villa*, Alarcón posits his own narrative as revealing to the reader those truths normally hidden to foreigners. Simultaneously, he discredits the written record of the official investigation by referring to the stolen money taken by the police but which never appears in the legal records (p. 31). By problematizing official discourse in opposition to the truth of testimony, Alarcón inserts *Cuando me muera quiero que me toquen cumbia* into the tradition of the nonfiction novel in Argentine literature, one that began with Rodolfo Walsh's work *Operación masacre* (2003), originally published in 1957 and a classic example of protest literature. In the prologue, Alarcón implies that his book should not be compared to the work of Walsh: "Perhaps it would have been better to reveal the identity of a murderer, the mechanics of a shooting, a message from the mafia, the network of power of a corrupt policeman, a *crime passionelle* committed with a well-sharpened blade" (p. 16). The phrase "mechanics of a shooting" harks back to Walsh's 1969 work *¿Quién mató a Rosendo?*, a meticulous investigation of the shooting of trade unionist Rosendo García. Despite Alarcón's implied suggestion that his work is distant from writings such as those of Walsh, he owes much to the latter's use of fictional techniques to relate factual events. That debt is evident, for example, in the way Alarcón builds up tension at the start of *Cuando me muera quiero que me toquen cumbia* in the style of a thriller:

> Sergeant Héctor Eusebio Sosa, alias "El Paraguayo," and corporals Gabriel Arroyo and Juan Gómez were travelling in patrol car 12179. Corporal Ricardo Rodríguez and Jorgelina Massoni, known, because of her methods, as "La Rambito" were in car 12129. The police sirens could be heard getting ever closer. (p. 30)

Similarly, his parody of official logic—"That means that to have killed el Frente, as he declared in court, Sosa would have had to have been at least three meters thirty centimeters high" (p. 32)—is very similar in terms of style, tone, and bathos to the following line from Walsh's *¿Quién mató a Rosendo?*: "For such acrobatic reasoning, you need to make Rosendo into a Nijinsky, who stands up, turns his back on the other group (the only way the bullet could enter his back perpendicularly), 'jump turns,' only then 'facing' his attackers and while the shot rings out that wounds him while his back is turned, still walks several steps and falls next to the tabletop" (2004, p. 107).

Alarcón himself retains a liminal position with regard to the *villa*. Initially he describes entering the shantytown as if it were some kind of jungle: "I penetrated the *villa*" (p. 34). And from the beginning he describes the *villa* as a seemingly impregnable territory, not only physically enclosed but also linguistically and socially foreign in terms of everyday codes and practices (p. 45). As the book progresses, his relationship with the *villeros* fluctuates: On one occasion, for example, he finds himself penniless when he is asked to help out at the hospital by donating some money (p. 112); on another, when Tincho plays at using him as a human shield, he admits to feeling like "a potential victim, a civilian carrying a few pesos" (p. 133). Ultimately, however, the moment of his full "integration" into the *villa* comes when he is caught in the crossfire of a shootout. Hearing a voice behind him, Alarcón turns to discover a 6-year-old boy who tells him that he is shaking. With reassuring confidence, Alarcón tells the boy not to worry, that it will all soon be over. In this moment of crisis, then, Alarcón expresses genuine compassion, constructing himself as a surrogate father to the petrified boy as part of his attempt to find a place of familiarity in the *villa*.

The outsider's desire to enter the *villa* is also evident in an earlier novel about shantytowns in Buenos Aires, Bernardo Verbitsky's 1957 novel, *Villa Miseria también es América* (Shanty Town is also America), in which urban dwellers fear that the shantytown will spill over into the city at large and disrupt its imagined order. Verbitsky, however, sees the *villa* as a site of positive values, particularly collective, socialist work (2003, p. 49). The key project, the sinking of a new well, becomes a metaphor for a return to an original, pure state (Verbitsky, 2003, p. 182). Verbitsky envisions in the shantytown a post-conquest Latin American utopian collectivity, a desire evident in the reference to Guaraní as a primal, almost mythic path to the linguistic soul of Latin America (Verbitsky, 2003, pp. 208–209).

Though Verbitsky's novel goes some way to writing the *villa* back into Buenos Aires, however, it ultimately reinforces the *villa*'s exclusion

from the city because it retains the ideal modern city as its civic reference. Far from simply promoting the *villa* as the source of a new set of
values, Verbitsky rather seeks to amalgamate the laws of the metropolis
with the community of the *villa*. Thus, Verbitsky employs the character
named "el Espantapájaros" (the Scarecrow), a former student left in the
villa after being tortured for assisting workers on a strike, as a choric
figure. Espantapájaros sees his torture as a point of affiliation with the *villeros*: "[T]he humiliation caused by the *picana* on his genitals was the same
that these people suffered daily" (Verbitsky, 2003, p. 97). Despite calling
the *villeros* brothers, however, Espantapájaros is never entirely integrated
precisely because he speaks of standing up *for* them: "And I will grow and
rise up, I will raise myself to be the scarecrow of the ruins, and I will
extend my arms, not to bless them, but to call upon them to follow me"
(Verbitsky, 2003, p. 64). Supplicating his disciples to follow him, he is the
figure of the consciousness-raising student-militant-intellectual, wishing
to fulfill an act of "proletarianization" by representing those around him
for the sake of the "people in all its purity" that he perceives exists in the
shantytown (Gorelik, 2003, pp. 38–39). So even if he reassures the reader
that "something of me will remain in this neighborhood" (Verbitsky, 2003,
p. 231), once Espantapájaros has achieved the necessary *self*-understand-
ing, he departs, leaving the *villa* behind.

Verbitsky's novel emerges from the legacy of the social realist literature that emerged in Latin America during the first half of the 20th
century. Drawing on the revaluation of realism opened up by debates
in the magazine *Contorno* (1953–1959) (Prieto, 2006, p. 325), it is no
coincidence that *Villa Miseria también es América* was published in the
same year as Rodolfo Walsh's *Operación masacre*, a work that fused literature and politics in unprecedented fashion. Even if Verbitsky did not
share Walsh's style, they were friends and both militant journalists (Prieto,
2006, p. 343), and Verbitsky's descriptions of the everyday blurs fiction
and journalism in similar fashion to Walsh (Perilli, 2004, p. 557). In her
discussion of "the seduction of margins," Jean Franco suggests that the
arrival of *testimonio*, to which writers like Verbitsky and Walsh were pre-
cursors, "provided sociologists, anthropologists, and literary critics with
an open window through which they could scrutinize guerrilla fighters,
slum dwellers, the indigenous, and blacks, some of whom were looked
to for love, solidarity, tactful understanding, and justification" (2002, p.
212). The difficulty faced by such literature, Franco argues, is that it runs
the risk of stripping the object of its own space.

Cuando me muera quiero que me toquen cumbia, even if it is not
a *testimonio* in the strictest sense of the word, does draw on *testimonio*'s

claim to truth and realism. The book expresses a sense of escape into the margins and in so doing brackets that space's imaginary *within* the *villa*, precisely reaffirming and restoring the "real" order of the metropolis. Thus, Alarcón's realism here emphasizes not the common of the *villa* but precisely the "irreality," the otherness, of the *villa*. Rather than using margins as "the subtle points of dissonance that disturb the world as it is presented to us" (Franco, 2002, p. 216), Alarcón precisely constructs the *villa* as a locale to escape to and return from, emphasizing his otherness from the *villa* even as he stresses his integration: "I saw myself submerged in another language and time, in another way of surviving and living until death itself" (p. 16). He is submerged in the *villa* but only in so far as the *villa* is a space with an "other" language, time, and forms of survival. Just as when Alarcón remarks near the end of the book that the story of El Frente "had always seemed a mythical scene worth ratifying" (p. 188), a statement that emphasizes his authoritative role as truth teller, by referring to his experience as "I saw myself," he constructs his time in the *villa* as a moment when he was other from himself. Like Espantapájaros, once he believes he has revealed the "secret" of the *villa*, he feels able to return to the city and so also to his "true" self.

Metrópolis in the Metropolis

Like Verbitsky, despite his attempt to unpack the mystery of the shantytown and draw it back into the city via narrative, Alarcón ultimately reinforces the detached position of the shantytown in the urban landscape, highlighting the difficulties of imagining a city in common. But as *cumbia villera*, the music of the shantytown, makes clear, it is just as often the inhabitants of the shantytown who do not want to be included in the rest of the city but who rather ratify and fortify the spatial, conceptual, and cultural boundaries between the two. In fact, both Alarcón and the musicians of *cumbia* employ similar forms of social realism to highlight the singular, almost unreal, qualities of the *villa*. A musical form that has its origins in the folklore music of Peru, Bolivia, and the northern provinces of Argentina; in salsa, merengue, and Colombian *cumbia*; in reggae, rap, and Argentine rock (Svampa, 2005, p. 179), the lyrics of *cumbia* are filtered through a concern with the social transformations brought about by the economic policies of the 1990s and the new millennium.

The recurring references to women in what is an overtly masculine genre, for example, can be tied to the transformation of the sexual politics of the *villa* brought about by increasing male unemployment stemming from privatization and a dying industrial economy. Women seeking work, predominantly in tertiary employment, unsettled the patriarchal male's belief in his own position as the breadwinning head of the family, one reason for the concern expressed over the new "liberty" of women. Such is the case in the song "No te hagas la nena de mamá" by Pibes Chorros, the lyrics of which instruct a woman not to play at being innocent since her mouth smells like semen. Transformations in the domestic sphere also meant that young people in the *villa* needed to construct new forms of belonging, one of the reasons why *cumbia* and the *villa* itself have been scrutinized as symptomatic of a problematic youth culture. The lyrics often romanticize lawlessness and laziness, concurrently presenting work as "a source of exploitation and, above all, as an activity belonging properly to idiots" (Martín, 2004, p. 8). The valorization of violence as an expression of courage and physical capability and of crime as an alternative to work is placed alongside a vehement hatred of the police, built on a long history of police repression of youth and of the widely acknowledged trigger-happy police force. "Hijo de yuta"[3] by Yerba Brava, for example, attacks the betrayal of the *villero* who follows in his father's footsteps to become a policeman. "Gatillo fácil" by Flor de Piedra is equally damning of the impunity enjoyed by "trigger-happy" cops. *Cumbia villera*, then, does not so much gaze nostalgically toward a lost past of strong masculinity, work, and lack of crime as reaffirm masculinity in a world without work, through sex, crime, and antiestablishment sentiment.

That aesthetic ideal has developed alongside a new set of values and codes as a strategy of defense against the rest of the city. The *cumbia* club, for example, has become a sphere of social belonging, collective dancing (rather than in couples), jumping up and down and the clapping of hands all generating an experience of togetherness. That togetherness, however, is often constructed around an "anti-anti-cumbia": "el que no hace palmas es un cheto" (the person not clapping is a snob) or "el que no baila es un anti-cumbiero" (the person not dancing is anti-*cumbia*) (Míguez, 2004, p. 80).[4] The opposition of snob-*villero* is made clear in "El vago fumanchú" by Damas Gratis, the lyrics of which sing about getting high and killing snobs. *Cumbia villera* shares many traits with rap and hip-hop. At the beginning of concerts given by Damas Gratis, the lead singer Pablo Lezcano often begins by telling the public that he wants to see "las palmas de todos los negros arriba y arriba" (the hands of all Blacks up in the air), a transformation of Blackness into resistance that mirrors the use of the nigga in hip-hop as a mode of opposition (Baldwin, 2004,

p. 166). Similarly, just as rap has placed the ghetto back into the urban imaginary, *cumbia* has reminded urban dwellers that the *villa* is very much part of the urban landscape. As Murray Forman has suggested, the social relations of the 'hood present in hip-hop "refutes the damning images of an oppressed and joyless underclass that are so prevalent in the media and contemporary social analyses" and communicate "the importance of places and the people that build community within them" (2004, p. 208). Upheavals in domestic spaces discussed above, therefore, are countered by an intensification of the role of the street as a site of social belonging. In the *villa* the street corner has become the mythic place of encounter and neighbors both the guardians and charges of criminals, in a territory where friend and neighbor are sacred relationships (Míguez, 2004, pp. 53–58).

Such urban transformations are by no means limited to Buenos Aires. Similar tropes of popular music genres and alterations of the city can be found throughout Latin America. Arlene Tickner has highlighted how hip-hop in Colombia, Cuba, and Mexico transforms the notion of "being" in the city, engaging with the everyday life of marginality in "an effort to 'be' in the city, to build 'niches' within the system, to create local forms of pleasure, and to (re)create everyday space" (2008, p. 127). Brazilian cities in particular are well known as places where music plays a hugely significant role in expressions of urban poverty and marginality. The *baile funk* clubs in Rio de Janeiro, for example, have the potential to function as cross-class, cross-racial spaces (Sneed, 2008, p. 76). Though each of these musical forms and spaces have their own particularities, they all engage with everyday life by providing linguistic and physical engagements with habits and daily experience and, furthermore, they all transform urban space both through their lyrics and by putting bodies into spaces.

Such transformations of urban space used to be found in clubs such as the now defunct New Metrópolis. Located in the busy hub of Pacífico, Metrópolis was orientated toward "música tropical," and *cumbia villera* in particular. By giving a space to *cumbia villera*, such clubs indicated how the cultural cartography of Buenos Aires incorporated the strains of the shantytowns into the city at large. Indeed, even though many inhabitants of Buenos Aires consider *cumbia* to be symbolic of the disruptive, chaotic tendencies of the *villa*, President Néstor Kirchner recognized the political need to affirm his affection for *cumbia* in August 2004 after his cabinet head, Alberto Fernández, suggested that the music inspired crime. Moreover, even though former journalist Andrew Graham-Yooll has argued that *cumbia* "is all part of the sound and life of the huge slums surrounding and now creeping into Buenos Aires" (2005, p. 175), *cumbia* nonetheless has a large following in the Argentine upper and middle classes. Just as working-class tango became popular throughout Argentine society, *cumbia* has become a major part of the Argentine music business—not least due, ironically, to the very rich kids ridiculed in venues such as Metrópolis.[5] By playing on the music's antiestablishment image, record companies made *cumbia* one of the most popular music forms in Argentina, from *villas* to the *barrios cerrados* of the wealthy. The group Yerba Brava, for example, sold 60,000 copies of the 2000 album *Corriendo la coneja* in 4 months (Barría, 2005).

Evaluating the inclusivity or exclusivity of *cumbia*, therefore, is a difficult task. Its deterritorializing force as a leading cultural form that originates from the shantytowns is undeniable, indicative of its ability to cross the territorial frontier of the *villa*. But, as Svampa observes, listening to *cumbia* as a member of the middle class runs the risk of reinforcing the stigmatization of the *villa* rather than creating affiliation with its inhabitants, since *cumbia* both legitimizes exclusion and marginality, and simultaneously constructs itself around a negative "us" (2005, pp. 179–180).[6] In terms of the urban imaginary, *cumbia* often enhances the inside/outside dichotomy between the city and *villa*. Moreover, by resorting to identities that reinforce territorial enclosure, dwellers from the shantytown who consume *cumbia* are expressing their discontent with a city that has always treated them as "others" and pushed them beyond its conceptual boundaries. Introducing a cultural *impasse* that is yet to be resolved, such dwellers highlight the fissures in the imagining of a city in common.

The Rotating *Villa*?

Both *cumbia villera* and *Cuando me muera quiero que me toquen cumbia* engage with the spatial territory of the *villa*. From El Frente's attempt to lose his pursuers in the interweaving, confusing passageways of the *villa*, to Alarcón's own incursion into what he describes as an initially hostile territory, the *villa* is a place in which frontiers and barriers, both physical and social, fluctuate and change according to use and origin. The deeper Alarcón penetrates into the physical space of the *villa*, he suggests, the closer he gets to reaching its core, its "truth," the same truth that *cumbia* musicians claim to reveal but which they believe outsiders will never understand. In contrast to these secret-bearing *villas* that are to be opened up and revealed in a manner that runs the risk of reinforcing spatial boundaries, a more productive reading of the space of the shantytown can be found in César Aira's 2001 novel *La villa*. Aira's novel relates the story of Maxi, a teenager who lives near a *villa* in Flores and who helps the *cartoneros* working around his house. Assisting them by pulling their carts, sometimes with *cartoneros* aboard, Maxi never sees his actions as an act of charity or solidarity: "[H]e did it and that was that" (p. 9). Even if Maxi sees walking as perfect exercise, emphasizing that the activity is not the same for him as the *cartoneros*, they still act in common when pulling the carts. Indeed, Maxi's body becomes a point of contact for different *cartonero* families. It is the act of putting his body to work with those of the *cartoneros* that creates a common tie. When Maxi sees the *villa* where the *cartoneros* live for the first time he is amazed by its magic but does not forget the poverty that resides there (p. 20). Without writing the poverty of the *villa* and yet still using the imaginative power of its space, Aira allows for a double move: the ability to feel wonder at the space of the *villa*—of imagining it—without denying the material reality of poverty.

The crucial quality of Aira's *villa* is that, in stark contrast to the *villa* of Alarcón, it has no center. Though all the streets and passageways of the *villa* go inward, unlike the grid pattern of the rest of the city, "not one arrived at the center, and . . . not one had an exit" (p. 35). It is not so much that the center of the *villa* is hidden, therefore, but rather that the center simply does not exist: "[W]hether illusion, whether confusion, he seemed to see, on the way to the inaccessible center, towers, domes, phantasmagorical castles, walls, pyramids, groves" (p. 36). The *villa*'s flickering lights make it seem fluid and shape-shifting (p. 128), and the lights come to play a crucial role in the novel and in the understanding of the space of the *villa* itself. As numbering the streets of the *villa* would have little use in a centerless, circular space with no beginning or end, the entrance to each street is marked by arrangements of lights that create a cipher. The advantage of this language of lights, particularly for the drug dealers, is that they can be shifted every night, the streets changing as the lights mutate. The system highlights how the shantytown overturns any externally imposed system of navigation, an affront, as it were, to the military's former practice of marking out the informal dwellings to be demolished by painting a number on the structure (Wagner, 2008, p. 27). Thus, when Inspector Cabezas, seeking the concealed Maxi and with his mind hazy from drugs, opens the door to the shack where he thinks the boy is hiding, all he finds is nothing: "It was a façade, behind which a desolate passage full of rain opened up, with other huts, near and far, lit up by the lightning. It was similar and different at the same time: outside, but also inside" (p. 167). Cabezas fails to realize that Maxi's protectors had changed the lights of the streets, the only means that Cabezas had of finding the right house.

The *villa* here, therefore, reveals space's fluid ability to turn in on itself, leading to the question presented toward the end of the novel: "Could the *Villa* 'rotate' then? Was it possible" (p. 168). The rotating *villa* with which the novel concludes is typical of Aira's use of fantasy. Like the *villa* itself, Aira's fiction, which transgresses strict genre boundaries, performs its own implosion of inside and outside, in this case within the field of literature (Porrúa, 2005, p. 25). Several commentators have pointed out how *La villa* fits within Aira's typical vision of literary production. Nancy Fernández suggests that the novel veers away from social critique to create "a fiction that is sufficient in and of itself" (2004, p. 99), a move exaggerated by the concluding acceleration in time, space, and action such that "the casual logic of the predictable" is dissolved (2004, pp. 101–102). In a similar vein, Cristina Guiñazú argues that Aira's "villa-text" presents "a challenge to the literary tradition that has addressed the same issue via realist-naturalist perspectives and approaches with the intention of creating corrective changes in the depicted situations" (2011, p. 2). And Annelies Oeyen notes that in *La villa* "there is a dissolution of the principals that guarantee the order and cohesion of the text" (2012, p. 88).

But the manner in which the *villa* is written in this novel does not only serve to reinforce the traditional reading of Aira as a writer who creates narrative machines that produce nothing except a literature that circulates (Montaldo, 2010, pp. 99–100). It also demonstrates how the disordered nature of the text can say something about the relationship between the city and shantytown. That is, the shantytown also disrupts the cohesion of the city, not as a space that sits outside the urban but rather as a space that is integral to it. In that sense, it is vital to remember that Aira "inverts common negative images" of the *villa* (Oeyen, 2012, p. 76). His novels demonstrate precisely what is dangerous about what is held in common by disturbing common imaginaries and reminding us of the constant need to revamp the shared way that we view the city. Aira deconstructs realism, but he also uses the encounter between Maxi and the dwellers of the shantytown, not to produce any false semblance of solidarity but simply—and powerfully—to produce a commons formed around mutual imaginative refashionings of territory itself.

Aira thus creates an alternative to those who formulate the *villa* as an outside space to the city, whether as a foreign, crime-ridden space threatening the ordered unity of the city, or, on the other hand, as a locale of resistance to the oppression and exclusions of the metropolis. In the latter vein, for example, Mike Davis has argued that slums will provide the future for the "myriad acts of resistance" that will challenge structural urban inequalities (2006, p. 202). Davis's take is an apocalyptic vision of the urban future: "Night after night, hornetlike helicopter gunships stalk enigmatic enemies in the narrow streets of the slum districts, pouring hellfire into shanties or fleeing cars. Every morning the slums reply with suicide bombers and eloquent explosions. If the empire can deploy Orwellian technologies of repression, its outcasts have the gods of chaos on their side" (2006, p. 206). Davis, of course, might be right to envision a dark future for the global city, though events in the past decade in Spain, Greece, and North Africa have hinted at other, equally potent forms of urban resistance. But it might also be possible to imagine the force of a shantytown as being something other than chaos, since the latter only fuels those who see the shantytown as a threat to the city, a space that is truly beyond the pale.[7] Certainly, the "irregularity" of the *villa* uses perceived unmappability to challenge the impositions of the rest of the city. But even in that challenge the *villa* remains vital to any attempt to imagine the urban future of Buenos Aires. At the very least, shantytowns are a reminder that we need to draw on an imaginary of commoning and recognize our mutual involvement in the common production of the city as a step toward overcoming urban disenfranchisement.

Epilogue

The days of 19 and 20 December 2001 marked a radical time in Argentine history. Though all commentators agree on the transformative *potential* of the manner in which the multitude took over the city and demanded change, whereas some have seen those days as a moment that transformed the nature of political expression (Colectivo Situaciones, 2002a; Dinerstein, 2014), others have seen them as a failed project cut short by the national-populist administrations of Néstor Kirchner and, subsequently, Cristina Fernández de Kirchner (Camacho, 2009; Svampa, 2014). Certainly, the 2003 elections that brought Néstor Kirchner to power do suggest that the constituent force of the multitude was tamed in a turn back to the people, and both Néstor Kirchner and Cristina Fernández have been highly successful in managing the raw power constituted to them in the wake of 2001. But the multitude did not disappear from Buenos Aires after 2001, its threat still evident in the anti-riot fences that were originally set up as temporary defenses but which became permanent fortifications around government buildings (Chronopoulos, 2011). Indeed, it was that being in common that emerged to welcome Néstor into the Plaza de Mayo after his victory in the 2003 election. Journalists covering the event noted that the crowd was comprised of a vast mix of political parties, political affiliations, and militant groups, and the newspaper *La Nación* highlighted the significance of the President elect moving through the crowd: "Kirchner broke protocol and drove his bodyguards crazy, crossing Calle Balcarce and approaching the hoardings that separated him from the public that was trying to greet him. By accident, a photographer banged Kirchner on the forehead, opening up a wound that he was forced to dress; from then on he accepted the recommendations of protocol" (cited in Sarlo, 2011, p. 195). That cut on the face was the mark of a constituent force that left on the president a reminder of its power.

Of course, the multitude is not inherently progressive. It too can act in ways that are themselves exclusionary, violent, and alienating. Precisely the same can be said, as this book has shown, about the commons. The history of Buenos Aires from the start of the military dictatorship in 1976 until the start of the new millennium reveals a range of approaches to commoning and the commons, many of which were mobilized as a means of shaping exclusive communities that turn their back on potential sites of shared belonging, a reminder that the commons should always be approached with caution. This book has also shown, however, that commons and commoning can confront enclosure and the loss of what is shared. It is of vital importance, particularly within overwhelming discourses and practices of fracture, fear, and immunization, to remind ourselves of the ongoing political potential of encounter and the importance of imagining alternative urban futures.

Looking at the commons of culture and the urban imaginary has highlighted the different material and conceptual ways in which the city has been inscribed between fragmentation and encounter. Culture and cultural imaginaries continue to be key sites for challenging neoliberal anomie. To take some examples from cinema alone, conflicts in the urban imaginary continue to be played out in the Argentine cultural sphere. Filmic approaches to the city in recent years have continued to express concern with the urban future. Pablo Trapero, for example, has produced two stark images of urban conflict. In *Carancho* (The Vulture; 2010), Buenos Aires is portrayed as a brutal dog-eat-dog world, in which rogue lawyers pray like vultures on citizens who suffer road accidents. The accident is a powerful metaphor for a wider collapse in urban order, and the state is a largely absent force in this shadowy, nighttime world in which citizens struggle to survive. The critique of the state is even more evident in his subsequent film, *Elefante blanco* (White Elephant; 2012). Set in Ciudad Oculta, a shantytown located in Capital Federal, the film focuses on the conflicts between the state, the priests working in the shantytown, and the urban poor. The pitched battle that takes place between police and shantytown dwellers occurs in front of the "Elefante blanco," the huge carcass of a semi-abandoned building that was designed to be the country's leading hospital. Originally planned in the 1920s, the structure is used in the film as a symbol of the systemic failure of the Argentine state to protect its citizens and, in particular, the urban poor. The abandonment of public urban structures is echoed in *La multitud* (The Multitude; dir. Martín M. Oesterheld, 2013), a documentary film that contrasts the large-scale construction of private tower blocks in Puerto Madero with the informal construction practices found next door in the shantytown Rodrigo Bueno. Focusing on the ruined projects of La Ciudad Deportiva, the sports complex designed for the football club Boca Juniors that sits alongside the shantytown, and of Parque de la Ciudad, an abandoned amusement park in Villa Lugano that is itself located next to housing blocks in poor state of repair, the film is a study, both aesthetic and social, of urban decay and decline. The panoramic and panning shots of abandoned spaces highlight how the city is failing the multitudes that inhabit it.

Other films take a more positive approach to urban communities. *Estrellas* (Stars; 2007) documents Julio Arrieta's successes as a talent agent for inhabitants of the shantytown in which he lives. Aside from his efforts to create a science-fiction film set in the shantytown, perhaps the most striking sequence occurs in the context of Arrieta's meeting with Alan Parker, who visited the shantytown in search of a set location for his film about Evita. Faced with the director's complaints about the cables that dominate the landscape, Arrieta points out that he can construct a shantytown street in an hour, just the way Parker wants. The local producer subsequently swindles Arrieta out of the deal, but to prove the point the directors of *Estrellas* include a scene in which a group of men build an entire shack in 2 minutes, 30 seconds (a stop watch is located at the bottom of the frame). The construction process is highly coordinated, and to prove the stability of the construction, various objects are thrown on the roof. Following these "tests," a family enters carrying household furniture, and they then occupy the shack and pose for a filmic portrait. It is a great moment of urban togetherness built around the trope of mutual construction practices. A similarly affirmative, though markedly different, take on urban exclusion can be found in *Medianeras* (2011), a love story about two neighbors overcoming their own self-imposed withdrawal from the city. Even if Buenos Aires is portrayed as chaotic, confusing, and overwhelming, it nonetheless provides the means for coming together. The seemingly liminal dead spaces between the apartment blocks, which appear to divide them, become modes of expression when the two characters simultaneously knock a hole in their respective sidewalls, disrupting the advertisements to discover each other. And yet, even here, the commons is less inclusive than it first appears: The urban encounter promoted here is less about meeting an other than about meeting a mirror image of white, middle-class angst.

In recent years, both Néstor Kirchner and Cristina Fernández have shown themselves to be astutely aware of the potential of culture and its role in shaping political imaginaries, evidenced, for example, by investments in state television and higher education. At the same time, the principal political opponent of the Kirchner administrations, Mauricio Macri, continued with projects that refurbished the image of the city, including the restoration of the Teatro Colón, the introduction of bicycle lanes, and the upkeep of pavements, all under the slogan of "haciendo Buenos Aires" (making Buenos Aires). But his comments at the time of the expulsion of those who tried to settle in Parque Indoamericana in 2008 that immigration was out of control and that "it would seem that the city of Buenos Aires has to look after bordering countries and that's impossible," demonstrate that these recyclings go hand in hand with an exclusionary vision of the city. It is not so much, therefore, that Macri used an "illusory Buenos Aires" as a "battering ram" against "the real city," as the group of left-wing intellectuals Carta Abierta put it (Carta Abierta, 2011), but that the mayor built his city on the basis of a set of very real and potent imaginaries—imaginaries that construct an urban future based on exclusion.

Recognizing the transformative and repressive potential of urban imaginaries, therefore, is vital for the ongoing process of seeking out inclusive urban futures. Buenos Aires remains a city of social, political, and cultural fragmentation and division, caught between Capital Federal and Gran Buenos Aires, between opposing political ideologies, and between perceptions of the Paris of South America and its growing "Latinamericanization." But in the interstices of these conflicting fragments Buenos Aires, like all cities, still emerges in common.

Notes

Introduction

1. Unless otherwise stated, all translations from the Spanish are mine.

Chapter 1

1. The suffix "-azo" in Spanish is used to aggrandize the original noun. In the cases referred to in this book—"Argentinazo," "Cordobazo," "siluetazo," "cacerolazo"—it is used to mark an event or manifestation of significant historical import. In the case of the two former examples there is also a fusion of space and time: the great events of Argentina or Córdoba.

2. *Piqueteros* are groups—principally of the organized unemployed—who use roadblocks as a means of social protest. An *asamblea barrial* is a form of informal political governance based on neighborhood organizations. A *cacerolazo* is a means of protest in which protagonists bang empty pots and pans as a symbol of discontent. Originating with the working and middle classes, in 2008 wealthy residents of Buenos Aires also used the *cacerolazo* to protest Cristina Fernández de Kirchner's proposal to increase taxes on agricultural production.

3. For other studies of urban fragmentation in cities around the world see, for example, Davis (1990, 1999), Marcuse and Van Kempen et al. (2000), Soja (2000), Low (2004), Coy (2006), and Jenks, Kozak and Takkanon (2008).

4. In a rather different lament for a lost Buenos Aires, Juan José Sebreli, in an extended essay written at the start of the new millennium for the second edition of his 1964 publication *Buenos Aires, Vida cotidiana y alienación*, wrote nostalgically about the loss of the traditional *barrio* and the transformation of the city center into a "nonplace" (2003, p. 254). He mourned the impossibility of being a flâneur in the city as a consequence of increases in traffic and traffic-orientated streets. Both street and café, Sebreli declared, archetypal sites of transit, discussion, and democracy, are dead or dying (2003, pp. 272–280). Alongside this lament for apparent political apathy and the death of public space, Sebreli simultaneously criticized *piqueteros* and the *carpa docente*, a campsite set

up in the Plaza de Mayo by teachers, for disrupting the city (2003, pp. 270–271). Democratic public space for Sebreli, it seems, should not include public protest that limits others' use of that space.

5. The urban population of Argentina in 2001 made up some 90% of the country's total population (Wagner, 2008, p. 17). Approximately 30% of the population currently lives in Buenos Aires.

Chapter 2

1. Other conflicts of note that took place over and through urban space in this period include the burning of the Jockey Club in 1953, in which Peronist supporters torched one of the establishment's most symbolic buildings; the bombing of the Plaza de Mayo in 1955 by a faction of the navy, an event that precipitated the downfall of Perón; and the conflict at Ezeiza in 1973, during which Perón's right-wing supporters opened fire on his left-wing supporters at the city's international airport, where both sides had gathered to celebrate the return of the former president after almost 20 years in exile.

2. The controversy shrouding the 1978 tournament only intensifies this "fictional" label. Accusations of doping were leveled at the Argentine team as a result of the submission of false urine samples (one player was found to be pregnant) (Burns, 2002, p. 49), and during the highly suspect Argentine 6–0 victory against Peru, which they needed to win by four clear goals to reach the final, just as the crucial fourth goal was scored a bomb exploded outside the house of Juan Alemann, the Finance Secretary who had questioned the levels of government spending for the tournament (Galeano, 2001, p. 178).

3. El Monumental, located in Bajo Nuñez, is now home to River Plate Football Club, whose nickname is none other than "the millionaires." La Bombonera, located in the working-class district of La Boca and the home of one of the two most widely supported clubs in Argentina, Boca Juniors, was not included as one of the chosen stadiums.

4. Exploiting these ties, the Argentine government announced during the 1978 World Cup its intentions to recover the islands in the Beagle Channel that an international court of arbitration had ruled belonged to Chile in 1977 (Kuper, 1994, p. 180), and in 1982 television coverage interspersed justifications for the Malvinas/Falklands invasion with images of the 1978 World Cup victory (Burns, 2002, p. 91).

5. The documentary film *Vida en Falcon* (dir. Jorge Gaggero, 2005) relates the life of a homeless man who lives in a clapped-out Ford Falcon, a metaphor, among other things, for the way the car has also become everyday. One group of artists has attempted to defamiliarize the car by placing its component parts on poles all painted white. The pieces are arranged in such a way that the viewer can walk through this deconstructed object via a central path. See Autores ideológicos (2013).

6. See also Kaminsky (2014).

7. The Movimiento Nacionalista Tacuara (MNT) was a Catholic, anticommunist and anti-Semitic right-wing group active from the mid-1950s to the mid-1960s. When it disbanded, many members then enrolled in left-wing Peronist guerrilla organizations, a point Saer notes elsewhere: "The ideology of [left-wing groups, particularly the famous Montoneros] was extremely shady: [M]any came from right-wing nationalist origins, like the group Tacuara, which was nationalist, ultra-Catholic, anti-Semitic and pro-Nazi" (2006, p. 185).

8. The Montoneras were the rural armed forces deployed by regional *cau-dillos* in 19th-century Argentina.

9. One telling gesture in terms of the continuity and difference between administrations was the 2004 ceremony in which Néstor Kirchner oversaw the portrait of Jorge Videla in the ESMA being taken down. Apologizing "on behalf of the national state for shamefully keeping silent about so many atrocities during twenty years of democracy" (Curia, 2004), Kirchner assumed responsibility for the acts of previous administrations at the same time as marking out his administration as different to both the dictatorship and previous post-dictatorship governments, a move that re-inserted the state in a memory commons that had largely been forged by human rights organizations. After the ceremony in the ESMA it emerged that the portrait was in fact a copy of the original, removed before Kirchner's arrival without the President's knowledge. The following day another image of Videla, an oil painting, was circulating over the Internet, accompanied by a text that attacked biased accounts of the 1970s (*Clarín*, 2004).

10. The submerged path inscribed with names echoes Maya Lin's Vietnam Veterans Memorial in Washington, D.C. (Huyssen, 2003, p. 108).

11. Already in 1977 the architectural magazine *summa* made a link between the military's architectural vision and disappearance by comparing Guillermo Laura, then secretary of municipal public construction, to Baron Haussmann (Silvestri & Gorelik, 2000, pp. 466–467). Haussmann's renovation of Paris in the 1860s not only demolished buildings to create wider avenues for shopping and transport but also aided the ability of the military to control the city in the event of a popular uprising.

12. In relation to the Obelisco, where the second *siluetazo* was held, Diana Taylor notes that on one occasion during the dictatorship, "a group of corpses–all dressed up in suits, with shoes dangling around their necks like neckties—was found tied around the Obelisk, . . . situated as *punto zero*, the dead-center of Buenos Aires" (1997, p. 98).

13. One notable exception to this demand was when a silhouette was placed lying down to refer to the dead body of Dalmiro Flores, a worker murdered by paramilitaries in December 1982 in front of the Cabildo in the Plaza de Mayo.

14. The *siluetazo*'s relationship to disappearance took an even more significant turn when members of the police arrived to remove some of the silhouettes, to which one Madre shouted: "That one you're pulling down is my son" (Flores, 2008, p. 99). The "disappearance" of works of memory is not uncommon: The 20th

anniversary of the *golpe militar* saw municipal authorities order the "cleaning-up" of the Avenida de Mayo, trashing the work of 40 artists who had created a "Bridge of Remembrance" (Feitlowitz, 1998, p. 190).

Chapter 3

1. The 19th-century dictator Juan Manuel de Rosas advocated federalism in opposition to the centralizing wishes of figures such as Domingo Faustino Sarmiento, who saw in Buenos Aires a symbol of European progress and enlightenment. Julio Cobos, Cristina Fernández de Kirchner's vice-President, cast a deciding vote in Congress against the government in July 2008 during a dispute with land-owning farmers over proposals to increase taxation on grain exports.

2. Carlos Gamerro's novel *Las islas* (1998) is a parody of Argentine nationalism that tackles the mythic narratives that are built around Malvinas and the belief that recovering the islands will restore national unity. It is set during the height of the neoliberal era, with references to surfaces, simulations, simulacra, reflections, and copies. The most telling simulacra of all is a computer game about the Malvinas War that contains within it a virus—Malvinas 140682 (14 June 1982 being the date of the Argentine surrender)—that means the British forces invade the mainland and eventually fly a Union Jack flag from the top of the Obelisco (1998, p. 150). *Las islas* is unusual in the close ties it makes between the myths of Malvinas and neoliberal Buenos Aires, symbolized by skyscrapers, shopping centers, and the homeless. At the conclusion of the novel, in a vision that demonstrates how Malvinas underpins the city's foundations, the protagonist describes how "a huge hand came down from heaven and, like someone preparing to remove a plaster, picked up the skin of the city from one point and pulled it off in one great tug to reveal underneath the desolate plain, the windswept pastures, the stone rivers, the rocks and the mud and the peat fields of the Malvinas" (1998, p. 541).

3. I would like to thank Mariana Santángelo for this last observation.

4. A "gorilla" is Argentine slang for an anti-Peronist, often one associated with the oligarchy and/or the military. Perón's Third Way was designed to tread a political path between the burgeoning gulf between U.S.-led capitalism and the communism of the Soviet Union.

5. The phrase here is a reproduction of the Peronist chant "Alpargatas sí, libros no" (*alpargatas* yes, books no). The chant was a cry for state investment in workers, and not intellectuals, the *alpargata* being an example of traditional, cheap Argentine footwear, similar to the French *espadrille*.

6. The 1974 version of *La guerra de los Antartes* was produced in extremely difficult circumstances. Oesterheld, living clandestinely, recited the narrative to Gustavo Trigo from a public telephone. The story was unfinished due to the closure of the newspaper *Noticias*, in which it was being published.

7. Solano López regularly turned his attention back to the city of this period, one that he had drawn for the famous *El eternauta*. The two pieces he contributed to Piglia's *La Argentina en pedazos*, adaptations of Rodolfo Walsh's *Operación masacre* and Germán Rozenmacher's *Cabecita negra*, and the short piece "Historia triste," written by his son Gabriel about a failed left-wing guerrilla during the dictatorship (*Fierro a fierro*, 1987, no.33), all depict this era.

8. *Parque Chas* includes several other references to the authors: In one episode, Barreiro's and Risso's names appear on a street sign as a marker of the story's authorship, and in "El libro" one of the passersby outside a bar window looks suspiciously like Barreiro.

9. The last military dictatorship played an important role in the history of Parque Chas: Osvaldo Cacciatore, the mayor of Buenos Aires during the dictatorship, stripped the neighborhood of its "barrio status" in 1976, status that was not restored until 2005. See Gobierno de la Ciudad de Buenos Aires (2015).

10. Prior to the 1976 coup, a banner was wrapped around the Obelisco with the phrase "El silencio es salud" (silence is healthy), ostensibly a campaign against excessive use of car horns but widely interpreted as a warning against freedom of expression. The Obelisco continues to be a sensitive space: In 2002, for example, Canadian artist Spencer Tunick photographed naked bodies around the monument, resulting in a lawsuit being brought against the artist and Aníbal Ibarra, then governor of Buenos Aires. Filing for "obscene exhibitionism," the lawyer Oscar Igounet claimed that the acts could misdirect "the natural sense of sexuality in children and young people caught unawares," not least because the participants with their "swinging and suspended organs, flaccid or erect" were "mixed one with the other, men with men, women with women and couples of different sexes." See *Clarín* (2002a) and *Clarín* (2002b). Ibarra was not deterred: In 2005 the Obelisco was sheathed with a giant condom for World Aids Day. See *Clarín* (2005a).

Chapter 4

1. In her study of private neighborhoods María Cecilia Arizaga has highlighted how the shopping center works as a key reference in the way children living in such residences map the city (2004).

2. The ties between the military dictatorship and shopping centers are also evident in the climax to Alejandro Agresti's 1996 film *Buenos Aires viceversa*, in which a homeless boy, who has befriended the daughter of a disappeared person, is shot by a security guard after the boy tries to steal a video camera during a visit to a shopping center.

3. Piñeiro's novel was adapted into a film in 2009 (*Las viudas de los jueves*, dir. Marcelo Piñeyro). Her later novel *Betibú* (2010) is also set in a gated community. Other Argentine texts set in gated communities include *Cara de queso*

(dir. Ariel Winograd, 2006), set in a Jewish *country*, and *Una semana solos* (dir. Celina Murga, 2007), about a group of children living in a gated community whose parents leave for a week. Luisa Valenzuela's earlier comic novel, *Realidad nacional desde la cama* (1990), uses a country club as the setting for an attempt by the military to return to power in post-dictatorship Argentina.

4. A stark visual representation of such harsh urban contrasts can be found in the opening sequence of Rodrigo Plá's 2007 film *La zona*, set in a gated community in Mexico City: The camera pans over the ordered, peaceful gardens of the affluent houses to the sound of chirping birds before eventually lifting up and over the surrounding wall to reveal the dark and ominous city lying alongside.

5. As the website of Estancias de Pilar states, "the urban planning, design and aesthetic restores the dynamic of 'towns', whose strong sense of identity differentiates them from shopping centers" (Estancias del Pilar, 2013). The inverted commas indicate the artificiality of the construction. What is also evident here, though, is the desire to recreate an "authentic" urban shopping experience rather than simply reproduce the experience of the shopping center (which is no longer regarded as a marker of exclusivity).

6. Aside from Nordelta in Buenos Aires, other examples include Alphaville in São Paulo and Colina and Lampa in Santiago de Chile.

7. The entry in *Nunca más* reads "Location: Quintana y Tapalqué (almost Naciones Unidas), four blocks from Avda. Gral. Paz, Partido de la Matanza, Provincia de Buenos Aires" (CONADEP, 2003, p. 110).

8. The title "El bonaerense" can mean both "The Man from the Province of Buenos Aires" or "The Police Officer from the Province of Buenos Aires."

9. Santiago Llach's brief poem "La raza" (The race) offers another take on the Obelisco. In the poem Germans celebrate victory in the European Cup by singing in English on Spanish television, causing the poet to wonder whether we could imagine "toda la negrada" (the whole gang) singing "we are the champions" around the Obelisco (2002, p. 11). A reflection on unstable national identities in globalized Europe, the use of the term "negrada" creates links to the city's white European aspirations undone by the Peronist "cabecita negras" (little black heads), all set to the backdrop of the Obelisco's symbolic whiteness.

Chapter 5

1. "Boca de lobo" translates roughly as "the lion's den" into English; however, whilst the translation retains the sense of danger, it loses the ominous, more sinister qualities of the Spanish phrase.

2. In the wake of Macri's successful re-election as the mayor of Capital Federal in 2011, one of Argentina's most famous rock stars, Fito Paez, wrote a polemical article in *Página 12* in which he stated that "half of Buenos Aires makes me sick," symbolic of the way that rock continues to think of Capital Federal (Paez, 2011). The point is emphasized by the fact that Manuel Quieto, a member

of the band Mancha de Rolando, wrote to PRO, Macri's party, to protest the use of their song "Arde la ciudad" as part of his victory celebrations. See *Perfil* (2011).

3. The 1995 explosion at the weapons factory in Río Tercero, Córdoba, was tied to suspicions of illegal arms trafficking to Croatia and Ecuador in which President Carlos Menem was later implicated. The 1991 Ley de Convertibilidad del Austral tied the Argentine currency to the U.S. dollar at the rate of 1:1. Gas del Estado, one of the country's largest state-owned enterprises, was privatized in 1992.

4. Gustavo Rearte's son has spoken of how prohibited films were sometimes screened clandestinely in Villa Celina during the 1960s, some including messages from the exiled Perón (Biaggini, 2014).

5. In a more recent article analyzing the Indian, the gaucho, the immigrant, the *cabecita negra,* and the shantytown dweller as those excluded from Buenos Aires, Incardona clarified this statement by referring to how Leopoldo Marechal's character Adán Buenos Ayres and Roberto Arlt's character Erdosain are both marginal figures that make a journey to the outer reaches of the city, representing in that sense a journey "from the border outwards, from the interior border to the exterior border" (Incardona, 2012). The decision by the Carris to move to a working-class neighborhood of Gran Buenos Aires discussed in Chapter 4 is another kind of journey to the Conurbano.

6. In a further hint to that wider urban literary geography, one chapter written in the form of a song in *Rock barrial* includes the line "¿Seguirá jugando en esa esquina / que a la noche es una boca de lobo?" (Is she still playing on that corner / that turns into a lion's den at night?) (2010b, p. 90). It is possible that Incardona read Chejfec's *Boca de lobo* while enrolled as a literature student at the Universidad de Buenos Aires, as the work was being read on the module Literatura Argentina II at that time.

Chapter 6

1. With the passing of the worst of the political crisis, the *piquete* was seen as an outmoded form of protest, preventing the city from returning to normality. See, for example, *Clarín*, 2005b. In a similarly significant shift, some *piquetero* groups also transformed themselves from independent, anti-state organizations into allies of the Kirchner administrations.

2. *Días de cartón* (dir. Verónica Souto, 2003).

3. Despite losing the 2003 elections, Macri eventually won the June 2007 mayoral elections and was re-elected in 2011. The Mayor of Buenos Aires is considered to be the third most influential political position in Argentina after the President and the Governor of the Province of Buenos Aires.

4. Though comparisons can be made between liquidacion.org and the global freecycle network (www.freecycle.org), liquidacion.org placed greater emphasis on the individual history of the collector, making the object inseparable from the recycler.

5. There have been other examples of *cartoneros* who, once in the public eye, appear to have moved beyond their *cartonero*/shantytown past (such as the transvestite Zulma Lobato) or for having talent despite being a *cartonero,* as in the case of the *cartonero* who sang on Crónica TV accompanied by a patronizing, snide host and the banner "He was a *cartonero*, he lives in poverty, he sings opera very well" ("Heaven music canta tema nuevo," 2009).

6. Paper has become even more contentious in Argentina ever since two companies, one Spanish (Ence) and one Finnish (Botnia), built new paper mills on the Uruguayan side of the Río Uruguay, with processing starting in 2007. Those living on the opposite side of the river in Argentina, together with environmental groups from both countries, have protested at the potential health hazard of these mills. To some extent, such demonstrations can be read as reactions against multinational companies treating Latin America as a garbage dump.

7. The back cover of *El carrito de Eneas* suggests that references such as that to the city "down there" align the narrator of the poem with President De la Rúa, looking down on the city from his helicopter as he fled the crowds on 20 December 2001.

8. *Días de cartón* (dir. Verónica Souto, 2003).

Chapter 7

1. Establishing a clear definition of a *villa* is complex. The notion that they are temporary residences, as implied by their original name "villas de emergencia," is incompatible with their current permanence. Neither are *villas* necessarily precarious dwellings built with discarded material on undeveloped areas of the city, as the two-story concrete houses now being built in some shantytowns indicate. Neighborhoods such as Fuerte Apache also have little in common with the traditional image of the physical appearance of the *villa.* One of the city's most troubled zones, it is comprised not of shacks but of crumbling tower blocks. It is crime, drug trafficking, and above all poverty, as well as its internal maze of apartments, that explains why Fuerte Apache is sometimes called a shantytown. That Fuerte Apache is now policed by the Gendarmería, the national border force that is also deployed for internal conflicts of significant national importance, only exaggerates the sense that the neighborhood is implicitly being pushed beyond the city's imaginary.

2. The notion of the *villa* as a rural space encroaching on the city reverses another trope of urbanity particularly evident during the boom of the modern city—that of the city encroaching on the rural. The idyllic countryside of Ricardo Güiraldes's1926 novel *Don Segundo Sombra*, for example, is placed in contrast to a dangerous, threatening city (Sarlo, 1988, p. 33).

3. "Yuta" is slang for the police. The wordplay in the song's lyrics makes reference to the rhyme of "yuta" and "puta" (bitch).

4. Such phrases echo the football chant made popular during the 1978 World Cup finals: "el que no salta es holandés" (the one not jumping is Dutch), later transformed into "el que no salta es un inglés" (the one not jumping is English) after the Falklands/Malvinas War.

5. The musician Kevin Johansen, whose work fuses different musical genres, languages, and styles, incorporated that transformation in his song "Cumbiera intelectual," which dealt with the *cumbia* boom. The song from the album *Sur o no sur* (2003) relates a meeting between a *cumbia* fan and a middle-class girl studying literature at university.

6. Like *cumbia*, rock bands also turn perceived negative traits into markers of identity, using names such as Viejas Locas, Callejeros, La Renga, Jóvenes Pordioseros, Bien Desocupados, No Demuestra Interés, and Intoxicados (Flachsland, 2006, p. 62).

7. In John Pilger's documentary film *The War on Democracy* (2006) an inhabitant of Caracas states that prior to the Chávez regime the shantytown in which she lives appeared on maps as a white space—that is, a shantytown literally beyond the pale.

Bibliography

Achugar, Hugo. (2009). On Maps and Malls. In R. Biron (Ed.), *City/Art: The Urban Scene in Latin America* (pp. 185–209). Durham, NC: Duke University Press.

Agamben, Giorgio. (1998). *Homo Sacer: Sovereign Power and Bare Life*. Stanford, CA: Stanford University Press.

———. (2005). *State of Exception*. Chicago, IL: University of Chicago Press.

Aguilar, Gonzalo. (2006). *Otros mundos: Un ensayo sobre el nuevo cine argentino*. Buenos Aires: Santiago Arcos Editor.

Aguiló, Ignacio. (2014). Tropical Buenos Aires: Representations of race in Argentine literature during the 2001 crisis and its aftermath. In C. Levey, D. Ozarow, & C. Wylde (Eds.), *Argentina Since the 2001 Crisis: Recovering the Past, Reclaiming the Future* (pp. 177–194). New York, NY: Palgrave Macmillan.

Aguirre, Osvaldo. (2003). Reportaje: Daniel Samoilovich. *La Capital*. Online: http://archivo.lacapital.com.ar/2003/08/03/Seniales/noticia_24541.shtml [Accessed 15 March 2015].

Ahrens, Jörn, & Arno Meteling. (2010). Introduction. In J. Ahrens & A. Meteling (Eds.), *Comics and the City: Urban Space in Print, Picture and Sequence* (pp. 1–16). New York and London: Continuum.

Aira, César. (2001). *La villa*. Buenos Aires: Emecé.

Alarcón, Cristian. (2003). *Cuando me muera quiero que me toquen cumbia: Vida de pibes chorros*. Buenos Aires: Norma.

Amin, Ash. (2008). Collective Culture and Urban Public Space. *City*, *12*(1), 5–24.

Amin, Ash, & Thrift, Nigel. (2002). *Cites: Reimagining the Urban*. Cambridge: Polity.

Andermann, Jens. (2011). *New Argentine Cinema*. New York, NY: I.B. Tauris.

Angotti, Tom. (2013). Urban Latin America: Violence, Enclaves, and Struggles for Land. *Latin American Perspectives*, *40*, 5–20.

Anguita, Eduardo. (2003). *Cartoneros: Recuperadores de desechos y causas perdidas*. Buenos Aires: Norma.

Appiah, K. Anthony. (2001). Cosmopolitan Reading. In V. Dharwadker (Ed.), *Cosmopolitan Geographies: New Locations in Literature and Culture* (pp. 197–227). New York, NY: Routledge.

Aprea, Gustavo. (2008). *Cine y políticas en Argentina: Continuidades y discontinuidades en 25 años de democracia.* Buenos Aires: Biblioteca Nacional and Universidad Nacional de General Sarmiento.

Arendt, Hannah. (1994). *Eichmann in Jerusalem: A Report on the Banality of Evil.* London: Penguin.

Arizaga, María Cecilia. (2004). Prácticas e imaginarios en el proceso de suburbanización privada. In B. Cuenya, C. Fidel, & H. Herzer (Eds.), *Fragmentos sociales: Problemas urbanos de la Argentina* (pp. 53–73). Buenos Aires: Siglo XXI.

Assmann, Jan. (2006). *Religion and Cultural Memory: Ten Studies.* Stanford, CA: Stanford University Press.

Atlas Ambiental de Buenos Aires. (n.d.). Online: http://www.atlasdebuenosaires. gov.ar/aaba/ [Accessed 12 November 2009].

Autores ideológicos. (2013). Autores ideológicos. Online: http://conti.derhuman. jus.gov.ar/2014/03/i-autores-ideologicos.shtml [Accessed 15 March 2015].

Baldwin, Davarian L. (2004). Black Empires, White Desires: The Spatial Politics of Identity in the Age of Hip-Hop. In M. Forman & M. Anthony Neal (Eds.), *That's the Joint!: The Hip-Hop Studies Reader* (pp. 159–176). New York, NY: Routledge.

Balzer, Jens. (2010). "Hully gee, I'm a Hieroglyphe": Mobilizing the Gaze and the Invention of Comics in New York City, 1895. In J. Ahrens & A. Meteling (Eds.), *Comics and the City: Urban Space in Print, Picture and Sequence* (pp. 19–31). New York, NY, and London: Continuum.

Barrantes, Guillermo, & Víctor Coviello. (2009). *Buenos Aires es leyenda 2: Mitos urbanos de una ciudad misteriosa.* Buenos Aires: Booklet.

———. (2010a). *Buenos Aires es leyenda: Mitos urbanos de una ciudad misteriosa.* 3rd edition. Buenos Aires: Booklet.

———. (2010b). *Buenos Aires es leyenda 3: Mitos urbanos de una ciudad misteriosa.* Buenos Aires: Booklet.

Barreiro, Ricardo, & Juan Giménez. (1992). *Ciudad.* Buenos Aires: Ediciones de la Urraca.

Barreiro, Ricardo, & Eduardo Risso. (2004). *Parque Chas.* Rosario: Puro Comic.

Barría, María Soledad. (2005).Cumbia villera: ¿El ruido de los olvidados?. Online: http://www.odonnell-historia.com.ar/registros/pdf/cumbia_villera8.pdf [Accessed 15 March 2015].

Barthes, Roland. (1993). *Camera Lucida.* London: Vintage.

Batlle, Diego. (1999). Mundo grúa. *La Nación.* Espectáculos, (17/06/99), p. 4.

BBC. (2008). Daniela Cott: From Rubbish to Riches. Online: http://www. bbc.co.uk/worldservice/outlook/2008/04/080402_model_outlook.shtml [Accessed 22 July 2009].

Beasley-Murray, Jon. (2002). Towards an Unpopular Cultural Studies. In S. Godsland & A. White (Eds.), *Cultura Popular: Studies in Spanish and Latin American Popular Culture* (pp. 27–45). New York, NY: Peter Lang.

———. (2005). The Common Enemy: Tyrants and Pirates. *South Atlantic Quarterly. 104*, 217–225.

———. (2010). *Posthegemony*. Minneapolis: University of Minnesota Press.

Bergero, Adriana J. (2008). *Intersecting Tango: Cultural Geographies of Buenos Aires, 1900–1930*. Pittsburgh, PA: University of Pittsburgh Press.

Berjman, Sonia. (n.d.). Parque Chas: El laberinto de Buenos Aires. Online: http://www.parquechasweb.com.ar/parquechas/historia/histo.htm [Accessed 15 March 2015].

Berman, Jessica. (2001). *Modernist Fiction, Cosmopolitanism, and the Politics of Community*. Cambridge: Cambridge University Press.

Bernades, Horacio. (1998a). La ciudad descarnada. *Clarín*. Cultura y Nación, (05/02/98), p. 8.

———. (1998b). El cine por asalto. *Los Inrockuptibles. 19*, 62–63.

Bernini, Emilio. (2003). Un proyecto inconcluso: Aspectos del cine contemporáneo argentino. *Kilometro 111. 4*, 87–105.

———. (2008). *Estudio crítico sobre* Silvia Prieto. Buenos Aires: Picnic.

Beverley, John, & Oviedo, José. (1995). Introduction. In J. Beverley & J. Oviedo (Eds.), *The Postmodernism Debate in Latin America* (pp. 1–17). Durham, NC: Duke University Press.

Biaggini, Martín A. (2014). Villa Celina entre 1955 y 1970. Online: http://historiadevillacelina.blogspot.co.uk/2014/02/villa-celina-entre-1955-y-1970.html [Accessed 15 March 2015].

Bilbao, Horacio. (2011). Rock callejero en la continuidad de una saga sobre el conurbano. *Revista Ñ*. Online: http://www.revistaenie.clarin.com/literatura/ficcion/Entrevista_Juan_Diego_Incardona_0_437356506.html [Accessed 15 March 2015].

Blaustein, Eduardo. (2001). *Prohibido vivir aquí: Una historia de los planes de erradicación de villas de la última dictadura*. Buenos Aires: Comisión Municipal de la Vivienda.

Blaustein, Eduardo and Zubieta, Martín. (1998). *Decíamos ayer: La prensa argentina bajo el proceso*. Buenos Aires: Colihue.

Blejmar, Jordana. (2012). *The Truth of Autofiction: Second-Generation Memory in Post-Dictatorship Argentine Culture*. Unpublished PhD dissertation. University of Cambridge.

Blejmar, Jordana, Natalia Fortuny, & Luis Ignacio García (Eds.), (2013). *Instantáneas de la memoria: Fotografía, dictadura y memoria en Argentina y América Latina*. Buenos Aires: Libraria.

Biron, Rebecca E. (2009). Introduction: City/Art: Setting the Scene. In R. Biron (Ed.), *City/Art: The Urban Scene in Latin America* (pp. 1–34). Durham, NC: Duke University Press.

Borsdorf, Axel, & Rodrigo Hidalgo. (2008). New Dimensions of Social Exclusion in Latin America: From Gated Communities to Gated Cities, the Case of Santiago de Chile. *Land Use Policy, 25,* 153–160.

Breccia, Enrique. (2007). *El Sueñero.* Buenos Aires: Doedytores.

Briceño-León, Roberto. (2007). Caracas. In K. Koonings & D. Kruijt. (Eds.), *Fractured Cities: Social Exclusion, Urban Violence and Contested Spaces in Latin America* (pp. 86–100). London and New York, NY: Zed Books.

Burns, Jimmy (2002). *Hand of God: The Life of Diego Maradona.* London: Bloomsbury.

Caldeira, Teresa Pires do Rio. (2000). *City of Walls: Crime, Segregation and Citizenship in São Paulo.* Berkeley, CA: University of California Press.

Calderón, Darío. (2006). El tiempo no para: Cuatro décadas y después. In A. Franco, G. Franco, & D. Calderón (Eds.), *Buenos Aires y el rock* (pp. 83–120). Buenos Aires: Gobierno de la Ciudad de Buenos Aires.

Calveiro, Pilar. (1998). *Poder y desaparición: Los campos de concentración en argentina.* Buenos Aires: Colihue.

Camacho, Jorge. (2009). A Tragic Note: On Negri and Deleuze in the Light of the "Argentinazo." *New Formations, 68,* 58–76.

Carassai, Sebastián. (2007). The Noisy Majority: An Analysis of the Argentine Crisis of December 2001 from the Theoretical Approach of Hardt & Negri, Laclau and Žižek. *Journal of Latin American Cultural Studies, 16*(1), 45–62.

Careri, Francisco. (2002). *Walkscapes: Walking as an Aesthetic Practice.* Barcelona: Editorial Gustavo Gili.

Carta Abierta (2011). Carta Abierta/9. Online: http://cartaabierta.org.ar/index.php/cartas-abiertas/109-cartas/carta-abierta-09/155-carta-abierta9 [Accessed 15 March 2015].

Ceresa, Constanza. (2014). Velocidad y desorientación en *Punctum* de Martín Gambarotta y *Silvia Prieto* de Martín Rejtman. *Studies in Spanish & Latin American Cinemas, 11*(2), 179–191.

Chatterton, Paul. (2010). Seeking the Urban Common: Furthering the Debate on Spatial Justice. *City, 14*(6), 625–628.

Chejfec, Sergio. (2009). *Boca de lobo.* Buenos Aires: Alfaguara.

———. (2002). Sísifo en Buenos Aires. *Punto de Vista, 72,* 26–31.

Chronopoulos, Themis. (2006). Neo-liberal Reform and Urban Space: The Cartoneros of Buenos Aires. *City, 10,* 167–182.

———. (2011). The Neoliberal Political–Economic Collapse of Argentina and the Spatial Fortification of Institutions in Buenos Aires, 1998–2010. *City, 15*(5), 509–531.

Ciudad de Buenos Aires. (2003). Plan de urbanización en villas y barrios carenciados. Online: http://www.cnvivienda.org.ar/nuevo/notas/CiudadBA_9.pdf [Accessed 26 January 2007].

Clarín. (2002a). Una denuncia penal por los desnudos. *Clarín.* Online: http://edant.clarin.com/diario/2002/04/09/s-03003.htm [Accessed 15 March 2015].

————. (2002b). Fotografiar gente desnuda en la calle no es un delito. *Clarín*. Online: http://edant.clarin.com/diario/2002/05/09/s-03801.htm [Accessed 15 March 2015].

————. (2004). Un nuevo capítulo por el retrato de Videla. *Clarín*. Online: http://www.clarin.com/diario/2004/04/01/p-01203.htm [Accessed 15 March 2015].

————. (2005a). El Obelisco amaneció cubierto con un preservativo. *Clarín*. Online: http://edant.clarin.com/diario/2005/12/01/um/m-01099864.htm [Accessed 10 January 2013].

————. (2005b). Para el Gobierno, los piqueteros "agotaron" los cortes de calles y puentes. *Clarín*. Online: http://edant.clarin.com/diario/2005/08/27/um/m-1041673.htm [Accessed 15 March 2015].

Cohen, Marcelo. (2001). *Los acuáticos: Historias del Delta Panorámico*. Buenos Aires: Norma.

Colectivo Situaciones. (2002a). *19 y 20: Apuntes para el nuevo protagonismo social*. Buenos Aires: De Mano en Mano.

————. (2002b). *Genocida en el barrio: Mesa de escrache popular*. Buenos Aires: De Mano en Mano.

Comisión Nacional sobre la Desaparición de Personas (CONADEP). (2003). *Nunca más*. Buenos Aires: Eudeba.

Contreras, Sandra. (2009). Economías literarias en la ficción argentina del 2000 (Casas, Incardona, Cucurto, Llinás). Actas del II Congreso Internacional Cuestiones Críticas. Online: www.celarg.org/int/arch_publi/contreras_acta.pdf [Accessed 15 March 2015], pp. 1–20.

Copertari, Gabriela. (2005). *Nine Queens*: A Dark Day of Simulation and Justice. *Journal of Latin American Cultural Studies*, 14(3), 279–293.

Corbatta, Jorgelina. (1999). *Narrativas de la guerra sucia en Argentina: Piglia, Saer, Valenzuela, Puig*. Buenos Aires: Corregidor.

Costa, Silvina. (2004). Martín Kohan: *Dos veces junio*. *Segundo poesía*. Online: http://www.segundapoesia.com.ar/2004/06/martin-kohan-dos-veces-junio/ [Accessed 10 January 2013].

Coy, Martin. (2006). Gated Communities and Urban Fragmentation in Latin America: The Brazilian Experience. *GeoJournal*, 66(1–2), 121–132.

Crinson, Mark. (2005). Urban Memory: An Introduction. In M. Crinson (Ed.). *Urban Memory: History and Amnesia in the Modern City* (pp. xi–xxiii). London and New York, NY: Routledge.

Crovara, María Eugenia. (2004). Pobreza y estígma en una villa miseria argentina. *Política y cultura*, 22, 29–45.

Curia, Walter. (2004). Kirchner en la ESMA: "En nombre del Estado, vengo a pedir perdón." *Clarín*. Online: http://www.clarin.com/diario/2004/03/25/p-00301.htm [Accessed 15 March 2015].

Curtoni, Rafael, Axel Lazzari, & Marisa Lazzari. (2003). Middle of Nowhere: A Place of War Memories, Commemoration, and Aboriginal Re-emergence (La Pampa, Argentina). *World Archaeology*, 35, 61–78.

Dalmaroni, Miguel. (2003). La moral de la historia: Novelas argentinas sobre la dictadura (1995–2002). *Hispamérica*, *32*(96), 29–47.

Dalmaroni, Miguel, & Merbilhaá, Margarita. (2000). "Un azar convertido en don": Juan José Saer y el relato de la percepción. In E. Drucaroff (Ed.), *Historia crítica de la literatura argentina, Volume 9: La narración gana la partida* (pp. 321–341). Buenos Aires: Emecé.

Damai, Puspa. (2005). Messianic-City: Ruins, Refuge and Hospitality in Derrida. *Discourse*, *27*, 68–94.

Davis, Mike. (1990). *City of Quartz: Excavating the Future in Los Angeles*. London and New York, NY: Verso.

———. (1999). *Ecology of Fear*. London: Picador.

———. (2006). *Planet of Slums*. New York, NY: Verso.

de Certeau, Michel. (1988). *The Practice of Everyday Life*. Berkeley, CA: University of California Press.

de la Torre, Lidia. (2000). La ciudad residual. In J.L. Romero & L.A. Romero (Eds.), *Buenos Aires: Historia de cuatro siglos*, 2nd edition (pp. 273–283). Buenos Aires: Altamira.

Del Sarto, Ana, Alicia Ríos, & Abril Trigo (Eds.), (2004). *The Latin American Cultural Studies Reader*. Durham, NC: Duke University Press.

De Santis, Pablo. (1992). *Historieta y política en los '80*. Buenos Aires: Letra Buena.

Deleuze, Gilles, & Félix Guattari. (1986). *Kafka: Towards a Minor Literature*. Minneapolis, MN: University of Minnesota Press.

Derrida, Jacques. (2001). *On Cosmopolitanism and Forgiveness*. London and New York, NY: Routledge.

Di Tella, Andrés. (1999). La vida privada en los campos de concentración. In F. Devoto & M. Madero (Eds.), *Historia de la vida privada en la Argentina. Volume 3: La Argentina entre multitudes y soledades: De los años treinta a la actualidad* (pp. 79–105). Buenos Aires: Taurus.

Diken, Bülent. (2005). City of God. *City*, *9*, 307–320.

Diken, Bülent, & Carsten Bagge Laustsen. (2005). *The Culture of Exception: Sociology Facing the Camp*. London and New York, NY: Routledge.

Dinerstein, Ana. (2001). Roadblocks in Argentina: Against the Violence of Stability. *Capital and Class*, *74*, 1–7.

———. (2003). "¡Que se Vayan Todos!": Popular Insurrection and the *Asambleas Barriales* in Argentina. *Bulletin of Latin American Research*, *22*(2), 187–200.

———. (2014). Disagreement and Hope: The Hidden Transcripts of Political Recovery in Argentina Post Crisis. In C. Levey, D. Ozarow, & C. Wylde (Eds.), *Argentina Since the 2001 Crisis: Recovering the Past, Reclaiming the Future* (pp. 115–133). New York, NY: Palgrave Macmillan.

Dirección General de Patrimonio. (2003). *Guía: Patrimonio cultural de Buenos Aires: Vol.1*. Buenos Aires: Dirección General de Patrimonio.

Dolina, Alejandro. (1988). *Crónicas del Ángel Gris*. Buenos Aires: Ediciones de la Urraca.

Dorfman, Ariel, & Armand Mattelart. (2005). *Para leer al Pato Donald: Comunicación de masa y colonialismo*. Buenos Aires: Siglo XXI.

Draper, Susana. (2009). Spatial Juxtaposition and Temporal Imagery in Postdictatorship Culture. *Journal of Latin American Cultural Studies, 18*(1), 33–54.

Duschatzky, Silvia, & Cristina Corea. (2002). *Chicos en banda: Los caminos de la subjetividad en el declive de las instituciones*. Buenos Aires: Paidós.

Enghel, Florencia, Cecilia Flachsland, & Violeta Rosemberg (2008). Jóvenes, memoria y justicia: El caso Cromañón y la comunicación en la era de la precariedad. Online: https://sites.google.com/site/alaicgtccs/florencia-enghel [Accessed 15 March 2015].

Enns, Anthony. (2010). The City as Archive in Jason Lutes's *Berlin*. In J. Ahrens & A. Meteling (Eds.), *Comics and the City: Urban Space in Print, Picture and Sequence* (pp. 45–59). New York and London: Continuum.

Escobar, Arturo. (2010). Latin America at a Crosswords. *Cultural Studies, 24*(1), 1–65.

España, Claudio. (1998). Con realismo. *La Nación*. Online: http://www.lanacion.com.ar/85484-con-realismo [Accessed 15 March 2015].

Esposito, Roberto. (2008). Immunization and Violence. Online: http://www.biopolitica.unsw.edu.au/sites/all/files/publication_related_files/esposito_immunization_violence.pdf [Accessed 15 March 2015].

Estancias del Pilar. (2013). El Pueblo. Online: http://www.estanciasdelpilar.com/pueblo/index.html [Accessed 15 March 2015]

Estrade, Juan María. (2007). La capital que no fue. Online: http://trasladodelacapital.blogspot.com/2007/10/la-capital-que-no-fue.html [Accessed 15 March 2015].

Feitlowitz, Marguerite. (1998). *A Lexicon of Terror: Argentina and the Legacies of Torture*. New York, NY: Oxford University Press.

Feld, Claudia, & Jessica Stites Mor (Eds.), (2009). *El pasado que miramos: Memoria e imagen ante la historia reciente*. Buenos Aires: Paidós.

Fernández, Nancy. (2004). Experiencia y lenguaje: Sobre "El tilo y La Villa," de César Aira. *Hispamérica, 97*, 93–102.

Fierro a fierro: historietas para sobrevivientes. (1984–1992). Buenos Aires: Ediciones de la Urraca.

Filc, Judith. (1997). *Entre el parentesco y la política: Familia y dictadura, 1976–1983*. Buenos Aires: Biblos.

Flachsland, Cecilia. (2006). El rock argentino y los restos de lo nacional y popular. *Ojo Mocho, 20*, 60–64.

Flores, Julio. (2008). Siluetas. In A. Longoni & G.A. Buzzone (Eds.), *El siluetazo* (pp. 83–106). Buenos Aires: Adriana Hidalgo Editora.

Fontana, Patricio. (2002). Martín Rejtman: Una mirada sin nostalgias. *Milpalabras, 4*, 81–88.

Forman, Murray. (2004). "Represent": Race, Space, and Place in Rap Music. In M. Forman & M.A. Neal (Eds.), *That's the Joint!: The Hip-Hop Studies Reader* (pp. 201–222). New York, NY, and London: Routledge.

Fornazzari, Alejandro. (2013). *Speculative Fictions: Chilean Culture, Economics, and the Neoliberal Transition*. Pittsburgh, PA: University of Pittsburgh Press.

Foster, David William (1998). *Buenos Aires: Perspectives on the City and Cultural Production*. Gainesville, FL: University Press of Florida.

Franco, Jean. (1999). Comic Stripping: Cortázar in the Age of Mechanical Reproduction. In M.L. Pratt & K. Newman (Eds.), *Critical Passions: Selected Essays* (pp. 405–425). Durham, NC: Duke University Press.

———. (2002). *The Decline and Fall of the Lettered City: Latin America in the Cold War*. Cambridge, MA: Harvard University Press.

Franco, Adriana. (2006). Yo vivo en una ciudad: Aires de época. In A. Franco, G. Franco, & D. Calderón. *Buenos Aires y el rock* (pp. 21–37). Buenos Aires: Gobierno de la Ciudad de Buenos Aires.

Freedman, Carl. (2000). *Critical Theory and Science Fiction*. Hanover, NH: University Press of New England.

Fuggle, Sophie & Elisha Foust (Eds.). (2011) *Word on the Street: Reading, Writing & Inhabiting Public Space*. London: IMLR [igrs books].

Fundación Metropolitana. (2004). Historia de la gestión de residuos sólidos en la Región Metropolitana Buenos Aires. *La Gran Ciudad*. Online: http://www.metropolitana.org.ar/archivo/lgc/04/insert.pdf [Accessed 6 September 2007].

GAC. (2009). *Pensamientos Prácticas Acciones*. Buenos Aires: Tinta Limón.

Galeano, Eduardo. (2001). *El fútbol a sol y sombra*. Buenos Aires: Catálogos.

———. (2003). *Las venas abiertas de América Latina*. Buenos Aires: Catálogos.

Gamerro, Carlos. (1998). *Las islas*. Buenos Aires: Simurg.

García Canclini, Néstor. (2001). *Consumers and Citizens: Globalization and Multicultural Conflicts*. Minneapolis, MN: University of Minnesota Press.

García Navarro, Santiago. (2008). Como el fuego que se desparrama por un tanque de nafta. In A. Longoni & G.A. Buzzone (Eds.), *El siluetazo* (pp. 333–364). Buenos Aires: Adriana Hidalgo Editora.

Garguin, Enrique. (2007). *"Los Argentinos Descendemos de los Barcos"*: The Racial Articulation of Middle Class Identity in Argentina (1920–1960). *Latin American and Caribbean Ethnic Studies, 2*(2), 161–184.

Gobierno de la Ciudad de Buenos Aires. (2015). Comunas. Online: http://www.buenosaires.gob.ar/comunas [Accessed 15 March 2015].

———. (2015). Barrios: Parque Chas. Online: http://www.buenosaires.gob.ar/laciudad/barrios/parque-chas [Accessed 15 March 2015].

Gociol, Judith, & Diego Rosemberg. (2003). *La historieta argentina: Una historia*. Buenos Aires: Ediciones Flor.

Goñi, Uki. (2002). *The Real Odessa: How Perón Brought the Nazi War Criminals to Argentina*. London: Granta.

Gorelik, Adrián. (2002). El paisaje de la devastación. *Punto de Vista, 74,* 5–8.

———. (2003). *Mala época*: Los imaginarios de la descomposición social y urbana en Buenos Aires. In A. Birgin & J. Trímboli (Eds.), *Imágenes de los noventa* (pp. 19–46). Buenos Aires: Zorzal.

———. (2004). *Miradas sobre Buenos Aires: Historia cultural y crítica urbana*. Buenos Aires: Siglo XXI.

———. (2006). Modelo para armar: Buenos Aires, de la crisis al boom. *Punto de Vista, 84,* 33–39.

———. (2009). Buenos Aires is (Latin) America Too. In R. Biron (Ed.), *City/Art: The Urban Scene in Latin America* (pp. 61–84). Durham, NC: Duke University Press.

Graham-Yooll, Andrew. (2005). *Cumbia villera*: The Sound of the Slums. *Index on Censorship. 3,* 174–177.

Grimson, Alejandro. (2008). The Making of New Urban Borders: Neoliberalism and Protest in Buenos Aires. *Antipode, 40*(4), 504–512.

Grimson, Alejandro, & Gabriel Kessler. (2005). *On Argentina and the Southern Cone: Neoliberalism and National Imaginations.* New York, NY, and London: Routledge.

Grüner, Eduardo. (2008). La invisibilidad estratégica, o la redención política de los vivos. In A. Longoni & G.A. Buzzone (Eds.), *El siluetazo* (pp. 285–308). Buenos Aires: Adriana Hidalgo Editora.

Grupo de Arte Callejero. (2001). Aquí viven genocidos. Online: http://gacgrupo.ar.tripod.com/aquiviven.html [Accessed 15 March 2015].

———. (2008). Blancos móviles. In A. Longoni & G.A. Buzzone (Eds.), *El siluetazo* (pp. 427–432). Buenos Aires: Adriana Hidalgo Editora.

Guber, Rosana. (2001). *¿Por qué Malvinas?: De la causa nacional a la guerra absurda.* Buenos Aires and Mexico City: Fondo de Cultura Económica.

Guillermoprieto, Alma. (1994). *The Heart that Bleeds: Latin American Now.* New York, NY: Knopf.

Guiñazú, Cristina. (2011). Recorridos y lecturas: *La villa* de César Aira. *Ciberletras,* 27. Online: http://www.lehman.cuny.edu/ciberletras/v27/guinazu.html [Accessed 15 March 2015].

Gusmán, Luis. (2006). *Villa.* Buenos Aires: Edhasa.

Hardin, Garrett. (1968). The Tragedy of the Commons. *Science, 162,* 1243–1248.

Hardt, Michael, & Negri, Antonio. (2000). *Empire.* Cambridge, MA: Harvard University Press.

———. (2004). *Multitude: War and Democracy in the Age of Empire.* New York, NY: The Penguin Press.

———. (2009). *Commonwealth.* Cambridge, MA: The Belknapp Press of Harvard University Press.

Harel, Isser. (1975). *The House on Garibaldi Street: The Capture of Adolf Eichmann.* London: André Deutsch

Harvey, David. (2008). The Right to the City. *New Left Review, 53,* 23–40.

———. (2011). The Future of the Commons. *Radical History Review, 109,* 101–107.

"Heaven music canta tema nuevo." (2009). Online: http://www.youtube.com/watch?v=Opk79l9kQ2g&feature=related (Accessed 15 March 2015).

Hirsch, Marianne. (1997). *Family Frames: Photography, Narrative and Postmemory.* Cambridge, MA: Harvard University Press.

Huyssen, Andreas. (2003). *Present Pasts: Urban Palimpsests and the Politics of Memory*. Stanford, CA: Stanford University Press.

Incardona, Juan Diego. (2007). *Objetos maravillosos*. Buenos Aires: Tamarisco.

———. (2009). *Rock barrial*. Buenos Aires: Mondadori.

———. (2010a). *Villa Celina*. Buenos Aires: Verticales de Bolsillo.

———. (2010b). *Rock barrial*. Buenos Aires: Norma.

———. (2012). Periferia. *Eterna cadencia*. Online: http://blog.eternacadencia. com.ar/archives/19181 [Accessed 15 March 2015].

Incorvaia, Ivana. (2012). Las *multitudes* en Raúl Scalabrini Ortiz: La configuración de una identidad colectiva en *El hombre que está solo y espera* y *Tierra sin nada, tierra de profetas*. Online: http://citclot.fahce.unlp.edu.ar/viii-congreso/actas-2012/Incorvaia-%20Ivana.pdf [Accessed 15 March 2015].

Irwin, Robert McKee, & Mónica Szurmuk. (2012). Cultural Studies in Graduate Programmes in Latin America. *Cultural Studies, 26*(1), 8–28.

Iveson, Kurt. (2006). Strangers in the Cosmopolis. In J. Binnie, J. Holloway, S. Millington, & C. Young (Eds.), *Cosmopolitan Urbanism* (pp. 70–86). London and New York, NY: Routledge.

James, Daniel. (1993). *Resistance and Integration: Peronism and the Argentine Working Class, 1946–1976*. Cambridge: Cambridge University Press.

Janoschka, Michael. (2005). El modelo de ciudad latinoamericana: Privatización y fragmentación del espacio urbano de Buenos Aires: El caso Nordelta. In M.W. Guerra (Ed.), *Buenos Aires a la deriva: Transformaciones urbanas recientes* (pp. 96–131). Buenos Aires: Biblos.

Jelin, Elizabeth. (2003). *State Repression and the Struggles for Memory*. London: Latin American Bureau.

Jelin, Elizabeth, & Susana G. Kaufman. (2000). Layers of Memories: Twenty Years After in Argentina. In T.G. Ashplant, G. Dawson, & M. Roper (Eds.), *The Politics of War Memory and Commemoration* (pp. 89–110). London and New York, NY: Routledge.

Jenks, Mike, Daniel Kozak, & Pattaranan Takkanon (Eds.), (2008). *World Cities and Urban Form: Fragmented, Polycentric, Sustainable?* London: Routledge.

Joseph, Jaime A. (2005). *La ciudad, la crisis y las salidas: Democracia y desarrollo en espacios urbanos meso*. Lima: Fondo Editorial de la Facultad de Ciencias Sociales and Alternativa: Centro de Investigación Social y Educación Popular.

Journal of Latin American Cultural Studies. (2007). *16*(2).

Kohan, Martín. (1999). El fin de una épica. *Punto de Vista, 64*, 6–11.

———. (2000). Historia y literatura: la verdad de la narración. In E. Drucaroff (Ed.), *Historia crítica de la literatura argentina, Volume 9: La narración gana la partida* (pp. 245–257). Buenos Aires: Emecé.

———. (2002). *Dos veces junio*. Buenos Aires: De Bolsillo.

———. (2004). La apariencia celebrada. *Punto de Vista, 78*, 24–30.

———. (2007). *Zona urbana: Ensayo de lectura sobre Walter Benjamin*. Madrid: Editorial Trotta.

Koonings, Kees, & Dirk Kruijt. (2007). *Fractured Cities: Social Exclusion, Urban Violence and Contested Spaces in Latin America*. London and New York, NY: Zed Books.

Korn, Guillermo. (2007). La ciudad crispada. *El río sin orillas*, 1(1), 28–33.

Kozak, Daniel. (2008). Assessing Urban Fragmentation: The Emergence of New Typologies in Central Buenos Aires. In M. Jenks, D. Kozak, & P. Takkanon (Eds.), (2008). *World Cities and Urban Form: Fragmented, Polycentric, Sustainable?* (pp. 239–258). London: Routledge.

Kuper, Simon. (1994). *Football Against the Enemy*. London: Orion.

Landsberg, Alison. (2004). *Prosthetic Memory: The Transformation of American Remembrance in the Age of Mass Culture*. New York, NY: Columbia University Press.

Lavaca. (2009). Decí Mu: Letras & hip hop. Online: http://lavaca.org/deci-mu/deci-mu-territorios-en-resistencia/ [Accessed 15 March 2015].

Lee, Shin, & Chris Webster. (2006). Enclosure of the Urban Commons. *GeoJournal, 66*, 27–42.

Lefebvre, Henri. (2008). *Critique of Everyday Life*. 3 volumes. New York, NY: Verso.

Lerer, Diego. (1999). Mundo grúa. *Clarín*. Espectaculos. (17/06/99), p. 9.

———. (2002). La ley de la frontera. *Clarín*. Espectáculos. (19/02/02), p. 6.

Lewkowicz, Ignacio. (2002). *Sucesos Argentinos: Cacerolazo y subjetividad postestatal*. Buenos Aires: Paidós.

———. (2004). *Pensar sin Estado: La subjetividad en la era de la fluidez*. Buenos Aires: Paidós.

Lictira, Josefina. (2001). La gente no es xenófoba: Está sola, perdida y necesita agarrársela con alguien. *Veintitres* (29/11/01), pp. 38–42.

Linebaugh, Peter. (2008). *The Magna Carta Manifesto*. Berkeley, CA: University of California Press.

Liquidación.org. (2013). Online: http://www.liquidacion.org/ [Accessed 15 March 2015].

Lizama, Jaime. (2007). *La ciudad fragmentada: Espacio público, errancia y vida cotidiana*. Santiago de Chile: Ediciones Universidad Diego Portales.

Llach, Santiago. (2002). *La raza*. Buenos Aires: Siesta.

Longoni, Ana. (2010). Arte y Política: Políticas visuales del movimiento de derechos humanos desde la última dictadura: Fotos, siluetas y escraches. *Aletheia*, 1(1). Online: http://www.aletheia.fahce.unlp.edu.ar/numeros/numero-1/pdfs/Longoni-%20Aletheia%20vol%201.%20n1.pdf [Accessed 15 March 2015]

Longoni, Ana, & Buzzone, Gustavo A. (2008). Introducción. In A. Longoni & G.A. Buzzone (Eds.), *El siluetazo* (pp. 5–58). Buenos Aires: Adriana Hidalgo Editora.

Lorenz, Federico. (2002). ¿De quién es el 24 de marzo?: Las luchas por la memoria del golpe de 1976. In E. Jelin (Ed.), *Las conmemoraciones: Las disputas en las fechas "in-felices"* (pp. 53–100). Madrid: Siglo XXI.

————. (2006). *Las guerras por Malvinas*. Buenos Aires: Edhasa.

Low, Setha. (2004). *Behind the Gates: Life, Security and the Pursuit of Happiness in Fortress America*. London: Routledge.

Magnani, Esteban. (2006). Pirámides. . . . *Página 12*, CASH supplement, (26/03/06), pp. 2–3.

Mallo, Alfonso. (n.d.). La obrera y el hombre anónimo. Online: http://www.bazaramericano.com/resenas.php?cod=288&pdf=si [Accessed 15 March 2015].

Malosetti Costa, Laura. (2007). *Pampa, ciudad y suburbio*. Buenos Aires: Fundación Osde.

Marcuse, Peter and Ronald van Kempen (Eds.), (2000). *Globalizing Cities: A New Spatial Order?* Oxford: Blackwell.

Martín, Eloísa. (2004). *"Aguante lo 'pibe'!"*: Redefinitions of "Youth" in Argentina. *Sephis*, 1(2): 5–10.

Masiello, Francine. (2007). Reading for the People and Getting There First. In E. G. Zivin (Ed.), *The Ethics of Latin American Literary Criticism* (pp. 201–216). New York, NY: Palgrave Macmillan.

————. (2012). Cuerpo y materia: Una lectura de la poesía contemporánea argentina, *Revista de Crítica Literaria Latinoamericana*, 76, 143–172.

Massetti, Astor. (2004). *Piqueteros: Protesta social e identidad colectiva*. Buenos Aires: FLACSO/Editorial de las Ciencias.

Massey, Doreen. (2005). *For Space*. London: Sage.

McClennen, Sophia A. (2011). What's Left for Latin American Cultural Studies?. *Minnesota Review*, 76, 127–140.

McShane, Ian. (2010). Trojan Horse or Adaptive Institutions?: Some Reflections on Urban Commons in Australia. *Urban Policy and Research*, 28(1), 101–116.

Meagher, Sharon M. (2010). Critical Thinking About the Right to the City: Mapping Garbage Routes. *City*, 14(4), 427–433.

Memoria Abierta. (2013). Mapa de lugares de detención transitoria y centros clandestinos de detención. Online: http://www.memoriaabierta.org.ar/ccd/ [Accessed 15 March 2015].

Menazzi, Luján. (2008). Construyendo al barrio: La postulación del barrio como territorio político durante la transición democrática. *Argumentos*. Online: http://revistasiigg.sociales.uba.ar/index.php/argumentos/article/view/65/60 [Accessed 15 March 2015].

Míguez, Daniel. (2004). *Los pibes chorros: Estigma y marginación*. Buenos Aires: Capital Intelectual.

Montaldo, Graciela. (2010). Un arte basado en la incorrección: El cuestionamiento de las instituciones en una vanguardia finisecular. In R. Carbone & A. Ojeda (Eds.), *De Alfonsín al Menemato (1983: 2001)* (pp. 94–106). Buenos Aires: Paradiso and Fundación Crónica General.

Monteleone, Jorge. (2003). Cartoneros de la cultura. *La Nación*, (05/10/03). Online: http://www.lanacion.com.ar/532782-cartoneros-de-la-cultura [Accessed 15 March 2015].

Moore, Sarah A. (2009). The Excess of Modernity: Garbage Politics in Oaxaca, Mexico. *The Professional Geographer*, *61*(4), 426–437.

Moreno, María. (2002a). Interview with Alejandro Kaufmann. *Journal of Latin American Cultural Studies*, *11*(2), 137–142.

———. (2002b). Interview with Horacio González. *Journal of Latin American Cultural Studies*, *11*(2), 143–149.

———. (2011). *La comuna de Buenos Aires: Relatos al pie del 2001*. Buenos Aires: Capital Intelectual.

Motta, Sara C. (2009). New Ways of Making and Living Politics: The Movimiento de Trabajadores Desocupados de Solano and the "Movements of Movements." *Bulletin of Latin American Research*, *28*(1), 83–101.

Negri, Antonio. (2002). The Multitude and The Metropolis. Online: http://www.generation-online.org/t/metropolis.htm [Accessed 15 March 2015].

———. (2003). Toni Negri en Buenos Aires. In A. Negri, G. Cocco, C. Altamira, & A. Horowicz (Eds.), *Diálogo sobre la globalización, la multitud y la experiencia argentina* (pp. 27–49). Buenos Aires: Paidós.

Negri, Antonio, & Giuseppe Cocco. (2003). El trabajo de la multitud y el éxodo constituyente, o el "quilombo argentino." In A. Negri, G. Cocco, C. Altamira, & A. Horowicz (Eds.), *Diálogo sobre la globalización, la multitud y la experiencia argentina* (pp. 51–69). Buenos Aires: Paidós.

Nouzeilles, Gabriela. (2005). Postmemory Cinema and the Future of the Past in Albertina Carris *Los Rubios*. *Journal of Latin American Cultural Studies*, *14*(3), 263–278.

Oesterheld, Héctor Germán and Alberto Breccia. (2006). *El Eternauta y otras historias*. Buenos Aires: Colihue.

Oesterheld, Héctor Germán and Francisco Solano López. (2008). *El eternauta*. Barcelona: Norma.

Oesterheld, Héctor Germán and Gustavo Trigo. (1998). *La guerra de los Antartes*. Buenos Aires: Colihue.

Oeyen, Annelies. (2012). La villa miseria como laberinto mágico: El caso *La villa* de César Aira (2001). *Bulletin of Hispanic Studies*, *89*(1), 75–90.

Onuch, Olga. (2014). "It's the Economy, Stupid," Or is it? In C. Levey, D. Ozarow, & C. Wylde (Eds.), *Argentina Since the 2001 Crisis: Recovering the Past, Reclaiming the Future* (pp. 89–113). New York, NY: Palgrave Macmillan.

Ostuni, Hernán et al. (n.d.). Politics, Activism, Repression and Comics in Argentina During the 1970s. Online: http://www.camouflagecomics.com/flash.php [Accessed 15 March 2015].

Osuna, Viriginia. (2007). Malvinas: El recuerdo indómito. *El río sin orillas*, *1*, 66–71.

Oszlak, Oscar. (1982). Los sectores populares y el derecho al espacio urbano. *Punto de Vista*, *16*, 15–20.

Oubiña, David. (2004). Between Breakup and Tradition: Recent Argentine Cinema. Online: http://sensesofcinema.com/2004/feature-articles/recent_argentinean_cinema/ [Accessed 15 March 2015].

Paez, Fito. (2011). La mitad. *Página 12*. Online: http://www.pagina12.com.ar/
diario/contratapa/13-172084-2011-07-12.html [Accessed 15 March 2015].

Page, Joanna. (2005). Memory and Mediation in *Los rubios*: A Contemporary
Perspective on the Argentine Dictatorship. *New Cinemas*, 3(1), 29–40.

———. (2009). *Crisis and Capitalism in Contemporary Argentine Cinema*. Durham, NC: Duke University Press.

Parisi, Alejandro. (2002). *Delivery*. Buenos Aires: Sudamericana.

Patiño, Roxana. (2006). Revistas literarias y culturales argentinas de los 80. *Ínsula*:
715–716.

Pauls, Alan. (2003). Ficción súbita. Suplemento Radar, *Página 12* (15/06/03). Online:
http://www.pagina12.com.ar/diario/suplementos/radar/9-793-2003-06-15.
html [Accessed 15 March 2015].

———. (2008). Malvinas 78. Suplemento Radar, *Página 12* (01/06/08). Online:
http://www.pagina12.com.ar/diario/suplementos/radar/subnotas/4639-
754-2008-06-03.html [Accessed 15 March 2015].

Pedroso, Osvaldo, ed. (2007). *Debates en la cultura argentina 2: 2005–2006*. Buenos Aires: Emecé.

Peña, Fernando. (2003). *Generaciones 60/90: Cine argentino independiente*. Buenos
Aires: Museo de Arte Latinoamericano de Buenos Aires (MALBA).

Peralta, Elena. (2005). "Villa Tour": Llevan a extranjeros a visitar un barrio
pobre porteño. *Clarín*. Online: http://edant.clarin.com/diario/2005/05/28/
laciudad/h-06215.htm [Accessed 15 March 2015].

Perfil. (2006). Alfonsín: "Me tendría que haber ido en carpa al sur." *Perfil*. Online:
http://www.perfil.com/contenidos/2006/10/18/noticia_0011.html [Accessed
15 March 2015].

———. (2011). La Mancha de Rolando no quiere que Macri use sus temas.
Perfil. Online: http://www.perfil.com/contenidos/2011/08/01/noticia_0029.
html [Accessed 15 March 2015].

Perilli, Carmen. (2004). Reformulaciones del realismo: Bernardo Verbitsky,
Andrés Rivera, Juan José Manauta, Beatriz Guido. In N. Jitrik (Series Ed.)
& Sylvia Saítta (Vol. Ed.) *Historia crítica de la literatura argentina, Volume
9: El oficio se arma*, (pp. 545–572). Buenos Aires: Emecé.

Perron, Jacques. (2003). Rafael Lozano-Hemmer. Online: http://www.fondation-
langlois.org/html/e/page.php?NumPage=361 [Accessed 15 March 2015].

Petrina, Alberto. (2006). La ciudad justicialista: La arquitectura de la revolución
peronista en la obra de Daniel Santoro. Online: http://www.danielsantoro.
com.ar/mundoperonista.php?menu=mundo&mp=5 [Accessed 15 March
2015].

Piglia, Ricardo. (1993). *La Argentina en pedazos*. Buenos Aires: Ediciones de la
Urraca.

———. (2000). Sobre el género policial. In *Crítica y ficción* (67–70). Buenos
Aires: Seix Barral.

Pinedo, Rafael. (2004). *Plop*. Buenos Aires: Interzona.

Piñeiro, Claudia. (2005). *Las viudas de los jueves*. Buenos Aires: Alfaguara.

———. (2010). *Betibú*. Buenos Aires: Alfaguara.

Podalsky, Laura. (2004). *Specular City: Transforming Culture, Consumption, and Space in Buenos Aires, 1955-1973*. Philadelphia, PA: Temple University Press.

Porrúa, Ana. (2005). César Aira: Implosión y juventud. *Punto de Vista, 81*, 24-29.

Porter, Dennis. (2003). The Private Eye. In M. Priestman (Ed.), *The Cambridge Companion to Crime Fiction* (pp. 95-113). Cambridge: Cambridge University Press.

Prieto, Martín. (2006). *Breve historia de la literatura argentina*. Buenos Aires: Taurus.

Puex, Nathalie. (2003). Las formas de la violencia en tiempos de crisis: Una villa miseria del Conurbano Bonaerense. In A. Isla & D. Míguez (Eds.), *Heridas urbanas: Violencia delictiva y transformaciones sociales en los noventa* (pp. 35-70). Buenos Aires: Editorial de las Ciencias.

Punto de Vista. (1978-2008). Buenos Aires.

Quintar, Aída, & Perla Zusman. (2003). ¿Emergencia de una multitud constituyente?: Resonancias de las jornadas de diciembre de 2001 en Argentina. *Iconos: Revista de Ciencias Sociales, 17*, 58-65.

Ramos Mejía, José M. (1977). *Las multitudes argentinas*. Buenos Aires: Editorial de Belgrano.

Reggiani, Federico. (n.d.). Comics in Transition: Representations of State Terrorism at the Beginning of the Democratic Period. Online: http://www.camouflagecomics.com/flash.php [Accessed 15 March 2015].

Rep (2005). *Rep hizo los barrios: Buenos Aires dibujada*. Buenos Aires: Editorial Sudamericana.

Richard, Nelly. (2012). Humanities and Social Sciences in Critical Dialogues with Cultural Studies. *Cultural Studies, 26*(1), 166-177.

Robben, Antonius C.G.M. (2000). The Assault on Basic Trust: Disappearance, Protest, and Reburial in Argentina. In A.C.G.M. Robben & M.M. Súarez Orozco (Eds.), *Cultures Under Siege: Collective Violence and Trauma* (pp. 70-101). Cambridge: Cambridge University Press.

Rodgers, Dennis. (2007). Managua. In K. Koonings & D. Kruijt (Eds.), *Fractured Cities: Social Exclusion, Urban Violence and Contested Spaces in Latin America* (pp. 71-85). London and New York, NY: Zed Books.

Rodgers, Dennis, Jo Beall, & Ravi Kanbur. (2012). Re-thinking the Latin American City. In D. Rodgers, J. Beall, & R. Kanbur (Eds.), *Latin American Urban Development into the Twenty First Century: Towards a Renewed Perspective on the City* (pp. 3-35). New York, NY: Palgrave Macmillan,

Romero, José Luis. (2005). *Latinoamérica: Las ciudades y las ideas*. Buenos Aires: Siglo XXI.

———. (2009). *La ciudad occidental: Culturas urbanas en Europa y América*. Buenos Aires: Siglo XXI.

Rothberg, Michael. (2009). *Multidirectional Memory: Remembering the Holocaust in the Age of Decolonization*. Stanford, CA: Stanford University Press.

Saer, Juan José. (1993). *Lo imborrable*. Buenos Aires: Alianza.

———. (1995). *Glosa*. Buenos Aires: Seix Barral.

———. (2006). *El río sin orillas: Tratado imaginario*. Buenos Aires: Seix Barral.

Salvatori, Samanta, María Elena Saraví, & Sandra Raggio. (n.d.). La política social de las topadoras: Erradicación de villas durante la última dictadura militar. Online: http://www.comisionporlamemoria.org/jovenesymemoria/docs/dossiers/16.PDF [Accessed 15 March 2015].

Samoilovich, Daniel. (2003). *El carrito de Eneas*. Buenos Aires: Bajo la luna.

Sampayo, Carlos and Francisco Solano López. (1998). *Evaristo*. Buenos Aires: Colihue.

Sarlo, Beatriz. (1988). *Una modernidad periférica: Buenos Aires 1920 y 1930*. Buenos Aires: Nueva Visión.

———. (1993). *Jorge Luis Borges: A Writer on the Edge*. New York, NY: Verso.

———. (1994). No olvidar la guerra de Malvinas: Sobre cine, literatura e historia. *Punto de Vista, 49*, 11–15.

———. (2003). Plano, repetición: Sobreviviendo en la ciudad nueva. In A. Birgin & J. Trímboli (Eds.), *Imágenes de los noventa* (pp. 125–149). Buenos Aires: Zorzal.

———. (2004). *Escenas de la vida posmoderna*. Buenos Aires: Seix Barral.

———. (2005). *Tiempo Pasado: Cultura de la memoria y giro subjetivo: Una discusión*. Buenos Aires: Siglo XXI.

———. (2008). Cultural Landscapes: Buenos Aires from Integration to Fracture. In A. Huyssen (Ed.), *Other Cities, Other Worlds: Urban Imaginaries in a Globalizing Age* (pp. 27–49). Durham, NC: Duke University Press.

———. (2011). *La audacia y el cálculo: Kirchner 2003–2010*. Buenos Aires: Sudamericana.

———. (2012). *Ficciones argentinas: 33 ensayos*. Buenos Aires: Mardulce.

Sarmiento, Domingo Faustino. (1963). *Facundo*. Buenos Aires: Losada.

Sasturain, Juan. (1980). Epílogo: La marginalidad no es un tigre de papel. In C. Trillo & G. Saccomanno. *Historieta: Historia de la historieta argentina* (pp. 185–189). Buenos Aires: Ediciones Record.

———. (1995). *El domicilio de la aventura*. Buenos Aires: Colihue.

Scalabrini Ortiz, Raúl. (1933). *El hombre que está solo y espera*. Buenos Aires: Anaconda. Online: http://www.labaldrich.com.ar/wp-content/uploads/2013/05/Scalabrini-Ortiz-Raul-El-Hombre-Que-Esta-Solo-Y-Espera-PDF.pdf [Accessed 15 March 2015].

———. (2009). *Tierra sin nada, tierra de profetas: Devociones para el hombre argentino*. Buenos Aires: Lancelot.

Schmitt, Carl. (2003). *The Nomos of the Earth in the International Law of the* Jus Publicum Europaeum. New York, NY: Telos Press.

Scholz, Pablo O. (2002). Historia de un país en emergencia. *Clarín*. Espectáculos. (11/04/02), p. 9.

Scobie, James R. (1964). *Argentina: A City and a Nation*. New York, NY: Oxford University Press.

Scorer, James. (2008). From *la guerra sucia* to "A Gentlemans Fight": War, Disappearance and Nation in the 1976–1983 Argentine Dictatorship. *Bulletin of Latin American Research, 27*(1), 43–60.

———. (2010). Once Upon a Time in Buenos Aires: Vengeance, Community and the Urban Western. *Journal of Latin American Cultural Studies, 19*(2), 141–154.

Sebreli, Juan José. (2003). *Buenos Aires, Vida cotidiana y alienación; Buenos Aires, Ciudad en crisis.* Buenos Aires: Sudamericana.

Semán, Pablo, & Pablo Vila. (2002). Rock Chabón: The Contemporary National Rock of Argentina. In W.A. Clark (Ed.), *From Tejano to Tango: Latin American Popular Music* (pp. 70–94). New York, NY, and London: Routledge.

Semán, Pablo, Pablo Vila, & Cecilia Benedetti. (2004). Neoliberalism and Rock in the Popular Sector of Contemporary Argentina. In D.P. Hernandez, H. Fernández L'Hoeste, & E. Zolov (Eds.), *Rockin' Las Americas: The Global Politics of Rock in Latin/o America* (pp. 261–289). Pittsburgh, PA: University of Pittsburgh Press.

Sen, Atreyee, & David Pratten. (2007). Global Vigilantes: Perspectives on Justice and Violence. In A. Sen and D. Pratten (Eds.), *Global Vigilantes* (pp. 1–21). London: Hurst.

Serra, Adolfo. (2002). Pablo Trapero, el director de *El bonaerense. Gente.* (24/09/02), pp. 82–85.

Siskind, Mariano. (2005). Sergio Chejfec. *Hispamérica, 100,* 35–46.

Silvestri, Graciela. (1999). Memoria y monumento. *Punto de Vista, 64,* 42–44.

———. (2000). Apariencia y verdad: Reflexiones sobre obras, testimonios y documentos de arquitectura producidos durante la dictadura militar en la Argentina. *Block, 5,* 38–50.

Silvestri, Graciela, & Adrián Gorelik. (2000). Ciudad y cultura urbana, 1976–1999: El fin de la expansión. In J.L. Romero & L.A. Romero (Eds.), *Buenos Aires: Historia de cuatro siglos,* 2nd edition (pp. 461–499). Buenos Aires: Altamira.

Sneed, Paul. (2008). Favela Utopias: The Bailes Funk in Rio's Crisis of Social Exclusion and Violence. *Latin American Research Review, 43*(2), 57–79.

Soja, Edward W. (2000). *Postmetropolis: Critical Studies of Cities and Regions.* Oxford: Blackwell.

Solnit, Rebecca. (2002). *Wanderlust: A History of Walking.* London: Verso.

Sosa, Cecilia. (2014). *Queering Acts of Mourning in the Aftermath of Argentina's Dictatorship: The Performances of Blood.* New York, NY: Tamesis.

Smulovitz, Catalina. (2003). Citizen Insecurity and Fear: Public and Private Responses in Argentina. In H. Frühling, J. S. Tulchin, & H. A. Golding (Eds.), *Crime and Violence in Latin America: Citizen Security, Democracy, and the State* (pp. 125–152). Washington, D.C.: Woodrow Wilson Center Press.

Stam, Robert. (1997). Hybridity and the Aesthetics of Garbage: The Case of Brazilian Cinema. Online: http://www.tau.ac.il/eial/IX_1/stam.html [Accessed 15 March 2015].

Sternberg, José Enrique. (2004). Tren Blanco: El tren de los cartoneros. Online: http://www.zonezero.com/exposiciones/fotografos/sternberg/indexsp.html [Accessed 15 March 2015].

Strasser, Susan. (1999). *Waste and Want: A Social History of Trash*. New York, NY: Metropolitan Books.

Subsecretaría de Desarrollo Urbano y Vivienda. (2012). Online: www.vivienda. gov.ar (Accessed 15 March 2015).

Svampa, Maristella. (2005). *La sociedad excluyente: La Argentina bajo el signo del neoliberalismo*. Buenos Aires: Taurus.

———. (2008). *Los que ganaron: La vida en los countries y barrios privados*. Buenos Aires: Editorial Biblos.

———. (2014). Revisiting Argentina 2001–13: From "¡Que se vayan todos!" to the Peronist Decade. In C. Levey, D. Ozarow, & C. Wylde (Eds.), *Argentina Since the 2001 Crisis: Recovering the Past, Reclaiming the Future* (pp. 155–173). New York, NY: Palgrave Macmillan.

Tappatá de Valdez, Patricia. (2003). El Parque de la Memoria en Buenos Aires. In E. Jelin & V. Langland (Eds.), *Monumentos, memoriales y marcas territoriales* (pp. 97–111). Madrid: Siglo XXI.

Taylor, Diana. (1997). *Disappearing Acts: Spectacles of Gender and Nationalism in Argentina's "Dirty War."* Durham, NC: Duke University Press.

Tella, Guillermo. (2005). Rupturas y continuidades en el sistema de centralidades de Buenos Aires. In M.W. Guerra (Ed.), *Buenos Aires a la deriva: Transformaciones urbanas recientes* (pp. 29–73). Buenos Aires: Biblos.

Ternavasio, Marcela. (2009). *Historia de la Argentina, 1806–1852*. Buenos Aires: Siglo XXI.

Terranova, Juan, ed. (2011). *Buenos Aires/Escala 1:1: Los barrios por sus escritores*. Buenos Aires: Editorial Entropía.

Thuillier, Guy. (2005). Gated Communities in the Metropolitan Area of Buenos Aires, Argentina: A Challenge for Town Planning. *Housing Studies, 20*(2), 255–271.

Tickner, Arlene B. (2008). Aquí en el Ghetto: Hip-hop in Colombia, Cuba, and Mexico. *Latin American Politics and Society, 50*(3), 121–146.

Torre, Juan Carlos. (2000). La ciudad y los obreros. In J.L. Romero & L.A. Romero (Eds.), *Buenos Aires: Historia de cuatro siglos*, 2nd edition (pp. 259–271). Buenos Aires: Altamira.

Tour Experience. (2007). http://www.tourexperience.com.ar [Accessed 17 January 2007].

Trigo, Abril. (2004). General Introduction. In A. Del Sarto, A. Ríos, & A. Trigo (Eds.), *The Latin American Cultural Studies Reader* (pp. 1–14). Durham, NC: Duke University Press.

Trillo, Carlos, & Guillermo Saccomanno. *Historieta: Historia de la historieta argentina*. Buenos Aires: Ediciones Record.

Trímboli, Javier. (2003). Una lectura de *Imágenes de los noventa*. In A. Birgin & J. Trímboli (Eds.), *Imágenes de los noventa* (pp. 187–208). Buenos Aires: Zorzal.

————. (2006). *Los rubios* y la incomodidad. Online: http://www.buenosaires.gob. ar/areas/educacion/cepa/conferencia_trimboli_los_rubios.pdf [Accessed 15 March 2015].

Valenzuela, Luisa. (1990). *Realidad nacional desde la cama*. Buenos Aires: Grupo Editor Latinoamericano.

Vanoli, Hernán, & Diego Vecino. (2010). Subrepresentación del conurbano bonaerense en la "nueva narrativa argentina": Ciudad, peronismo y campo literario en la argentina del bicentenario. *Apuntes de investigación del CEC-YP, 17*, 259–274.

Vazquez, Laura. (2010). *El oficio de las viñetas: La industria de la historieta argentina*. Buenos Aires: Paídos.

Velazco, Carlos A. (1965). El pardo Meneses. *Revista Panorama*. April. Online: http:// www.magicasruinas.com.ar/revdesto041a.htm [Accessed 15 March 2015].

Verardi, Malena. (2009). El nuevo cine argentino: Claves de lectura de una época. In I. Amatriain (Ed.), *Una década de nuevo cine argentino (1995-2005): Industria, crítica, formación, estéticas* (pp. 171–189). Buenos Aires: Ciccus.

Verbitsky, Bernardo. (2003). *Villa miseria también es América*. Buenos Aires: Editorial Sudamericana.

Vezzetti, Hugo. (2002). *Guerra, dictadura y sociedad en la Argentina*. Buenos Aires: Siglo XXI.

Viñas, David. (1998). Los "Aguafuertes" como autobiografismo y colección. In R. Arlt, *Obras: Tomo II* (pp. 7–32). Buenos Aires: Losada.

Virno, Paolo. (2004). *A Grammar of the Multitude*. Los Angeles: Semiotext(e).

Wagner, Raúl Fernández. (2008). *Democracia y ciudad: Procesos y políticas urbanas en las ciudades argentinas (1983-2008)*. Buenos Aires: Universidad Nacional de General Sarmiento and Biblioteca Nacional.

Walsh, Rodolfo. (2003). *Operación masacre*. Buenos Aires: Ediciones de la Flor.

————. (2004). *¿Quién mató a Rosendo?* Buenos Aires: Ediciones de la Flor.

Whitelocke, John. (1808). *The Trial at Large of Lieutenant General Whitelocke, Late Commander in Chief of the Forces in South America, by a General Court Martial, Held at Chelsea Hospital on Thursday January 28 1808 and Continued by Adjournment to Tuesday March 15*. London: R. Faulder and Son.

Whitson, Risa. (2011). Negotiating Place and Value: Geographies of Waste and Scavenging in Buenos Aires. *Antipode, 43*(4), 1404–1433.

Williams, Gareth. (2002). *The Other Side of the Popular: Neoliberalism and Subalternity in Latin America*. Durham, NC: Duke University Press.

Williams Castro, Fatimah. (2013). Afro-Colombians and the Cosmopolitan City: New Negotiations of Race and Space in Bogotá, Colombia. *Latin American Perspectives, 40*, 105–117.

Wolf, Sergio. (2002). Las estéticas del nuevo cine argentino: El mapa es el territorio. In H. Bernades, D. Lerer, & S. Wolf. (Eds.), *El nuevo cine argentino: Temas, autores y estilos de una renovación* (pp. 29–39). Buenos Aires: Tatanka.

Wood, Nancy. (1999). *Vectors of Memory: Legacies of Trauma in Postwar Europe*. Oxford and New York, NY: Berg.

Wortman, Ana (2002). Vaivenes del campo intelectual político cultural en la Argentina. In D. Mato (Ed.), *Estudios y Otras Prácticas Intelectuales Latinoamericanas en Cultura y Poder* (pp. 327–338). Caracas: Consejo Latinoamericano de Ciencias Sociales (CLACSO) and CEAP, FACES, Universidad Central de Venezuela.

Zibechi, Raúl. (2003). Genealogía de la revuelta: Argentina: La sociedad en movimiento. La Plata: Letra libre.

Filmography

5 pal' peso. Dir. Raúl Perrone. 1998.
Bolivia. Dir. Adrián Caetano. 2001
Buenos Aires viceversa. Dir. Alejandro Agresti. 1996.
Cara de queso. Dir. Ariel Winograd. 2006.
Carancho. Dir. Pablo Trapero. 2010
City of God. Dir. Fernando Meirelles and Kátia Lund. 2002.
Crónica de una fuga. Dir. Adrián Caetano. 2006.
Días de cartón. Dir. Verónica Souto. 2003.
El abrazo partido. Dir. Daniel Burman. 2004.
El bonaerense. Dir. Pablo Trapero. 2002.
Elefante blanco. Dir. Pablo Trapero. 2012.
El tren blanco. Dir. Nahuel García, Sheila Pérez Giménez and Ramiro García. 2003.
El viaje. Dir. Fernando Solanas. 1992.
Espejo para cuando me pruebe el smoking. Dir. Alejandro Fernández Mouján. 2005.
Estrellas. Dir. Federico León and Marcos Martínez. 2007.
Fuckland. Dir. José Luis Marqués. 2000.
Graciadió. Dir. Raúl Perrone. 1997.
Labios de churrasco. Dir. Raúl Perrone. 1994.
La fiesta de todos. Dir. Sergio Renán. 1979.
La hora de los hornos. Dir. Fernando Solanas. 1968.
La multitud. Dir. Martín M. Oesterheld. 2013.
La zona. Dir. Rodrigo Plá. 2007.
Las viudas de los jueves. Dir. Marcelo Piñeyro. 2009.
Los rubios. Dir. Albertina Carri. 2003.
Luna de Avellaneda. Dir. Juan José Campanella. 2004.
Mala época. Dir. Various. 1998.
Medianeras. Dir. Gustavo Taretto. 2011.
Mundo grúa. Dir. Pablo Trapero. 1999.
Nueve reinas. Dir. Fabián Bielinsky. 2000.

Pizza, birra, faso. Dir. Bruno Stagnaro and Adrián Caetano. 1997.

Rapado. Dir. Martín Rejtman. 1992.

Silvia Prieto. Dir. Martín Rejtman. 1999.

Tan de repente. Dir. Diego Lerman. 2002.

The War on Democracy. Dir. John Pilger. 2006.

Tire dié. Dir. Fernando Birri. 1960.

Un oso rojo. Dir. Adrián Caetano. 2002.

Una semana solos. Dir. Celina Murga. 2007.

Vida en Falcón. Dir. Jorge Gaggero. 2005.

Index